ENCYCLOPEDIA OF LANGUAGE AND EDUCATION

Encyclopedia of Language and Education

VOLUME 6: KNOWLEDGE ABOUT LANGUAGE

The volume titles of this encyclopedia are listed at the end of this volume.

Encyclopedia of Language and Education

Volume 6

KNOWLEDGE ABOUT LANGUAGE

Edited by

LEO VAN LIER

Monterey Institute of International Studies
Monterey, California
USA

and

DAVID CORSON

The Ontario Institute for Studies in Education
University of Toronto
Canada

KLUWER ACADEMIC PUBLISHERS

DORDRECHT / BOSTON / LONDON

Library of Congress Cataloging-in-Publication Data

P
40.8
.E52
1997
v. 6

ISBN 0-7923-4933-4 (PB)   ISBN 0-7923-4641-6 (HB)
ISBN 0-7923-4936-9 (PB-SET)   ISBN 0-7923-4596-7 (HB-SET)

Published by Kluwer Academic Publishers,
P.O. Box 17, 3300 AA Dordrecht, The Netherlands

Sold and distributed in the U.S.A. and Canada
by Kluwer Academic Publishers,
101 Philip Drive, Norwell, MA 02061, U.S.A.

In all other countries, sold and distributed
by Kluwer Academic Publishers Group,
P.O. Box 322, 3300 AH Dordrecht, The Netherlands.

TABLE OF CONTENTS

VOLUME 6: KNOWLEDGE ABOUT LANGUAGE

*(eds), Encyclopedia of Language and Education,
...t Language, v–vi.*

GENERAL EDITOR'S INTRODUCTION

ENCYCLOPEDIA OF LANGUAGE AND EDUCATION

This is one of eight volumes of the Encyclopedia of Language and Education published by Kluwer Academic. The publication of this work signals the maturity of the field of 'language and education' as an international and interdisciplinary field of significance and cohesion. These volumes confirm that 'language and education' is much more than the preserve of any single discipline. In designing these volumes, we have tried to recognise the diversity of the field in our selection of contributors and in our choice of topics. The contributors come from every continent and from more than 40 countries. Their reviews discuss language and education issues affecting every country in the world.

We have also tried to recognise the diverse interdisciplinary nature of 'language and education' in the selection of the editorial personnel themselves. The major academic interests of the volume editors confirm this. As principal volume editor for Volume 1, Ruth Wodak has interests in critical linguistics, sociology of language, and language policy. For Volume 2, Viv Edwards has interests in policy and practice in multilingual classrooms and the sociology of language. For Volume 3, Bronwyn Davies has interests in the social psychology of language, the sociology of language, and interdisciplinary studies. For Volume 4, Richard Tucker has interests in language theory, applied linguistics, and the implementation and evaluation of innovative language education programs. For Volume 5, Jim Cummins has interests in the psychology of language and in critical linguistics. For Volume 6, Leo van Lier has interests in applied linguistics and in language theory. For Volume 7, Caroline Clapham has interests in research into second language acquisition and language measurement. And for Volume 8, Nancy Hornberger has interests in anthropological linguistics and in language policy. Finally, as general editor, I have interests in the philosophy and sociology of language, language policy, critical linguistics, and interdisciplinary studies. But the thing that unites us all, including all the contributors to this work, is an interest in the practice and theory of education itself.

People working in the applied and theoretical areas of education and language are often asked questions like the following: 'what is the latest research on such and such a problem?' or 'what do we know about such

L. van Lier and D. Corson (eds), Encyclopedia of Language and Education,
Volume 6: Knowledge about Language, vii–ix.
© 1997 Kluwer Academic Publishers. Printed in the Netherlands.

and such an issue?' Questions like these are asked by many people: by policy makers and practitioners in education; by novice researchers; by publishers trying to relate to an issue; and above all by undergraduate and postgraduate students in the language disciplines. Each of the reviews that appears in this volume tries to anticipate and answer some of the more commonly asked questions about language and education. Taken together, the eight volumes of this Encyclopedia provide answers to more than 200 major questions of this type, and hundreds of subsidiary questions as well.

Each volume of the Encyclopedia of Language and Education deals with a single, substantial subject in the language and education field. The volume titles and their contents appear elsewhere in the pages of this work. Each book-length volume provides more than 20 state-of-the-art topical reviews of the literature. Taken together, these reviews attempt a complete coverage of the subject of the volume. Each review is written by one or more experts in the topic, or in a few cases by teams assembled by experts. As a collection, the Encyclopedia spans the range of subjects and topics normally falling within the scope of 'language and education'. Each volume, edited by an international expert in the subject of the volume, was designed and developed in close collaboration with the general editor of the Encyclopedia, who is a co-editor of each volume as well as general editor of the whole work.

The Encyclopedia has been planned as a necessary reference set for any university or college library that serves a faculty or school of education. Libraries serving academic departments in any of the language disciplines, especially applied linguistics, would also find this a valuable resource. It also seems very relevant to the needs of educational bureaucracies, policy agencies, and public libraries, particularly those serving multicultural or multilingual communities.

The Encyclopedia aims to speak to a prospective readership that is multinational, and to do so as unambiguously as possible. Because each book-size volume deals with a discrete and important subject in language and education, these state-of-the-art volumes also offer authoritative course textbooks in the areas suggested by their titles. This means that libraries will also catalogue these book-size individual volumes in relevant sections of their general collections. To meet this range of uses, the Encyclopedia is published in a hardback edition offering the durability needed for reference collections, and in a future student edition. The hardback edition is also available for single-volume purchase.

Each state-of-the-art review has about 3000 words of text and most follow a similar structure. A list of references to key works cited in each review supplements the information and authoritative opinion that the review contains. Many contributors survey early developments in their topic, major contributions, work in progress, problems and difficulties, and future directions for research and practice. The aim of the reviews, and of the Encyclopedia as a whole, is to give readers access to the international literature and research on each topic.

David Corson
General Editor Encyclopedia of Language and Education
Ontario Institute for Studies in Education of the University of Toronto
Canada

INTRODUCTION

In this volume, editors and contributors have sought to bring together a representative collection of articles that all deal with a central theme: the role of knowledge about language (or, as it is often called, metalinguistic knowledge) and awareness of language in education.

The papers included move well beyond the usual discussions about the explicit teaching of formal aspects of language as part of language development in schools. In fact, all contributions advance the notion that an awareness of and information about the forms (grammar, style, pronunciation, etc.) of language are useful, or even necessary. However, all contributions also look further than traditional prescriptive grammar rules, vocabulary lists, spelling tests, and so on. Rather, what is emphasized is the varied nature of language knowledge, and the multiple ways in which such knowledge can be part of educational experiences and human growth. The variety of language knowledge and experiences presented in these pages reflects the broad view of language that is adopted here for educational purposes. As Maturana and Varela put it in their fascinating book *The tree of knowledge*, "every reflection . . . invariably takes place in language, which is our distinctive way of being human and being humanly active" (1992: 26).

Using language, in the spirit of this collection, is not primarily a matter of uttering or writing messages that conform to rules of grammar, diction, spelling and rhetorical structures of standard language. First and foremost, using language, and using it consciously and deliberately, means expressing our humanity and collaborating with others in the construction of our common reality. The demands of "proper" or "standard" language are surely an important part of educational reality, but they need not overshadow all other facets of language. This is a constant danger when prescriptive grammar is inculcated in classrooms by grammar teachers through "innumerable acts of correction", as Bourdieu puts it (1991).

Debates about language are often heavily skewed towards issues of correctness, proper usage, the "right" way to say and write words. Language mavens in newspapers and magazines field questions from readers about *who* versus *whom*, *I* versus *me*, the use or abuse of *irregardless* and *hopefully*, and the right pronunciation of *short-lived* and *harassment*. Although such discussions are interesting, they are not very different

L. van Lier and D. Corson (eds), Encyclopedia of Language and Education,
Volume 6: Knowledge about Language, xi–xvi.
© 1997 Kluwer Academic Publishers. Printed in the Netherlands.

from discussions about proper ways of dressing, eating, or behaving at funerals. In other words, public discussions about language tend to focus on linguistic etiquette rather than on other substantive issues (I leave aside, for the moment, debates about language policy, such as whether or not English should be the official language of the US, or if African-American children should be allowed to use black English or Ebonics in the classroom). There are exceptions to this, for example in the work of Deborah Tannen about language use between men and women, Richard Lutz's descriptions of "doublespeak" in politics, and Richard Lederer's amusing books on language fun and games (Tannen, 1986; Lutz, 1989; Lederer, 1990).

The central mission of this volume, from the perspective of the editors, is to promote a broader awareness of language, its uses and its abuses, its strengths and its fragility, its social and its private functions, its power and its playfulness.

Greater knowledge about language will not solve all the social and educational problems we face in many countries around the globe. However, as many of the contributions show, if we look at language carefully and respectfully, without being blinded by superficial questions of right or wrong, we can make educational experiences richer and more efficient for learners in different classrooms, in schools, and at work.

When we ask children about their best and worst subjects in school, they will very often include language (native and foreign) among their most difficult and hateful (i.e., "boring") subjects. Yet, these same children, out of school, will entertain you with word games, puns, examples of slang expressions, deadly accurate imitations of regional or foreign accents, and a thousand testimonials of keen language interest and skill. This illustrates a deep paradox about language and education: even though language is fascinating to children and grownups alike, and a constant focus of attention and comment, in school it is often stripped of precisely those things that make it interesting. It is almost a general rule that language is interesting when it is used, but boring when it is taught. Of course, everything can be taught badly, and conversely, everything can be taught well, and this volume addresses the diverse ways in which language can be and is taught well, in different parts of the world.

To teach language well requires an awareness of what it is and does, an awareness that it is more than words or sentences that are either right or wrong. It also requires a genuine effort to teach language *across the curriculum*, that is, to agree on a common language philosophy in the school, a common commitment to assist learners in finding a personal, strong, effective voice to speak in. These are difficult tasks. First, they require a broad definition of language (such as that proposed by *ecolinguistics*, or *ecological linguistics*, e.g. Makkai (1993), Mühlhäusler (1996)), second, they require synchronization and collaboration across disciplines and school departments, in a school culture which appears increasingly "balkanized", in the words of Andy Hargreaves (1994). Detailed proposals for language policy across the curriculum have been made in various countries (see, e.g., Corson, 1990). The contributions by Donmall, van Essen, Corson and Goodman show how difficult such changes in practice can be. Brumfit and Wright and Bolitho offer some suggestions about teacher education in this respect.

In reaction to old-style grammar teaching, with its parsing and diagramming of sentences and endless drills and rules, many approaches to language teaching have tried to be anti-grammar or grammar-less, but, as a recent thematic issue of *English Journal* (1996) argues, the pendulum has now once again swung back to the inclusion of grammar teaching, at least in English as a native language instruction in the US. Whether or not a similar pattern of grammar-rejection followed by a grammar-return has occurred in second and foreign language teaching is not quite so clear. Certainly, there have been – and are – methods which advocate a focus on communication or fluency, and others which focus on solid formal instruction and accuracy, but these appear to have existed side by side, or occasionally in competition, over the last few decades. There is also a third, and rather recent, trend which proclaims that the era of packaged methods is over, and which proposes alternative ways of organizing teaching (Kumaravadivelu, 1994; van Lier, 1996).

What really is knowledge about language? How is it used by a learner, and how is it promoted by a teacher? How much of this knowledge is explicit, and how much is implicit? How much of it is "knowing that", and how much is "knowing how"? I suggest that there may be a significant difference between *metalinguistic knowledge* and *language awareness*, and that both types are necessary and produce an essential tension. The former is what you come up with if you test or interview people, because it is limited to that which can be expressed in technical words, or metalanguage; the latter accompanies and guides the conscious language user's language use, but is not easily amenable to explicit scrutiny or comment. The former may be the tip, the latter the submerged bulk of the iceberg of language knowledge.

The contributions to this volume examine a number of aspects of knowledge about language in this wider sense. It has been our particular aim to show, not so much in any single review as across the entire range, that explicit knowledge of formal features of language, critical sociolinguistic analysis and artistic appreciation all relate to one another, and that a responsible and rich language education cannot dispense with any of them.

There are still a number of questions to which no clear answers are currently available. In second language acquisition, for example, the extent to which negative evidence, that is, explicit correction, or explanation of linguistic phenomena, is necessary or beneficial, still requires a great deal of research (see Ellis, this volume; see also Doughty, Fotos). A recently concluded study at the Centre for Language in Language Education of Lancaster University (Alderson, Clapham & Steel, 1997) concludes that there is little relationship between metalinguistic knowledge and language proficiency. Of course, the last word has not been said about this issue. If we consider metalinguistic knowledge as a set of tools, we should not conclude that having more tools is always better. To use an analogy, we do not call someone a better carpenter just because he or she has more tools or a larger toolbox. However, that does not mean that carpenters can do without tools. What matters is how they are used, and teaching metalinguistic knowledge may be very different from learning how to use it. Further, as mentioned above, language awareness and language knowledge may be two quite different things. We can look forward to more research like that of Alderson et al., in the hope that some of these questions can be answered.

Another area of much current debate is the appropriate balance, for each child, between creative (Whole Language) and formal (Phonics) approaches to the acquisition of literacy. As the reviews by Goodman, Nicholson and Sandra show, neither wholesale, uncritical implementation of a particular method, nor its summary rejection (as is often the tenor of public discussions of the whole language – phonics issue) are appropriate decisions in education. A similar either-or debate, equally unhelpful, is sometimes witnessed in the UK and elsewhere between two interpretations of language awareness: explicit grammatical knowledge on the one hand, and critical awareness on the other. The reviews by van Essen, Donmall and others in the first section of the volume clearly illustrate the futility of such debates.

Late in the production of this volume the Ebonics controversy erupted in the US. The various voices in this debate illustrate, perhaps more powerfully than anything written in this volume, the need for higher levels of awareness about language for all people, not just students on school benches and their teachers. The review by Corson in this volume gains increased significance in the light of the Ebonics debate (see also Fillmore (1997), Long (1997), van Lier (1997), and the review by Corson in Volume 1 on non-standard varieties and educational policy, which discusses the Ebonics debate).

An area that needs increasing attention is that of the relationship between language education and technology. Even though it is stereotypically assumed that computers and other electronic systems lead to impoverished communication, it can be demonstrated that careful planning and design can actually lead to enhanced and enriched communication through the use of technology (Crook, 1994). However, technology can also have the opposite effect – that of reducing communication and increasing the inequality of educational opportunity (Tyack & Cuban, 1995). The research of these issues, and their relation to communication in schools and classrooms, should be a priority, though it is beyond the scope of this volume.

Let us, by way of conclusion, summarize on what it has been possible to bring together in this volume. We have traced the history of language awareness and knowledge about language (van Essen, Donmall, Walmsley, Gombert), looked in detail at classrooms to see how language is treated (DeFazio, Papaeftymiou-Lytra, Tsui), examined specific types of class-rooms (Ellis, Jones) and academic subjects (Fettes, Zabalbeascoa), from literacy (Goodman, Nicholson, Sandra) to academic writing (Clark & Ivanic, Maylath, Wallace), the teaching of argument (Freedman, Mitchell, Costello), discussed teacher development (Brumfit, Wright & Bolitho) and critical social issues (Corson, Wortham), and looked at communication in the multilingual work place (Malcolm).

As this volume – and the Encyclopedia of Language and Education as a whole – shows, language is the central means by which education is conducted and constructed, and its development itself is also one of the major goals of education. Everything schools aim to achieve depends in large measure on language, on the effectiveness of its use in instruction, its contribution to the well-being of students, and the students' command of language in cognitive, academic, social and personal ways. Equality and excellence in education, in all subject areas, can only be achieved through a profound understanding of language, and through equality and excellence in language education.

REFERENCES

Alderson, J.C., Clapham, C. & Steel, D.: forthcoming, 'Metalinguistic knowledge, language aptitude and language proficiency', *Language Teaching Research* 1(2).

Bourdieu, P.: 1991, *Language and Symbolic Power*, Cambridge, MA: Harvard University Press.

Corson, D.: 1990, *Language Policy Across the Curriculum*, Clevedon: Multilingual Matters.

Crook, C.: 1994, *Computers and the Collaborative Experience of Learning*, London: Routledge.

Doughty, C.: 1991, 'Second language instruction does make a difference: Evidence from an empirical study on SL relativization', *Studies in Second Language Acquisition* 13, 431–469.

English Journal: 1996, *The Great Debate (Again): Teaching Grammar and Usage* 85(7).

Fillmore, C.J.: 1997, 'A linguist looks at the Ebonics debate', *TESOL Matters* 17(1), 13–14, 16.

Fotos, S.: 1994, 'Integrating grammar instruction and communicative language use through grammar consciousness-raising tasks', *TESOL Quarterly* 28(2), 323–346.

Hargreaves, A.: 1994, *Changing Teachers, Changing Times: Teachers' Work and Culture in the Postmodern Age*, New York: Teachers College Press.

Kumaravadivelu, B.: 1994, 'The postmethod condition: (E)merging strategies for second/foreign language teaching', *TESOL Quarterly* 28(1), 27–48.

Lederer, R.: 1990, *The Play of Words: Fun and Games for Language Lovers*, New York: Simon & Schuster.

Long, M.: 1997, *Ebonics, Language, and Power*, University of Hawaii Working Papers in ESL, 15.1.

Lutz, W.: 1989, *Doublespeak*, New York: Harper Collins.

Makkai, A.: 1993, *Ecolinguistics: ¿ Toward a New **Paradigm** for the Science of Language?* London: Pinter Publishers.

Maturana, H. & Varela, F.J.: 1992, *The Tree of Knowledge: The Biological Roots of Human Understanding*, Boston: New Science Library.

Mühlhäusler, P.: 1996, *Linguistic Ecology: Language Change and Linguistic Imperialism in the Pacific Region*, London: Routledge.

Tannen, D.: 1986, *That's Not What I Meant: How Conversational Style Makes or Breaks Relationships*, New York: Ballantine Books.

Tyack, D. & Cuban, L.: 1995, *Tinkering Toward Utopia: A Century of Public School Reform*, Cambridge, MA: Harvard University Press.

van Lier, L.: 1996, *Interaction in the Language Curriculum: Awareness, Autonomy, and Authenticity*, London: Longman.

van Lier, L.: 1997, *Critical Language Awareness and Language Use in Multilingual Classrooms: A Social-Interactionist Perspective*, unpublished paper.

Section 1

Historical and Theoretical Issues

ARTHUR VAN ESSEN

LANGUAGE AWARENESS AND KNOWLEDGE ABOUT LANGUAGE: AN OVERVIEW

'Language Awareness' (henceforth: LA) has become a buzzword in language education. This does not mean that everybody in the profession knows what it means, let alone that one knows what its origins and implications are. For this reason a number of educational linguists from all over Europe got together in London in late 1991 to try and establish what the term stands for. At this mini round-table (I was one of those present) broad agreement was reached on the following working definition of LA: '. . . a person's sensitivity to and conscious awareness of the nature of language and its role in human life' (James & Garrett, 1992, p. 8). I shall use this definition as a point of reference throughout this chapter. LA and 'Knowledge about Language' (henceforth: KAL) will be used interchangeably unless stated otherwise.

In the following sections I propose to deal with the evolution and trends in LA. The survey will be chiefly limited to the Germanic language area and will adopt a largely European perspective, as elsewhere LA studies seem to be only just taking off (cf. Candelier, 1992). In the last but one section I shall take up some of the current problems and difficulties experienced in the field of LA. In the final section we shall look at some potential directions in research and educational practice.

EARLY HISTORY OF LA

Ever since Wilhelm von Humboldt (1767–1835) apprised the linguistic world of his belief that language is not so much a product (*ergon*) as a process (*energeia*) which manifests itself in the ever repetitive effort of the individual mind to suit the collective medium that language is to the expression of one's thoughts ('[Die Sprache] ist nemlich die sich ewig wiederholende Arbeit des Geistes, den articulirten Laut zum Ausdruck des Gedankens fähig zu machen' [Steinthal, 1884, pp. 262–3]), language pedagogues who derived their inspiration from Humboldt have wondered whether this mental effort could somehow be aided. This is how early modern LA was born. But how to go about it?

In the prevailing pedagogical climate of the nineteenth century, dominated by a deductive methodology of teaching in which the inculcation of grammar rules was rife, it was by no means easy for the reformers to

L. van Lier and D. Corson (eds), Encyclopedia of Language and Education,
Volume 6: Knowledge about Language, 1–9.
© *1997 Kluwer Academic Publishers. Printed in the Netherlands.*

implement the Humboldtian precepts. For one thing because Humboldt himself had not expressed himself as unequivocally as one would wish. For example, while Humboldt had said that just because native language acquisition is largely a matter of arousing our language faculties it cannot really be taught or learnt, he had at the same time made allowance for external influences ('[Die Sprache] ist zugleich nicht bloss passiv, Eindrücke empfangend, sondern [...] modificirt durch innere Selbstthätigkeit jede auf sie geübte äussre Einwirkung.' [Steinthal, 1884, pp. 247–8]) such as 'practice' (*Übung*, cf. Steinthal, 1884, p. 285), which might foster the growth of language competence. For another thing there was no appropriate methodology, one that besides enjoyed sufficient scholarly prestige. Phonetics and neogrammarian research seemed to offer these. Both sciences were primarily concerned with studying the speech of individuals ('language' was really an abstraction) through the senses, by 'observation' or by 'self-observation' (i.e. introspection). Both favoured an inductive methodology, both resorted to associationist psychology.

By and large these views were also adopted by the early proponents of LA (cf. Hildebrand, 1867, *passim*; Jespersen, 1904, pp. 125–41; Sweet, 1899, pp. 236–55). Oblivious of Humboldt's ambivalence, they seemed to assume that *conscious* reflection on language form and language use would automatically benefit the workings of the learner's *intuitive* linguistic sense). This is a perennial issue in LA to which we will return in the last but one section.

THE TWENTIETH CENTURY: MAJOR CONTRIBUTIONS

Not surprisingly, in an age dominated by the deductive grammar-translation method, LA has remained a phenomenon on the periphery of the language teaching arena. Refinements of the original LA theory were introduced by Gabelentz (Gabelentz, 1901), who devoted a chapter of his work *Die Sprachwissenschaft* to knowledge of language (*Sprachkenntniss*), who made a distinction between unconscious acquisition and conscious learning, and one between LA in the teaching of the native and of another language. Gabelentz played down the importance of translating (except as an LA tool) and made out a strong case for what we would now call 'educational linguistics' (Gabelentz, 1901, p. 71).

It is not unlikely that Harold Palmer (1877–1949) was influenced by Gabelentz. In any case, both Palmer (1917) and (1922), but especially the latter show a close affinity with Gabelentz's views on LA. In two separate chapters Palmer (1922) elaborated on the distinction between our 'spontaneous capacities for acquiring speech' and our 'studial capacities of language studies'. The former operate unconsciously ('subconsciously' in Palmer, 1917) in the acquisition of one's mother tongue and in the natural acquisition of any subsequently learnt language, the latter are conscious strategies which are mobilised whenever artificial learning tasks like reading and writing are involved. Palmer made much of the latter capacities: '... it would be either unwise or impossible to proceed by the sole aid of nature or by the reconstruction of natural conditions' (Palmer, 1922, p. 22).

Inspired by developments in Germany around 1900 Holland began to evolve its own brand of LA. It formed part of a broader movement for the emancipation of native language education. Not only because of its relevance to our topic but also because of its intrinsic interest I should like to quote from one of this movement's central publications (Van den Bosch, 1903): '[it is our aim] to turn the youngster into a keen observer and a shrewd judge [of language use by] teaching him how to compare and how to distinguish, [by making him] find things out for himself' so that through a process of growing awareness and increasing self-confidence that will continue throughout life, he will become the 'authoritative controller of his own language use'. *What* was to be observed was the immediate language reality of the learners. It was the teacher's role to provide guidance to his pupils.

These quotations bespeak a close affinity with the current British movement for Critical LA (henceforth: CLA) especially if one compares them with a recent statement by a prominent protagonist of CLA that if LA is to affect the pupil's competence in a positive way it should incorporate 'the important principle that critical language awareness should be built from the existing language capabilities and experience of the learner. The experience of the learner can, with the help of the teacher, be made explicit and systematic as a body of knowledge which can be used for discussion and reflection ... ' (Fairclough, 1992, p. 16). Like their modern British CLA counterparts, the Dutch reformers also had an ideological axe to grind: they emphasized the social responsibility of teachers as citizens. Language education was seen as a language liberation movement.

There is another parallel between CLA and the early Dutch LA movement: neither want LA work to be conducted as an isolated activity, as a kind of mini-course in linguistics taught across the curriculum, but as an integral part of any normal language class. This is a marked difference with 'ordinary' British LA (cf. Hawkins, 1984).

During the 1930s, LA received renewed attention in Germany and Holland from Drach (1937) and Langeveld (1934), both important monographs, continuing and refining the earlier LA work.

The last two works to be mentioned in this section are: Royen (1947) and Stutterheim (1954). To appreciate the proper significance of the former, it should be compared with a British book on LA that appeared almost forty years later: Hawkins (1984). Both books aim at an adult readership (primary school teachers or prospective teachers), both books are primarily concerned with the teaching of the national language, either to native speakers or to speakers of other languages. Both books have roughly the same aims and cover roughly the same topics, including language comparison. Even in their definitions of the aims of LA the authors use similar wordings (cf. Hawkins, 1984, pp. 4–5; Royen, 1947, p. 5). Royen was the first to take a much broader view of LA than had up till then been usual. For example, it included a discussion of language diversity. Where Royen and Hawkins would have parted company is on the question of whether LA should be dealt with in an integrative way or as a separate element on the school curriculum. Royen preferred the former.

Stutterheim (1954) very appropriately bore the title *Taalbeschouwing en Taalbeheersing* (ie. language awareness and language competence). It was a well-documented empirical study focusing on the question as to whether in the teaching of reading the explicit attention given to language structure has any positive effect on the pupils' interpretation of what they read and, if so, how this knowledge of grammar can be brought to bear on the pupils' linguistic competence. On the basis of his evidence, Stutterheim's answer was a qualified 'yes'. For further discussion, see Van Essen (1995).

CURRENT WORK IN LA

After LA studies had been in abeyance for about three decades there was a resurgence of interest in the 1980s, without any obvious link with the earlier Humboldtian tradition. This renewed interest arose out of a universal disenchantment over the way languages (but especially the mother tongue) were taught in schools and academic institutions. Calls for reform had been heard from the early 1960s onwards. These demands had been expressed most clearly and consistently in the UK and had resulted in a new and detailed teaching programme called *Language in Use* in which the functional linguist Michael Halliday had also had a hand. The aim of the course was defined as 'to develop in pupils and students awareness of what language is and how it is used and at the same time, to extend their competence in handling the language' (Doughty et al., 1971, pp. 8–9).

Subsequent studies carried out in the UK and elsewhere have demonstrated that there is a close correlation between the home background of the learner and underachievement, with 'adult time' as an important predictor of school failure. These findings pointed to the need for a much greater awareness among teachers as well as parents, of how children's use of language and the school's attitude to language interact to affect learning (Hawkins, 1984, pp. 16–17). It was thought that LA, as a separate subject in the school curriculum and as a course for parents, would cater to just this need.

What would this 'new' element do? It would provide a common ground for discussing language issues in a common vocabulary, thus bridging the gap between English, ethnic minority mother tongues, foreign languages (including 'dead' languages), and English as a second language. It would offer a forum where language diversity could be discussed, so that linguistic prejudice and parochialism could be challenged. On top of that it would seek to give learners confidence in grasping the formal patterns in language, especially as such insight had been shown to be a key element in foreign language learning aptitude. Contrastive procedures could be helpful in bringing out any differences (Hawkins, 1984, p. 4).

Observe that the above is rather a statement of what LA does than what it is. (The definition quoted earlier, put forward in 1985 by the British Consortium of Centres for Language Awareness, quite legitimately, states its *nature*). It is also obvious that Hawkins takes a broad view of LA (not just attending to the language system, but to the socio-cultural function of language), in the way that Royen (1947) did.

The next important landmark in the history of recent LA was the appearance of Ronald Carter's reader *Knowledge about Language and the Curriculum* (Carter, 1990). It is a collection of sixteen accessible essays designed to boost teachers' confidence and to provide them with the theoretical basis on which they may organize their classroom practice. An analysis of each of the articles is beyond the scope of the present survey and a brief discussion of the chief aims and the main assumptions underlying this reader must therefore suffice. The book falls into two parts: part one addresses issues of KAL (i.e. knowledge about language) for learners in primary and secondary schools. Issues addressed are: the interface hypothesis, syllabus content, LA methodologies, and KAL and its relationship to CLA (see Clark and Ivanic, Wallace, both in this volume). Part two is predominantly concerned with teachers' KAL and treats such matters as: early language development, the four skills, multilingualism, language and social groups, spoken and written language.

It is extremely difficult to extract a definition of KAL from this book; none of the authors seems willing to commit her/himself. On p. 23 there occurs a kind of paraphrase of KAL: 'Knowing things about language. Being interested in and informed about language'. This statement is modi-fied on p. 27, where it is said that the 'most important kind of knowledge about language is implicit knowledge'. For further discussion, see the next section.

Following Halliday, the authors take a functional view of language. This means that there is a preponderant concern with language variation, and the uses and functions of language are stressed *vis-à-vis* the forms of language. Emphasis is placed on the description of language in social contexts rather than on that of isolated decontextualised bits of language. CLA is promoted: being more explicitly informed about the sources of attitudes to language, about its uses and misuses, about how language is used to manipulate, can 'empower' learners to see through language to the ideologies that particular stylistic choices embody. On top of this KAL should promote experiential learning, exploratory and reflective encounters with language.

The LINC (i.e. Language in the National Curriculum) project, of which the book under review is the outgrowth, aims at enhancing teachers' understanding and KAL in relation to processes of teaching and learning. KAL will provide them with a shared frame of reference in which to discuss language issues, and assist them in discussing such issues with parents (Carter, 1990, pp. 3–4).

Recent American studies dealing with LA are Rutherford (1987) and van Lier (1995). van Lier, perhaps unwittingly, continues the Dutch tradition. His book aims at helping learners and teachers to understand how language is used as a tool, how it relates to life's central activities, from learning to thinking to social relationships. Employing LA activities, the book is in itself a LA-raising exercise. It deals with a variety of LA and CLA aspects.

In the context of second language grammar teaching, Rutherford (1987) uses the term 'grammatical consciousness-raising' to denote the processes whereby the learner raises grammatical operations to the level of consciousness. Rutherford convincingly shows that a grammatical syllabus need not rule out a process approach. On the contrary it would nicely dovetail with a discourse process approach (cf. McCarthy & Carter, 1994).

PROBLEMS AND PRACTICAL DIFFICULTIES

In this section we shall address the moot question of the relationship between consciously learned and unconsciously used knowledge (see also the contributions by Ellis and Gombert in this volume). Many workers in the field (e.g. Richmond [in Carter, 1990]; Stainton, 1992) would hold that LA is concerned with explicit or conscious knowledge (and this is how we defined it in the introduction) and 'knowledge about language' (KAL) rather with implicit or unconscious knowledge. In the latter case it would border on 'linguistic sense', or Chomsky's knowledge of language, and it would be the teacher's job to help the learner's implicit knowledge of language to develop. But here an important epistemological question arises: what **is** the difference between conscious and unconscious knowledge if we can help the latter to develop by means of the former? Does one not thus create a learner who can say '**What** I must know I can describe explicitly, but **how** I get to know it I cannot tell. Cannot tell because (a) I cannot analyse what I am doing or (b) I do not care to analyse it'. Does this not mean then that the teacher has to go about the development of implicit knowledge in a haphazard way, leaving it to chance for it to actually develop? Or does he have to create the 'rich linguistic environment' known from the Chomskyan linguistics of the 1960s or the level of comprehensible input known in the literature as 'i + 1' (e.g. Krashen, 1982)? Further, is implicit knowledge perhaps the final product of an explicit process?

Is it appropriate to call 'knowledge' a process? To make matters even more complex, some researchers (Butzkamm, 1993, pp. 101–104; Green & Hecht, 1993, p. 140) postulate a whole range of (interrelated) levels of awareness.

Be this as it may, the questions of levels of awareness or of whether there is any seepage between conscious and unconscious knowledge (known as the Interface Hypothesis) or of whether there is also an **intuitive** awareness that the learner cannot explicitly articulate (Nicholas, 1992), cannot be resolved here and now. But at least one comes in for somewhat closer scrutiny here: the Interface Hypothesis. This hypothesis, launched by Krashen (1982, p. 83) holds that there is no interface between conscious and unconscious knowledge, that conscious knowledge can therefore never become unconscious knowledge, so that 'learning' and 'acquisition' are entirely independent of one another. The non-interface position thereby rejects any useful role for conscious LA activities.

Other researchers (for a review, see Larsen-Freeman & Long, 1991, p. 324), on the other hand, uphold the interface position, believing that carry-over of *some* sort does take place. They point to empirical evidence to substantiate this claim (for a discussion, see James & Garrett, 1992, p. 243ff.) As we noted above this question cannot be settled conclusively until it is made clear what is meant by (un)conscious knowledge.

Another big problem is the diversity of interpretations and implementations of LA in schools. A lesson may be drawn from the ostensible failure of LA experiments in three comprehensive schools in the Netherlands (see Diephuis, 1986, p. 57ff.). As a possible cause of their lack of success I may point to the existence at these schools, alongside each other, of a LA element calling for the explicit comparison of the learner's native language with other languages, and a communication oriented unilingual language pedagogy, ignoring if not banning, such comparison. In any event, it was left to the learners to reconcile the two opposing viewpoints. But any attempt to introduce LA into a school's curriculum without resolving the potential disparity between the two approaches may prove counterproductive. This is far from a peripheral issue. It is a crucial one, which curriculum developers and teachers alike need to monitor carefully.

FUTURE DIRECTIONS IN RESEARCH AND PRACTICE

The reader who, after these reflections, remains sceptical about the value of LA work should bear in mind that much of what today constitutes received educational wisdom or is common practice in the language classroom has never been evaluated for its effectiveness. In the past, many successful educational innovations started as hunches, intuitions, or inspirations, or indeed as oracular statements by gurus (cf. James & Garrett, 1992, p. 307).

Does this mean we do not have to evaluate LA work? No. What it does mean is first of all that LA is to be firmly implanted in teacher education, and that a workable definition should be agreed on by all concerned. Besides, LA must be seen to *work*. Research and evaluation (preferably in the workaday conditions of the classroom) go hand in hand here. Any evaluation of LA work done before 1992 was reported in the reader by James & Garrett (1992). More recently most (evaluation of) LA work has appeared in *Language Awareness*, a journal with an international editorial board, founded at the round table referred to in the introduction, and published by Multilingual Matters in the UK.

James & Garrett (1992, p. 307) point to the 'major benefit' that might accrue from a positive evaluation of LA work: the proof with which to convince sceptical colleagues of its value. The establishment of national and regional centres for LA may be an important step in the dissemination of information about LA, in uniting authorities and teachers on a definition, and in helping teachers to overcome any misgivings about LA. But the setting up of such centres will require extra funding. And will this be forthcoming?

It has been argued that LA is just the means to an end, never the end itself. And that, whatever it is that is raised to consciousness, is not to be regarded as an artifact or object of study to be memorised by the learner and to be recalled by him/her whenever sentences are to be produced. Rather, what is raised to the level of consciousness is not so much the product (Humboldt's *ergon*) as aspects of the process (Humboldt's *energeia*) (cf. Rutherford, 1987, p. 104). LA activities should aim to be consistent with this principle.

Conscious language learning has, traditionally, been focused on the 'nuts and bolts' of language (i.e. phonology, morphology, syntax, discourse) emphasizing formal correctness. But full mastery of a language, any language, can only come as a result of understanding its nature and function, of being aware of what it is and what it does, for us and for others (van Lier, 1995). It is unlikely that such understanding will evolve by mere exposure to the language. At least some things will have to be taught explicitly and learned consciously.

In the meantime research carried out under experimental conditions could give us interesting sidelights on the differences between conscious 'learning' and unconscious 'acquisition' (cf. McLaughlin, 1987, p. 22).

University of Groningen
The Netherlands

REFERENCES

Butzkamm, W.: 1993, *Psycholinguistik des Fremdsprachenunterrichts* (second edition), Francke Verlag, Tübingen/Basel.

Candelier, M.: 1992, 'Language awareness and language policy in the European context: A French point of view', *Language Awareness* 1(1), 27–32.

Carter, R.: 1990, *Knowledge about Language and the Curriculum*, Hodder & Stoughton, Sevenoaks.

Diephuis, R. (ed.): 1986, *Language Awareness: wat is dat?*, SLO, Enschede.

Doughty, P. et al. (eds.): 1971, *Language in Use*, Edward Arnold, London.

Drach, E.: 1937, *Grundgedanken der deutschen Satzlehre*, Diesterweg, Frankfurt/Main.

Fairclough, N. (ed.): 1992, *Critical Language Awareness*, Longman, London.

Green, P.S. & Hecht, K.: 'Language awareness of German pupils', *Language Awareness* 2(3), 125–142.

Hawkins, E.: 1984, *Awareness of Language: An Introduction*, Cambridge University Press, Cambridge.

Hildebrand, R.: 1867, *Vom deutschen Sprachunterricht in der Schule und von deutscher Erziehung und Bildung überhaupt*, Tauchnitz, Leipzig.

James C. & Garrett, P.: 1992, *Language Awareness in the Classroom*, Longman, London.

Jespersen, O.: 1904, *How to Teach a Foreign language*, Allen & Unwin, London.

Krashen, S.: 1982, *Principles and Practice in Second Language Acquisition*, Pergamon Press, Oxford.

Langeveld, M.J.: 1934, *Taal en Denken*, Wolters, Groningen.

Larsen-Freeman, D. & Long, M.H.: 1991, *An Introduction to Second Language Acquisition Research*, Longman, London.

McCarthy, M. & Carter, R.: 1994, *Language as Discourse: Perspectives for Language Teaching*, Longman, London.

McLaughlin, B.: 1987, *Theories of Second Language Learning*, Edward Arnold, London.

Nicholas, H.: 1992, 'Language Awareness and Second Language Development', in C. James & P. Garrett (eds.), *Language Awareness in the Classroom*, Longman, London, 78–95.

Palmer, H.E.: 1917, *The Scientific Study and Teaching of Languages*, Harrap, London.

Palmer, H.E.: 1922, *The Principles of Language Study*, Harrap, London.

Royen, G.: 1947, *Taalkundig inzicht voor school en leven*, Zwijsen, Tilburg.

Rutherford, W.E.: 1987, *Second Language Grammar: Learning and Teaching*, Longman, London.

Stainton, C.: 1992, 'Language awareness: Genre awareness – A focused review of the literature', *Language Awareness* 1(2), 109–121.

Steinthal, H. (ed.): 1884, *Die sprachphilosophischen Werke Wilhelm's von Humboldt*, Dümmler, Berlin.

Stutterheim, C.F.P.: 1954, *Taalbeschouwing en taalbeheersing*, Meulenhoff, Amsterdam.

Sweet, H.: 1899, *The Practical Study of Languages*, Dent, London.

Van den Bosch, J.H.: 1903, 'Methodologie van het moedertaal-onderwijs in de eerste klasse h.b.s. en gymnasium', *Taal en Letteren* 13, 145–158.

Van Essen, A.J.: 1995, 'Language awareness in Holland: Evolution and trends', *Toegepaste Taalwetenschap in Artikelen* 51, 9–26.

Van Lier, L.: 1995, *Introducing Language Awareness*, Harmondsworth, Penguin Books.

Von der Gabelentz, G.: 1901, *Die Sprachwissenschaft*, Tauchnitz, Leipzig.

JOHN WALMSLEY

PEDAGOGICAL GRAMMAR: FROM PRESCRIPTIVE TO DESCRIPTIVE

The interest in Pedagogical Grammars or Grammar (PG) reflects a growing sensitivity to the role which grammars play at the point of interaction between the learner, the material to be learned, and the teacher. Among the issues which engage the attention of applied linguists and teachers are whether PG should be descriptive or prescriptive, the proper relation between PG and other kinds of grammar, the psycholinguistic foundations for learning via explicit grammar teaching, the nature and choice of the object to be taught (linguistic selection), and the macro- and micro-organization of a grammar. Attention has to be divided between what people argue ought to be done (theory), what people do in practice, and attempts to answer the above questions empirically (research) (see reviews by Shirai and by Schachter in Volume 4).

EARLY HISTORY

It is probably safe to assume that all or most early grammars (Greek and Latin) started from some pedagogical purpose. Although later grammars were written for teaching Latin or Greek as second – and not only as first – languages, it was some centuries before grammars were produced explicitly with the non-native user in mind.

The Renaissance, and the advent of printing, gave a strong impetus to this development. Most early descriptions of vernacular languages were written with the aim of facilitating communication between travellers, merchants, etc. The rapid increase in the production of grammars during the sixteenth and seventeenth centuries was perceived in Europe as a source of terminological, theoretical, and methodological confusion. In England, Henry VIII decreed that only one grammar – Lily's – should be licensed for teaching Latin in schools. In Germany, the same perception led not to a single imposed solution for the Holy Roman Empire, but to conscious attempts to didacticise grammar – i.e. to strip it to its essentials, and to 'harmonize' or unify the grammatical terminology (and with it the grammatical categories) used to teach different languages. One may see in this period, then, early attempts to produce PGs designed to accommodate the requirements of the learner, in contradistinction to conventional grammars, which simply recorded 'the facts'.

L. van Lier and D. Corson (eds), Encyclopedia of Language and Education,
Volume 6: Knowledge about Language, 11–20.
© 1997 Kluwer Academic Publishers. Printed in the Netherlands.

The vernaculars were not universally installed as curriculum subjects in European schools and universities until the nineteenth century. This development accentuated the gap between descriptive grammars and the requirements of schools. Curtius wrote his Greek grammar explicitly, 'to make fruitful for practical teaching purposes at least some of the results from comparative linguistics' (Curtius, 1852, p. iv). Viëtor was one of the first to concentrate on the tensions between 'scientific grammar' and PG in his paper 'Scientific grammar and English teaching' (Viëtor, 1880).

FROM 1900 TO THE PRESENT

The main developments in theory were concerned with the relation between grammar and lexicon, the nature of first and second language acquisition, the elimination of error, and the nature of PG and its relations with other disciplines.

The most influential tendency in grammar during the first half of this century was the divorce of syntax from meaning. In PG this led to an emphasis on structure and associationist or behaviourist methods, which was reinforced by developments in psychology. In Halliday et al. (1964) a clear distinction was drawn between *lexis* and *grammar*, and related to the distinction between open and closed lexical classes or sets. This accentuated the distinction between grammar and lexicon. An exception to this trend was Palmer (1938), who recognized that lexemes, too, have grammar, and that major lexical items cannot be learned successfully in isolation from the structures they control.

Language acquisition research was to sharpen the distinction between behaviourist and mentalist views of how language is acquired. Indirectly, it led to two different approaches, still identifiable, one of which has crystallized into PG. The first locates the linguistic material on the level of *objectives*, and embeds these in systematic progression in different *content*. PG by contrast makes the linguistic material the object of study, on the assumption that some kind of transfer will take place from conscious knowledge to linguistic competence (the Teachability Hypothesis). At this stage, however, the task of PG was seen as providing exercises to develop habits, rather than descriptions or explanations of language.

Structuralism made its influence felt in the Contrastive Structure Series (Chicago University Press). Based on the old hypothesis that any two languages share much in common, so that teaching can be concentrated on areas of difference, this series provided contrastive accounts of the grammar and phonologies of pairs of languages. Theoretical and practical difficulties with this approach led to Contrastive Analysis being superseded by Error Analysis (EA) – research into the *actual* errors made by second language acquirers – and a comparison of these with errors made by native acquirers. Similarities between these patterns across speakers of different languages resulted in the Developmental Hypothesis (DH), according to which learners/acquirers with different mother tongues pass – on the basis of their 'in-built syllabus' (Corder, 1967) – through largely similar stages of acquisition.

The 60s saw serious attempts to test empirically the efficacy of conscious learning (Cognitive Code) as opposed to habit-formation (Audio-visual) theories. The fact that neither could be shown to have a decisive advantage suggests that effective teaching may be due more to the individual teacher rather than to the method. It was also during the 60s that Pedagogical Grammar itself began to emerge as a focus of attention (Mossel, 1960).

The new focus on PG led to vigorous discussion of definitory, curricular, and typological issues. Among the issues debated were what PG actually is (or should be); its relation to descriptive linguistics on the one hand and classroom texts on the other; how PG should be approached (from linguistics or from education); and what other kinds of grammar PG could be related to ('didactic grammar', 'school grammar', 'reference grammar,' etc.).

Major directions in research were signalled by attempts to reorganize syllabuses along notional-communicative lines on the one hand, and to produce PGs as material for the teacher, if not the learner, on the other (Edmondson et al., 1977). Whether the material thus presented was intended to be wrapped in some other content, or made the object of direct study by the learner, is not always stated. Rutherford and Sharwood Smith by contrast, propagated the necessity of 'consciousness raising' (CR) in language learning (Rutherford, 1987; Sharwood Smith, 1981). PG in this sense stands in conflict with the Developmental Hypothesis, and research was carried out to find out how resistant the 'in-built syllabus' is to the teaching of items in an order different from that of the DH (Hahn, 1982; Pienemann, 1989).

Prescriptivism, too, became an issue during this period, but the topic suffered from a lack of focus. For some, it concerned the choice of a variety of a language as a model for teaching. For others, it meant a teacher's reluctance to correct a learner's utterance, because 'She catched a cold' is as good as 'She caught a cold' (Quirk, 1990, p. 9). Superficial liberalism of this kind must be seen not only from the teacher's but also the learner's point of view: if language teaching is business, at least as much respect needs to be paid to the rights of the customer as to what the teacher wants to teach.

RECENT WORK

In recent years several typologies for PG have been put forward. The features proposed to distinguish PGs include whether the grammar is associated with a course book or not; whether it is intended for the hands of the teacher or for self-instruction; and what its chief aims are – correct speech, enhanced communication through analysis, the development of the conventional 'four skills', or the teaching of grammar *per se*.

The need to prescribe has been associated by a number of authors with the emancipatory function of a standard variety (Quirk, 1990). Complicating the picture is the fact that – certainly as far as foreign language teaching (FLT) is concerned – one can associate prescriptive attitudes with grammars which have been written on either a prescriptive or a descriptive basis.

Beyond the question of the use to be made of a grammatical description lie the questions of what is to be described and how. The variety to be chosen as model is a matter for the authors, publishers, or countries concerned. But the question of how the object is to be described is increasingly a subject of debate. Viëtor's (1880) sketch exhausted itself in phonology and inflection: it never got as far as syntax. In this century, the sentence – ('the largest unit over which constructional relations hold', Matthews, 1981, p. 29) – as opposed to the *word* has become the main focus of attention. Recently, however, the sentence itself has come under attack, with the result that greater emphasis is laid on communicative, functional, or notional categories. There seems to be growing agreement that future grammars are going to be increasingly discourse or function orientated. The most comprehensive and fruitful model of linguistic description proposed so far seems to be that developed by Halliday, which permits grammatical choices to be related to the ideational, interpersonal and textual (meta-) functions of language.

These developments find their reflection in a diversity of practical grammars. The differences become apparent at both the macro (organization of the grammar) and the micro (presentation) level. The *Larousse* grammar (Chevalier et al., 1964) exhibits a traditional organization – even including historical information and examples – but is distinguished by its clear layout, with rule and example set off by the type. Leech and Svartvik work from meaning to form, and from concepts to discourse – a feature they share with the COBUILD grammar. Nevertheless, both concentrate predominantly on relations within the sentence and say little about the organization of larger units of discourse or text(s). Graustein (1976) starts from the 'dialectic of both system and social activity', but the movement towards discourse remains largely a gesture ('communication types'). Werlich (1976), on the other hand, is almost unique in the direction of its presentation: from context, via text-type, text-group and text-form to composition.

Murphy (1985) is self-instructional and course-independent. Its layout, with brief explanations facing related exercises on opposite pages, reflects its pedagogical intentions. In starting from forms, Murphy presupposes knowledge of the grammatical subsystems to be practised, which are largely restricted to the parts of speech and associated grammatical categories (tense, mood etc.) Both the COBUILD grammar (1990) and Downing & Locke (1992) pay attention to pedagogical considerations. This comes out particularly clearly in the COBUILD grammar both in its concern with terminology and in the manner of address (second person 'you'; cf. Zimmermann & Wissner-Kurzawa, 1985). On the micro level, the text is carefully constructed round concise statements, with subheadings in the margins and informative 'Usage notes'.

Downing & Locke (1992) is probably one of the most complete current exemplars of PG for students. It exhibits a clear, function based approach which allows it to work from systematic presentations of meanings in discourse to the forms which express them. Each module contains an initial summary, a discursive presentation, and exercises. Since answers are included, as in Murphy (1985), the book can be used self-instructionally.

In some areas, the results of empirical research flow into the construction of actual grammars; in other respects, the production of grammars seems to proceed parallel to – but not immediately influenced by – ongoing research. Most of the grammars mentioned were produced on the assumption that conscious knowledge about language enhances the capacity to apply it in communicative practice. However, views differ as to how effective the teaching of grammar can be in foreign language learning. Empirical results are still too sparse to permit definite conclusions to be drawn. Current research concentrates chiefly on the possible interplay between formal instruction and second language development. In this 'dual competence' model (Sharwood Smith, 1981; cf. Ellis, 1988), the issue turns on the transfer or conversion of conscious knowledge into skills which can be applied in actual language use. However, care has to be taken to identify just what it is that is being influenced. Evidence suggests that the effectiveness of formal instruction differs according to whether the developmental sequence ('route of acquisition'), proficiency, or speed of acquisition ('rate') is examined. While it appears that proficiency and rate of learning can be influenced, the 'inbuilt syllabus' (as revealed in the developmental sequence) seems to be remarkably robust. There nevertheless remains a widespread view that formal instruction has a useful contribution to make to the language learning process. For this to be convincingly demonstrated, greater attention probably needs to be paid to the balance of available speech in the learner's environment inside and outside the institutional setting ('pure' vs. 'impure') and (within the institutional setting) to the varying uses of language ('communicative' vs. 'model').

From a practical point of view, complaints are made that whereas scholars, when assessing a grammar, concentrate on the nature of the linguistic theory, the contextualization of sentences, the balance between speech and written language, and the accommodation of communicative intentions, users (teachers, learners and parents) are more interested in how easy it is to access information in the grammar, the relationship between rule and example, and whether the text is easily understood. Significantly, the user group seems to be much interested in the elimination of error, less so in whether the rules are accurate or plausible.

At the macro organizational level, the index is a tool of fundamental importance for the grammar user. But a considerable amount is also known about the presentation of information at the micro level. The nature and packaging of rule and example and the relations between them, the size of paragraphs, when to emphasize context and when not, have all been commented on. From the user's point of view, the terminology should be as uncomplicated and conventional as possible, and should be clearly defined.

UNRESOLVED PROBLEMS

The fact that the discipline has to date largely skated round the problem of defining PG has its consequences for research. Unstated assumptions leave the way open to different and even conflicting strategies. Further, the point at which research results are turned into strategy depends crucially upon the assumptions underlying the research. Certain of these areas remain largely unexplored. One such is the question of the relationship between linguistic theory and PG. With few exceptions (e.g. Halliday's grammar, mentioned above) the two strands develop side by side with little or no apparent contact. The history of FLT, however, shows that changes in linguistic theory do leave their mark on language teaching, even if the time and manner are not always predictable. The consequences of different theories of grammar for PG – and their associated terminologies – thus remains an unresolved problem. One result seems to be that only fragmentary descriptions are offered as examples of how the various theories would treat the material: scarcely any PG to date has come up with a comprehensive alternative syllabus for teaching a foreign language from scratch.

The Teachability Hypothesis constitutes a second area of uncertainty. One can divide the views into two broad camps: the proponents of the 'interface' hypothesis (Sharwood Smith, 1981), and their opponents (e.g. Krashen, cf. Ellis, 1988 – and see the contribution by Ellis, this volume). The issues have become so involved that it is difficult to see how the question can be empirically investigated. In those areas where research has led to reasonably reliable results (on e.g. the route, proficiency, and rate of learning/acquisition), a number of unanswered questions still remain. Even though 'classroom learners in general do better than street learners', the results do not explain why this should be so. And the research on comparative rates of learning leaves uncomfortable gaps. While there have been some comparative studies of different methods, there has been little interest in comparing the effectiveness of any method as against no method at all.

Despite the fact that formal instruction seems to have little influence upon the route learners follow when acquiring language, Nunan (1994) argues for it, claiming that other considerations – psycholinguistic or pedagogical – play a role when instruction is being planned. One might also argue that PG might serve different purposes at different stages of learning (initial – intermediate – advanced). Finally, the effectiveness of PG may differ according to whether spoken or written discourse is the focus of attention.

A final area of uncertainty concerns the mode of presentation and teaching. Conventionally, rules have a significant function in PG. If, however, as has been argued, rules are scarcely ever foolproof and may even be counterproductive, a new area of uncertainty opens up – namely, what do learners actually do with the information we feed to them? How do they move from 'skill-getting' to 'skill-using' (Rivers & Temperley 1978)? And what do they do when it leads to wrong results?

FUTURE DIRECTIONS

It has been observed that PG does not have a coherent research programme (Odlin, 1994). Not unlike some other disciplines, such as Applied Linguistics, PG seems to define itself differently in different environments. While there is much to be said for adopting a nonprescriptive attitude to the definition of PG, it must also be recognized that without a purposeful definition the label is available for unrestrained use for marketing purposes, regardless of the content of the work being marketed. Further, even if a consensus is not essential, it is incumbent on every researcher or author to make explicit the assumptions which underlie their concept of PG. A clear understanding of the postulated role of PG is a prerequisite for purposeful research strategies.

One area in which change is becoming apparent is in the starting point for grammatical description. It is not enough simply to put a description of some grammatical phenomenon on the table and to teach from it. The teaching can only be as accurate as the description it is based on. PG has developed in the context of a broader swing away from Structuralism and towards Universalism and Notionalism (Walmsley, 1994). PG descriptions made under the influence of Structuralism start from the form and work towards meaning. The danger of this approach lies in the fact that while many worthwhile insights are obtained, they are too often not systematically connected: one arrives at almost as many meanings as contexts. It is worth considering in how far an accomplished PG presentation could work instead from a constrained notional description – in the sense of Jespersen (1924) – towards the forms expressing the meanings. A parallel shift in emphasis in descriptive grammar, from syntax to the lexicon, may also prove fruitful for PG. Since members of the major form-classes possess individual lexical properties, it may prove easier to present the classes concerned on a notional semantic basis than in terms of conventional syntax (cf. Dixon, 1991).

A second area of development shows greater emphasis being placed on the spoken language, in the tradition of Palmer (1924), and a continued move towards discourse-, data- or corpus-driven grammars, in the tradition of Quirk et al. (1985). A number of new publications in these areas by Brazil, Carter, and McCarthy and others have either appeared or are expected to appear shortly (e.g. Carter & McCarthy, 1994; Mindt, 1995, the COBUILD family of grammars).

A third area of interest and in need of research concerns the nature of the learning process. We need to know more about how instruction based on the acknowledged differences between L1A and L2A can be integrated into users' competence, and ultimately performance. How do they make use of positive and negative evidence, and how do they react to various feedback transforms? We need to learn more about the difficulties L2 learners face, and the information they require to overcome them, particularly in view of the difficulties they have in recognizing a given usage – of their own, or someone else's – in terms of a rule – 'analyzing a token in terms of a type' (Odlin, 1994, p. 316). Since grammars, too, are textbooks, PG might also profit from the research which has been done into the accessibility of texts in other subjects (Davies & Greene, 1984). This question, though, on the level of the micro organization of PG, presupposes one particular interpretation of the role of PG.

Finally, if the relationship between prescription and description is not to suffer further misinterpretation, then PG needs properly trained practitioners. To be effective, these practitioners require a sound foundation in linguistics to optimize the quality of the linguistic description, a solid background in second language acquisition research in order to be able to apply the most appropriate methods, and pedagogical skill – the ability to teach PG in engaging ways (Nunan, 1994; and cf. also the contribution by Ellis in this volume).

University of Bielefeld
Germany

REFERENCES

Carter, R. & McCarthy, M.: 1994, *Language as Discourse: Perspectives for Language Teaching*, Longman, London.

Chevalier, J.C., Arrivé, M., Blanche-Benveniste, C. & Peytard, J.: 1964, *Grammaire Larousse du Français Contemporain*, Larousse, Paris.

Collins COBUILD English Grammar: 1990, J. McH. Sinclair (ed.), William Collins, London & Glasgow.

Corder, S.P.: 1967, 'The significance of learners' errors', *International Review of Applied Linguistics* V, 161–169.

Curtius, G.: 1852, *Griechische Schulgrammatik*, Tempsky, Prague.

Davies, F.I. & Greene, T.: 1984, *Reading for Learning in the Sciences*, Oliver & Boyd, Edinburgh.

Dixon, R.M.W.: 1991, *A New Approach to English Grammar, on Semantic Principles*, Clarendon Press, Oxford.

Downing, A. & Locke, P.: 1992, *A University Course in English Grammar*, Prentice-Hall, New York.

Edmondson, W., House, J., Kasper, G. & McKeown, J.: 1977, *A Pedagogic Grammar of the English Verb. A Handbook for the German Secondary Teacher of English*, Narr, Tübingen.

Ellis, R.: 1988, *Classroom Second Language Development*, Prentice-Hall, New York.

Graustein, G. et al.: 1976, *English Grammar. A University Handbook*, VEB Verlag Enzyklopädie, Leipzig.

Hahn, A.: 1982, *Fremdsprachenunterricht und Spracherwerb: linguistische Untersuchungen zum gesteuerten Zweitsprachenerwerb*, Passau, Diss.

Halliday, M.A.K., McIntosh, A. & Strevens, P.D.: 1964, *The Linguistic Sciences and Language Teaching*, Longman, London.

Jespersen, O.: 1924, *The Philosophy of Grammar*, George Allen & Unwin, London.

Matthews, P.H.: 1981, *Syntax*, Cambridge University Press, Cambridge.

Mindt, D.: 1995, *An Empirical Grammar of the English Verb. Modal Verbs*, Cornelsen, Berlin.

Mossel, R.: 1960, 'Pédagogie des langues étrangères et linguistique', *International Review of Education* 6, 309–317.

Murphy, R.: 1985, *English Grammar in Use*, Cambridge University Press, Cambridge.

Nunan, D.: 1994, 'Linguistic theory and pedagogic practice', in T. Odlin (ed.), 253–270.

Odlin, T. (ed.): 1994, *Perspectives on Pedagogical Grammar*, Cambridge University Press, Cambridge.

Palmer, H.E.: 1938, *A Grammar of English Words*, Longmans, Green & Co., London.

Palmer, H.E.: 1924, *A Grammar of Spoken English, on a Strictly Phonetic Basis*, Heffer, Cambridge.

Pienemann, M.: 1989, 'Is language teachable? Psycholinguistic experiments and hypotheses', *Applied Linguistics* 10, 52–79.

Quirk, R.: 1990, 'Language varieties and standard language', *English Today* 6, 3–10.

Quirk, R., Greenbaum, S., Leech, G.N. & Svartvik, J.: 1985, *A Comprehensive Grammar of the English Language*. Longman, London.

Rivers, W. & Temperley, M.: 1978, *A Practical Guide to the Teaching of English*, Oxford University Press, London.

Rutherford, W.: 1987, *Second Language Grammar: Learning and Teaching*, Longman, Harlow.

Sharwood Smith, M.: 1981, 'Consciousness-raising and the second-language learner', *Applied Linguistics* II, 159–168.

Viëtor, W.: 1880, 'Die wissenschaftliche Grammatik und der englische Unterricht', *Englische Studien* III, 106–124.

Walmsley, J.B.: 1994, 'Parameters or continuum? English grammatical thought since Henry Sweet', in G. Blaicher & R. Glaser (eds.), *Anglistentag 1993 Eichstätt. Proceedings*, Niemeyer, Tübingen, 100–115.

Werlich, E.: 1976, *A Text Grammar of English*, Quelle & Meyer, Heidelberg.

Zimmermann, G. & Wissner-Kurzawa, E.: 1985, *Grammatik: lehren – lernen – selbst lernen*, Hueber, Munich.

B. GILLIAN DONMALL-HICKS

THE HISTORY OF LANGUAGE AWARENESS IN THE UNITED KINGDOM

The term 'Language Awareness' (LA) came into widespread use in the United Kingdom in the early 1980s. A definition of the term was produced by the working party on LA of the National Congress on Languages in Education (NCLE), cited in the report of its work (Donmall, 1985), as follows: "Language Awareness is a person's sensitivity to and conscious awareness of the nature of language and its role in human life". During the four-year lifetime of this working party (1982–1986) and for some time after, the term, with this definition, was understood and used widely in schools and local education authorities in England, to an extent in Wales, Scotland, and Northern Ireland, also in some departments in institutions of Higher Education, which included Applied Linguistics, Education, Classics, and, though to a lesser extent in the Higher Education sector, English and Modern Languages. The Association for Language Awareness (ALA), whose formation in 1992 marked the culmination of the work of many in this field, defines LA as "explicit knowledge about language, ... conscious perception and sensitivity in language learning, language teaching, and language use" (1996 publicity sheet of the Association). These definitions point to the far-reaching implications of LA for the individual not only within Education but also in all areas of life.

DEVELOPMENTS UP TO 1986 AND MAJOR CONTRIBUTIONS

Language Awareness (LA) developed rapidly from an unknown term to one in common usage, with goals widely understood and shared by people involved in all areas of language. Several factors served to bring it about. First was the work of some noted academics such as Carter, Doughty, Halliday, Hawkins, Perera, Sinclair, and Tinkel. Second was the report of the Bullock Committee, *A Language for Life* (1975), which had a major impact on schools, third was the existence of the National Congress on Languages in Education (NCLE) as a facilitating body, fourth, the existence of government funding for NCLE, and finally, the willingness of teachers and academics to commit of their time and energies.

The report of the Bullock Committee which investigated the teaching of English became a major force in alerting the teaching profession as

L. van Lier and D. Corson (eds), Encyclopedia of Language and Education,
Volume 6: Knowledge about Language, 21–30.
© 1997 Kluwer Academic Publishers. Printed in the Netherlands.

a whole to the importance of language for the entire school curriculum, with proposals for language education programmes and for the training of teachers to carry them out.

In 1976, the National Congress on Languages in Education (NCLE) had been set up with the particular goal of building bridges between the disparate language groups which historically had operated alone. LA came into being as a direct result of cooperation and collaboration between those groups under the NCLE umbrella.

The Language Awareness working parties set up by NCLE (1981–1986) solicited papers to further the theoretical underpinning of LA. In addition, they responded to the groundswell of enthusiasm amongst teachers by promoting the LA work of seven 'core' schools, by carrying out a survey in England to ascertain where LA initiatives of any kind were in operation (it was widespread throughout England and there was also significant work in parts of Wales, Scotland, and Northern Ireland) and by producing a series of newsletters. They drew up an annotated bibliography, a programme for the evaluation of LA courses and a list of speakers, and organised a conference in Leeds. The first cycle of work was published in book form under Donmall's editorship in 1985.

The coining of the new term, Language Awareness, marked out a new interest in language and by mid-1986 it had acquired the dimensions and features of a movement, whose goals were to promote LA as a field worthy of study in its own right, as a vital factor in the teaching and learning of all subjects in the curriculum and as the area of commonality of the discrete language fields. In the affective domain, schools sought to overcome prejudice and bring about an appreciation of the richness and diversity of British languages other than English, also to overcome problems aroused by difference, e.g. between the language of home and school. In sum, LA was viewed as an enabling field, designed to facilitate people's access to one another through language, to make available the language to talk about language, and to reduce jargon. Its starting point was the removal of barriers, which was to remain its essence.

Methodological approaches for the teaching and learning of LA, built on foundations laid by Tinkel, were widely agreed among teachers. Indeed, one of the strengths of the LA movement lay in the fact that practising schoolteachers perceived sufficient benefits in it to find teaching time for it within existing subject allocations even though it was not a GCSE (General Certificate of Secondary Education) examination subject.

Ventures included: LA courses in secondary school as an introduction to learning a specific language or as part of an English as Mother Tongue programme, LA as part of children's language development in primary schools, LA work bridging the gap between primary and secondary school, sixth form LA courses, LA as a particular feature in language-across-the-curriculum programmes, and LA as an element of a preparation for parenthood course. In addition, the Oxford and Cambridge Schools Examination Board piloted an AO examination entitled *Principles of Language*.

Teacher enthusiasm was not matched by knowledge and skills to lead LA courses. NCLE therefore supported a working party, chaired by Christopher Brumfit, to examine implications for teacher training to put right this deficit (Brumfit, 1988: see the reviews by Brumfit in this volume and by Widdowson in Volume 4).

During this period schools were at the forefront of developments and teachers were the driving force. However, there were interesting developments in Higher Education too, such as the degree course in Applied Language at Brighton Polytechnic.

LA at home was complemented by initiatives abroad. Contact was made with groups working similarly in Holland and New Zealand, for example. A less positive picture from Australia pointed to pitfalls which the UK would do well to avoid. In particular, LA should not be regarded as a means to resolving problems in foreign language learning (Quinn & Trounce, 1985, p. 132–141).

LATER DEVELOPMENTS AND MAJOR CONTRIBUTIONS: THE NEXT DECADE

(a) *The National Consortium of Centres for Language Awareness and the Association for Language Awareness*

In the summer of 1986, the working parties of NCLE ceased to exist. On their recommendation, a Centre for LA was set up with Gillian Donmall at King's College, London (later at the University of Derby), which became the fulcrum of a network of centres in England, Wales, Scotland, and Northern Ireland, known as the National Consortium of centres for Language Awareness (NCcLA), set up to further the movement by supporting local initiatives, by promoting LA as an item for inclusion in the National Curriculum which was being prepared, and by fostering LA as a recognised academic field.

In October, 1991, in response to developments abroad, NCcLA organised a European symposium in London, which was sponsored by the Goetheinstitut, the British Council and the French Embassy. It brought together 14 language experts from countries in Europe. Views on LA were aired, a shared understanding of the term was reached, and equivalent terms in 6 other languages were found (editorial, *Language Awareness* 1,1,3). Participants expressed support for the development of a European network of LA centres.

In 1992, NCcLA set up an international professional association, called the Association for Language Awareness (ALA), and inaugurated a new journal, *Language Awareness*, published by Multilingual Matters. The editorial of the first edition of the journal set out progress made in the first decade of LA's existence and scope for its future.

The Association has organised biennial international conferences on LA (Bangor, 1992; Plymouth, 1994; Dublin, 1996) and produces the journal (editor Peter Garrett). An LA database is currently being set up on Internet and an annotated LA bibliography has been updated by Richard Aplin and published in the second volume of the journal.

Although it was not formally disbanded, at the inception of the Association, NCcLA ceased to be active.

(b) *The broader national scene and the LINC project*

On the schools front the requirements of the National Curriculum were being planned. Both the Kingman Committee, which carried out a further investigation of the teaching of English (1988), and the National Curriculum Committee for English, chaired by Brian Cox (1989), made a conclusive case for pupils to learn about language as a part of all classroom work. Both recognised that, in order for it to be carried out as a separate profile component, teachers would have to receive the necessary training. They gave their support to this.

There followed a multi-million pound project, funded by the government, called Language in the National Curriculum (LINC), which was directed by Ronald Carter of the University of Nottingham. Its purpose was to draw up programmes, produce materials and to carry out a nationwide in-service teacher training project on a cascade model, following the Kingman recommendations, commencing with representatives chosen by every local education authority in the country. The project lasted three years. On its completion in 1992, however, the then Minister of State for Education exercised his right to refuse to allow publication of the materials. Stated reasons for this had to do with anxieties that materials intended for teachers might get into pupils' hands with damaging effects.

Despite this setback the project has had a significant impact. Carter has edited a book entitled *Knowledge about Language and the Curriculum: The LINC reader* (1990) which is complemented by the book *Looking into Language: Classroom approaches to KAL* (eds. Bain, Fitzgerald & Taylor, 1992). Materials published by the University of Nottingham together with training programmes are in use in many In-service and Initial Teacher Training courses (INSET and ITT) in this country and abroad. Classroom teaching materials related to the above are in use in a number of schools. However, LA has not assumed the significant place in the National Curriculum requirements for English (i.e. for pupils up to the age of 16) that Kingman, Cox, Carter and others had anticipated; the freestanding module which Cox had considered possible has not come into being. Neither has the anticipated coordinated approach to the training of teachers in regard to language for which LINC was the preparation, but the need has been recognised.

In contrast to the pre-16 situation, however, interest in language study in its own right at post-16 level is reflected in a burgeoning of A-level English language examinations.

With regard to Modern Foreign Languages (MFLs), the role for LA in the learning of another language envisaged in early proposals for MFLs in the National Curriculum has not been recognised in current requirements.

Whilst it may be argued that all LA work is, by its nature and intentions, critical, there have been some publications specifically on critical LA (see Clark and Ivanic, this volume; Wallace, this volume and reviews by Pennycook and by Janks in Volume 1 and by Norton in Volume 8).

On the research front, work is taking place in the field of learning styles, notable among which is the research of Sabine Jones at the University of Ulster at Coleraine carried out with undergraduate students of German which has led to experiential learning, raising awareness about communication and examining interactions within the learner. (See the review by Jones in this volume.)

Corpus linguistics is throwing up insights into language use based on multi-millions of examples. Statements about language in use can now be based on information, not theory, overcoming intuitions about language which have often been wrong. Rules are being discovered which license freedom of usage rather than avoidance of error.

The influence of LA in this decade can be found in a number of different areas. Examples include LA as a topic on the M.Ed. module *Modern Languages in the Curriculum* at the Queen's University, Belfast, and the B.Ed. Hons. Specialist option in Language at Trinity and All Souls College, Leeds and an LA module as part of the MFLs degree course at the University of Derby. In schools there have been projects such as 'LA across the curriculum' carried out by Terry Lamb at Highgate Wood School, and investigative work such as that carried out by Jim Anderson focusing on the John Roan School, Greenwich into the potential of LA as a focus for cross-curricular work in the secondary sector. *The Minus One to Five* project in Huntingdon, Cambridgeshire, is bringing together health and social services and Education staff to raise the awareness of parents about the early language needs of babies and to involve young mothers in activities to respond to them (Downes, 1994). Without the 'home' for LA since NCcLA ceased to be active, however, it is not possible to give a comprehensive overview of the current scene.

SOME WORK IN PROGRESS

1. *Language Awareness bibliography*
   A further bibliography of LA publications is being produced by Richard Aplin of the School of Education, University of Leicester, on behalf of ALA, annotated and arranged in new format, which will be available for purchase from the Association.

2. *Language Awareness database*
   A database of people's teaching and research interests in LA has been set up by Mike Scott on the Internet, under the address: http://www.liv.ac.uk/~ms 2928/ala.html. It is available for access now.

3. *Language Awareness and Corpus Analysis of Texts: University of Liverpool*

   (a) LA and patterns of lexis for the nonspecialist language user
       The work of Michael Hoey and Mike Scott aims to discover patterns of lexis in text, and to make effective applications to nonlinguists. Scott's work concerns in particular the category 'key word', something language users are aware of and rely on (Scott, 1996). This work looks to find ways of supporting them, e.g. in determining whether their use of key words is effective. Hoey's work leads to applications, e.g. in summarising (Hoey, 1991).

   (b) LA and the form of business communications
       The DIRECT project (Development of International Research in English for Commerce and Technology) is carried out by the University of Liverpool and the Catholic University of São Paolo, Brazil and addresses the form of business communications. The LA aspect of it concerns beliefs within the business community about the terminology in, and format of, their communications. This has led to a number of Working Papers surveying communication problems and the format and use of document types.

4. *Corpus Linguistics: Projects of COBUILD (Collins Birmingham University International Language Database)*
   COBUILD was founded in 1980 by Professor John Sinclair of the English Department of the University of Birmingham in collaboration with the publishing house, Collins, to set up and use a large corpus of naturally occurring English as a basis for descriptions of the language. The corpus is currently being extended from 200 to 300 million words. It has produced an array of publications directed to the raising of awareness about language, primarily of advanced learners of English as a second or foreign language (e.g. raising

awareness about collocational and grammatical patterning). Materials and resources are now being developed for native speakers as well. Work is also being carried out on language in specific contexts which sensitises learners to register-specific language.

5. A book is in preparation by Walter Grauberg, formerly Director of the Language Centre and Head of the Department of Linguistics at the University of Nottingham, now retired, to which LA is central. It brings together observations on the nature of language and the process of language learning with particular reference to British learners of French and German and explores implications for teaching. Grauberg describes the role of linguistic awareness as an aspect of the contribution which learning a foreign language can make to education at school. The book is likely to be published by Multilingual Matters.

PROBLEMS AND DIFFICULTIES

The secondary school sector had been a major driving force in the early days of LA, but the tightly prescribed programmes of the National Curriculum which do not include LA, increased administrative workloads, and loss of morale amongst many teachers have sapped energies and reduced opportunities for them to continue their work.

LA has been misunderstood by some, through its promotion of study of language, to mean a reversion to poor practices of the past; in the case of English, the categorising of parts of speech based on sentence structure as an end in itself; in the case of MFLs, the learning of rules about grammar with little or no association with communicative goals. Such fears may account in part for the exclusion of LA from the National Curriculum for both English and MFLs.

A current concern of government is to ensure that children in school learn to speak Standard English (SE) well, with a good performance according to long-held grammatical practice, together with knowledge of grammatical terms, since a fall in standards has been ascertained. However, government does not favour the LA approach to achieving this goal (inter alia) put forward by Kingman and Cox and taken by the LINC project, and this may be one reason for the refusal to publish the LINC materials.

Following removal of government support funding, NCLE has ceased to operate. The disappearance of this forum which expressly sought to bring together people from all language fields and Education sectors has removed a significant support from LA whose roots were founded in the pooling of ideas and expertise.

FUTURE DIRECTIONS

LA is now viewed by many as a field of study in its own right. The English term 'Language Awareness' is widely known and understood at home and abroad and equivalent terms are in use in some other languages. There is an international association for LA, the Association for Language Awareness, and an LA journal. Research into a number of aspects of LA is being carried out.

Solutions need to be found for the problems and difficulties experienced. Pupils' high performance in Standard English is a goal widely shared; differences of view exist as to the optimum method of achieving it. The LA approach is backed by sufficient weight of expert authority to encourage serious reconsideration of it.

Loss of LA from the MFLs classroom and emphasis on use of the target language alone mean that insights gained into the nature and functioning of language through the learning of another are not brought out, also that awareness of the given language and how it functions are not directly assisting the learning of it. In monolingual classrooms, teachers' and learners' beliefs as to what has been learnt may vary. Research carried out by Rod Ellis described in the article *Uptake as Language Awareness*, in the Language Awareness journal (4,3, 1995) and research into consciousness in second language acquisition, of which a review is given by Nick Ellis in the same edition of the journal, should inform future teaching and learning methods.

Practice in the initial training of teachers has varied to an extent between institutions despite measures taken by professional bodies to establish broad comparability. The government intends to take action to ensure that teachers are efficiently trained to carry out the requirements of their profession and to eliminate 'trendiness'. This assumption of responsibility by the government offers the opportunity to ensure comparability, with a core of standard content in courses, incorporating best practice and research findings. It offers, too, the opportunity to reconsider inclusion of a LINC-type scheme for language.

Amongst the 16–18 age group in schools, there has been a burgeoning of interest in language, expressed in a rapid rise in numbers choosing to follow new courses in English language at Advanced level. In order to respond to the desire to pursue these studies post-A-level, there is a need for innovative degree courses, since most degrees currently available for English focus on English literature, degrees in MFLs rarely include study of language per se and degrees in linguistics remain heavily theoretical.

Since the emphasis within National Curriculum requirements as they currently exist is placed on discrete subject areas, language as a cross-curricular linking field has commanded little recent attention. It may re-emerge as pressures related to the introduction of the National Curriculum abate.

The LA movement placed emphasis on each individual and his or her unique relationship with language (see original definition of LA). Donmall (1991) emphasised the importance of recognising this in the process of learning another language. Exploration of the individual's sensitivity of thought and feeling extends pure knowledge about language (i.e. knowledge as something separate from the learner, which the learner acquires) into the personal realm of the emotions. This field is open to further exploration.

Some early LA courses which placed emphasis on appreciation of those languages which, together with English, constitute the wider UK speech community, gave rise to improved performance in MFLs by pupil members of those communities. Recognition by government, Education professionals and the public at large of those languages and the skills of their speakers, and of the benefits of performance skills in MFLs, which are promoted by LA work, together with acknowledgement of the importance of language for all UK citizens, may serve to enhance the country's performance as a polyglot nation performing on the world stage.

The Open University
England

REFERENCES

Bain, R., Fitzgerald, B. & Taylor, M. (eds.): 1992, *Looking into Language: Classroom Approaches to KAL*, Hodder & Stoughton, London.

Borg, S.: 1994, 'Language awareness as methodology', *Language Awareness* 3(2), 61–72.

Brumfit, C.J. (ed.): 1988, *Language in Teacher Education*, National Congress on Languages in Education, Brighton.

Brumfit, C.J. (ed.): 1995, *Language Education in the National Curriculum*, Blackwell, Oxford.

Bullock, Sir A., (Chairman): 1975, *A Language for Life*, Report of the Committee of Inquiry appointed by the Secretary of State for Education and Science, Her Majesty's Stationery Office, London.

Carter, R.A. (ed.): 1990, *Knowledge about Language and the Curriculum: The LINC Reader*, Hodder & Stoughton, London.

Cox, C. B.: 1991, *Cox on Cox, an English Curriculum for the 1990s*, Hodder & Stoughton, London.

Donmall, B.G.: 1984, 'The developing role of language awareness as a response to problems posed by linguistic diversity', *European Journal of Education* 19(1), 25–37.

Donmall, B.G. (ed.): 1985, *Language Awareness*, NCLE Papers and Reports 6, Centre for Information on Language Teaching and Research, London.

Donmall, B.G.: 1991, 'My Word!': 'The learner, the modern foreign language and language awareness', *Language Learning Journal* 3, 2–6.

Downes, P.: 1994, 'Pre-school progress', *Trends* 3(8), 7–8.

Doughty, P., Pearce, J. & Thornton, G.: 1971, *Language in Use*, Edward Arnold, London.

Ellis, N.C.: 1995, 'Consciousness in second language acquisition: A review of Fikeld studies and laboratory experiments', *Language Awareness* 4(3), 123–146.

Ellis, R.: 1995, 'Uptake as language awareness', *Language Awareness* 4 (3), 147–160.

Francis, G.: 1993, 'A corpus-driven approach to grammar: Principles, methods and examples', in M. Baker, G. Francis & E. Tognini-Bonelli, *Text and Technology: in Honour of John Sinclair*, Benjamins, Amsterdam, 137–156.

Halliday, M.A.K.: 1975, *Learning How to Mean*, Edward Arnold, London.

Hawkins, E.W.: 1979, 'Language as curriculum study', in G. Perren (ed.), *The Mother Tongue and Other Languages in Education*, Papers & Reports of the National Congress on Languages in Education, Centre for Information on Language Teaching and Research, London.

Hawkins, E.W.: 1984, *Awareness of Language: an Introduction*, Cambridge University Press, Cambridge.

Hoey, M.: 1991, *Patterns of Lexis in Text*, Oxford University Press, Oxford.

Perera, K.: 1979, 'The language demands of school learning', *Open University Supplementary Reading Course no. 232 (Language Development)*, Open University Press, Milton Keynes.

Perera, K.: 1993, 'Incorporating language study in an English curriculum', *The Australian Journal of Language and Literacy* 16, 25–34.

Perera, K., Collis, G. & Richards, B. (eds.): 1994, *Growing Points in Child Language*, Cambridge University Press, Cambridge.

Quinn, T. & Trounce, M.: 1985, 'Some aspects of Australian experience with language awareness courses', in B.G. Donmall (ed.), *Language Awareness*, NCLE Papers and Reports 6, Centre for Information on Language Teaching and Research, London.

Scott, M.: 1996, *WordSmith Tools*, Oxford University Press, Oxford.

Sinclair, J. McH.: 1982, 'Linguistics and the teacher', in R. Carter (ed.), *Linguistics and the Teacher*, Routledge & Kegan Paul, London.

Sinclair, J. McH. (ed.): 1987, *Looking Up: An Account of the COBUILD Project in Lexical Computing*, Collins, London.

Tinkel, A.J.: 1981, 'The relationship between the study of language and the teaching of languages', in *Issues in Language Education, NCLE Papers and Reports* 3, CILT, London, 106–123.

Tinkel, A.J.: 1985, 'Methodology related to language awareness work', in B.G. Donmall (ed.) *Language Awareness*, Centre for Information on Language Teaching and Research, London, 37–44.

Tinkel, A.J.: 1988, *Explorations in Language*, Cambridge University Press, Cambridge.

PATRICK J.M. COSTELLO

THE THEORY AND PRACTICE OF ARGUMENT IN EDUCATION

Learning to argue is one of the central objectives of education. Whether it be conducting a formal debate, participating in a group discussion, speaking in public in a variety of situations, writing an essay, a critique or a persuasive appeal, the ability of the student to employ argument and to anticipate and evaluate the arguments of others will generally be an important measure of achievement (Costello & Mitchell, 1995). This chapter examines the theory and practice of argument in primary, secondary, and tertiary education. I begin by charting early developments in this field and by examining the key ideas of initial contributors to it. This is followed by a discussion of the work of some major contributors to date. Having presented a review of research in progress, I shall examine problems and difficulties associated with the theory and practice of argument. Finally, some likely future directions in research and practice will be explored (also see the review by Mitchell).

EARLY DEVELOPMENTS

The debate about the theory and practice of argument in education has a long and varied history. For example, although the relationship between argument and classical rhetoric was a close one, the latter had '... no clear guidance on the question of how to put together an argument' (Andrews, 1995, p. 12). While Aristotle, in the *Rhetoric*, argues that 'a speech has two parts. It is necessary to state the subject, and then to prove it', the *Ad Herennium*, a Roman manual of rhetoric, suggests that 'the most complete and perfect argument ... is that which is comprised of five parts: the Proposition, the Reason, the proof of the Reason, the Embellishment, and the Resumé' (Andrews, p. 12).

Many contemporary contributors to the debate about the theory and practice of argument in education have examined problems associated with the latter. For example, Dixon & Stratta (1982, p. 42) suggest that 'It's time that we English teachers asked ourselves what we hope pupils will learn from the activity. Is it going to be a debating skill, an ability to hold your ground, come what may? Or is the emphasis rather on thinking – on reasoning to discover what it is you think and feel about such an issue, and to present a considered, personal viewpoint?'

L. van Lier and D. Corson (eds), Encyclopedia of Language and Education,
Volume 6: Knowledge about Language, 31–39.
© *1997 Kluwer Academic Publishers. Printed in the Netherlands.*

The authors argue that teachers of English are so uncertain about what they are attempting to achieve that they either ignore the teaching of argument or suggest that such teaching is not properly the province of the English lesson. In suggesting that change is required both in terms of classroom practice and methods of assessment, Dixon and Stratta conclude: '... for really searching Argument, examiners will need to turn to course work and new forms of questions, where pupils have time to discover, clarify and have second thoughts about what they do think and feel, and the grounds for their beliefs (or recommendations)' (pp. 53–54).

Similarly, other authors refer to problems such as students' inability to write arguments (Freedman & Pringle, 1984), while Clarke (1984) refers to the reading of argument in schools as 'an area of neglect'. Freedman and Pringle's research, conducted in Ontario, examined the narrative and argumentative writing of 500 students in grade seven and eight classes. All students completed two written assignments, one focusing on narrative and the other on argument. In order to evaluate the arguments presented, the authors proposed the following criteria:

First, the whole piece of discourse must be unified by either an implicit or (more commonly) an explicitly stated single restricted thesis ... Secondly, the individual points and illustrations must be integrated within a hierarchic structure so that each proposition is logically linked not only to the preceding and succeeding propositions but also to the central thesis and indeed to every proposition within the whole text (p. 74) (see also Andrews, Costello & Clarke, 1993; Andrews, 1995).

Having analysed the scripts presented, Freedman and Pringle found that 98 per cent of students were capable of incorporating narrative structure within their stories, while only 12.5 per cent were able to fulfill the authors' criteria for argumentation.

MAJOR CONTRIBUTIONS

Given the difficulties cited above, it became evident to many practitioners in primary, secondary, and tertiary education that there was a need to build on the insights developed in earlier work (see, for example, Buchmann, 1988; Andrews, 1989; Berrill, 1990; Wilkinson, 1990; Clarke & Sinker, 1992; Weston, 1992; Oléron, 1993) and to conduct further research into both the theory and practice of argument. To this end, two major projects were undertaken in Britain, by researchers at Hull University. The first, entitled 'Improving the Quality of Argument, 5–16', was directed by Richard Andrews and Patrick Costello and funded by the Esmée Fairbairn Charitable Trust. It took place over two years and involved the participation of twenty primary and secondary schools. The final report (Andrews, Costello & Clarke, 1993) examines some of the theoretical issues underpinning the research and contains accounts provided by teachers who participated in it, together with numerous examples of children's work and an independent evaluation of the project. The main objectives for the research were to:

> identify existing practice in primary and secondary schools regarding the teaching and learning of argument;
>
> examine the relationship between spoken and written argument;
>
> explore the relationship between argument, cognitive development, and thinking skills;
>
> identify problems in the teaching and learning of argument;
>
> devise materials, approaches, and strategies to improve the quality of argument.

The approach adopted in the project involved practitioner research. Teachers formulated their own objectives, detailed plans and assessment procedures for gauging improvement in argument. This work was supported by the project's two directors whose task it was to record progress and, on occasion, to contribute to classroom activities. Primary school projects focused on themes such as: 'Bias in historical documents'; 'Ways of seeing the world'; 'Exploring forms of written argument in the junior school'; and 'The prevention of school-based bullying'. Secondary schools worked on topics such as: 'Gender: from the rhetoric to the reality'; 'The video as argument' and 'Women in literature.'

The second project, entitled 'The Teaching and Learning of Argument in Sixth Forms and Higher Education', was funded by the Leverhulme Trust. Directed by Richard Andrews, this three-year, empirical study was undertaken by the project's Research Fellow, Sally Mitchell. The research focused on the place of argument at sixth form (for students aged sixteen to nineteen years) and higher education level, using an ethnographic methodology. It examined the nature of argument, its role in learning, and its form in various academic contexts. In the final report of the project (Mitchell, 1994), the author also offers an analysis of work produced in a number of disciplines and offers suggestions to improve the quality of students' argument.

Following the completion of the above projects and a dissemination of their findings at an international conference, two books were produced. The first, by Andrews (1995), explores his own doctoral research in this field and some of the findings of the Esmée Fairbairn and Leverhulme research. The second, edited by Costello & Mitchell (1995), is a collection of papers on the theory and practice of argument produced by speakers at the above conference. The contributors to the volume, from Australia, Britain, Canada, and the USA, represent a range of disciplinary perspectives and adopt a variety of approaches. Some offer theoretical discussion of the forms and functions of argument within social, philosophical, historical, and rhetorical contexts, while others undertake critical analyses of spoken and written argument and show how these are part of the learning process. Several authors provide ideas for developing the skills of argument.

In concluding this section, I should like to summarise (from the intro-duction to Costello & Mitchell, 1995), what I perceive to be some of the key themes or ideas that underpin much of the research which has taken place in this field. Firstly, the notions of 'competition' and 'consensus' are central to understanding the nature of argument. Competition suggests the work argument does to set a position or person apart; consensus, the work it does to bring positions together.

Secondly, argument, unlike formal logic, is a social operation, a partic-ular mode of communication which is oriented to context and to purpose. It functions, as the terms 'competition' and 'consensus' suggest, both to create and to challenge positions and to form and break apart agreement and identity. It is at once generative and coercive. These are qualities which do not neatly divide between consensus and competition but are potentially present in each. The clue is in the voices that are heard: who speaks? to whom? to what purpose and effect?

Thirdly, there is a sense that argument can be defined by what it does, as well as by what it, more abstractly, is. It initiates change, it transforms the significance of material, it enables reflection and action, it brings diver-gent voices together in interaction, it signals belonging within a certain community, it seeks to persuade, to publicise, to win. So, to answer the question 'what is argument?' entails asking a number of others: what does argument do? who does it? with or to whom? where? and why?

WORK IN PROGRESS

Two major pieces of research on the theory and practice of argument in education are taking place at the present time. The first, a three-year project entitled 'The Role of Higher Education for the Professions: Three Case Studies in Education, Management and Nursing', began in 1994 and is being undertaken by Dorothy Harris at the North East Wales Institute of Higher Education, in Wrexham, Wales. In offering a rationale for the focus of her research, Harris (1996, pp. 3 and 6–7) argues as follows:

The essential task is to seek a way of determining the features of academic argument to facilitate the formulating, analysing and assessing of the students' own arguments and to help them to do the same with the arguments they meet in the course of their studies.
Argument is an important aspect of the discourse of the professions of education, manage-ment and nursing. Managers in a modern organisation find themselves operating in many forums for argumentation . . . The process of making decisions and advocating and defend-ing them means continual use of argument as a mode of discourse with audiences both within the organisation and external to it. Nursing entails the use of reasoning processes to determine action appropriate to the information available for each individual case. It also involves persuading others of the benefits of such action. More recent views of the nursing role include the nurse as advocate for the patient or relative and the nurse as the equal of the doctor, articulating opinions on patient care. Teachers are also engaged in reasoning to diagnose appropriate strategies and techniques for pupil learning. They must also be

persuasive in presenting material in the classroom and effective advocates in their contact with parents, colleagues, governors and agents of local and national government.

The second project, funded by the Leverhulme Trust and based at Middlesex University, London, is entitled 'Improving the Quality of Argument in Higher Education'. This research is described in more detail in the contribution by Mitchell in this volume.

The relationship between argument and critical thinking is a close one and is the subject of much current research. Following the work of Matthew Lipman and his colleagues in the 'Philosophy for Children' movement (see Lipman, 1991, 1993), Philip Cam (1995, p. 1), a philosophy lecturer at the University of New South Wales, argues for 'the introduction of philosophy as a means of placing thinking firmly at the centre of primary education' and has produced a textbook that examines the role of philosophical inquiry in the classroom. Similarly, Robert Fisher (1996) has developed a programme to enhance thinking, learning, and language skills in children aged seven to eleven years, through the use of thirty multicultural stories. Richard Fox (1996) also uses stories to develop thinking skills in pupils aged nine to thirteen years. At a more advanced level, Peter Phelan & Peter Reynolds (1996) examine the relationship between argument and evidence, as a means to improve the critical thinking abilities and argument skills of undergraduate students.

Research is also being undertaken by Bowen & Costello (1996) into the teaching of argument in values education. This is taking place through a series of six books entitled collectively *Issues in Personal, Social and Moral Education*. The first two of these, on the themes *Deadly Habits?* (which considers problems associated with smoking, alcohol, and drugs) and *The Rights of the Child* have been published together with a teachers' handbook. Other titles are *Animal Rights, Family Values, Our Sexist World* and *Sport – Winners and Losers*. The series is intended for use both with children in primary schools and pupils with special educational needs in secondary education. Central to this programme is a concern to promote pupils' abilities to reason and to argue well. To this end, a schema for assessing progress in argument, developed as part of the Esmée Fairbairn research project referred to above, has been included in the teachers' handbook.

PROBLEMS AND DIFFICULTIES

In considering the theory and practice of argument in education, several problems arise. The first concerns the nature of scholarship in this field. Given that proficiency in argument is an important indicator of success at all levels in education, it is not surprising that academics from a variety of disciplines have sought to contribute to the debate about how the quality of people's thinking and argument might be improved (see Fisher,

1988; Trapp & Schuetz, 1990; Govier, 1992; Kuhn, 1991, 1992; Phelan & Reynolds, 1996). While such an eclectic approach is to be welcomed, especially since it has led both to a rich cross-fertilisation of ideas and to an emphasis in research on what academic disciplines have in common rather than on what makes them distinctive, yet the very range of perspectives on and approaches to argument is itself problematic.

For those scholars who are willing to contribute to the debate about the teaching and learning of argument, there is no agreed, common frame of reference from which to work. Coming from such diverse academic and pedagogical traditions as philosophy, linguistics, rhetoric, logic, critical thinking, the teaching of English, science, religious education etc., it is not surprising that significant disagreement should exist about the *nature* of argument, about its forms and functions, let alone about how students' argument skills might be improved in educational settings.

Secondly, there is the perennial problem of the relationship between educational theory and practice. I suggest that we need satisfactory answers to the following questions if research in this field is to have a major impact in our schools, colleges and universities:

To what extent does theorising about 'argument' actually lead to improvements in teaching and learning?

Is such theorising accessible to teachers in schools?

Does educational research seek to respond to teachers' own concerns about the teaching and learning of argument?

Are the skills of argument transferable across disciplinary boundaries?

Why teach argument at all?

Is teaching argument a good thing? Why?

Is there a relationship between one's ability to think and to argue well and a corresponding disposition to behave well?

Thirdly, the lack of continuity between different levels in the educational system is likely to mean that improving the quality of students' argument will continue to be an important but sporadic activity, limited to individual or group initiatives, for the foreseeable future. By way of illustration, it is notable that, while at the early stages of schooling, argument is thought about as an oral, exploratory, philosophical activity, permeating children's experience, at later levels other factors begin more strongly to shape its nature and practice. For example, at secondary and tertiary levels, learning comes increasingly to be dominated by disciplinary content, by standard forms of writing and ways of doing (speech accordingly is less emphasised and less valued in assessment terms). Subject boundaries at these levels begin to impose rules and limitations on the ways in which language is used and argument shaped, expressed, and legitimated. The view of academic disciplines as discrete entities, with their own rules of procedure, and the emphasis on writing as the dominant mode of expression, have militated against the holistic view of 'argument' that pertains at the primary level, with inevitable consequences for its development in secondary and tertiary education.

Even in countries where curriculum continuity is assured, to some extent, by the existence of a national curriculum, the prognosis for teaching and learning argument is not necessarily a healthy one since, by their very nature, such curricula tend to encourage conformity rather than creativity. To the extent that governments or their representatives either dictate or contribute significantly to the development of educational policy and curriculum provision at a national level, this is likely to have adverse consequences for schools in terms of their ability and/or willingness to provide contexts within which the teaching and learning of argument may take place. The amount of time which is usually devoted to the teaching and assessment of the specified content of a national curriculum may seriously inhibit the promotion of an activity – argument – which frequently entails the questioning and transformation of content (Costello & Mitchell, 1995).

FUTURE DIRECTIONS

In looking ahead to likely future directions for research and practice, I would suggest that the following areas require further exploration:

1. The relationship between gender and argument. Are there spoken and written forms of argument which are preferred by girls/boys and in which they perform better than their peers of the opposite sex? (See Andrews, Costello & Clarke, 1993; Sargeant, 1993; Mann, 1993).
2. An exploration of cultural variations in the discourse norms used in argument (Mitchell, 1994; Corson, 1993).
3. The role of argument in teacher education. To what extent is the ability to reason and to argue well an essential prerequisite of the notion of 'the reflective practitioner'?
4. Argument and higher education. Should teaching the skills of argument be regarded as essential to all academic disciplines? Should some level of expertise in argument be regarded as essential to the notion of 'graduateness'?
5. What is the relationship between argument and critical thinking? What is the contribution of each to the development of citizens?
6. Argument and early years education. Are infant school children capable of learning to reason, to argue, to philosophise? Should the skills of argument be taught in infant schools? Should young children be introduced to philosophy?
7. Argument and conflict resolution. What goals motivate arguments? What are the outcomes of arguments? How do we get into and how may we resolve arguments? (Trapp & Schuetz (1990). To what extent can teaching the skills of argument contribute to conflict resolution?

Future research into the theory and practice of argument should continue to focus on educational provision at all levels. In teaching children how to think, reason, and argue for themselves, we need to begin early (in the infant school if possible). To leave such teaching to the later years of secondary education, or to tertiary education, is to disadvantage children both as learners and as citizens.

North East Wales Institute of Higher Education
Wales

REFERENCES

Andrews, R. (ed.): 1989, *Narrative and Argument*, Open University Press, Milton Keynes.

Andrews, R.: 1995, *Teaching and Learning Argument*, Cassell, London.

Andrews, R., Costello, P.J.M. & Clarke, S.: 1993, *Improving the Quality of Argument, 5–16: Final Report*, Esmée Fairbairn Charitable Trust/University of Hull.

Berrill, D.: 1990, 'What exposition has to do with argument: Argumentative writing of sixteen-year-olds', *English in Education* 24(1), 77–92.

Bowen, M. & Costello, P.J.M: 1996–7, *Issues in Personal, Social and Moral Education*, Independence Educational Publishers, Cambridge.

Buchmann, M.: 1988, 'Argument and contemplation in teaching', *Oxford Review of Education* 14(2), 201–214.

Cam, P.: 1995, *Thinking Together: Philosophical Inquiry for the Classroom*, Hale & Iremonger, Sydney.

Clarke, S.: 1984, 'An area of neglect', *English in Education* 18 (2), 67–72.

Clarke, S. & Sinker, J.: 1992, *Arguments*, Cambridge University Press, Cambridge.

Corson, D.: 1993, *Language, Minority Education and Gender: Linking Social Justice and Power*, Multilingual Matters, Clevedon.

Costello, P.J.M. & Mitchell, S. (eds.): 1995, *Competing and Consensual Voices: The Theory and Practice of Argument*, Multilingual Matters, Clevedon.

Dixon, J. & Stratta, L.: 1982, 'Argument: What does it mean to geachers of English?', *English in Education* 16(1), 41–54.

Fisher, A.: 1988, *The Logic of Real Arguments*, Cambridge University Press, Cambridge.

Fisher, R.: 1996, *Stories for Thinking*, Nash Pollock Publishing, Oxford.

Fox, R.: 1996, *Thinking Matters: Stories to Encourage Thinking Skills*, Southgate Publishers, Devon.

Freedman, A. & Pringle, I.: 1984, 'Why students can't write arguments', *English in Education* 18(2), 73–84.

Govier, T.: 1992, *A Practical Study of Argument* (third edition), Wadsworth Publishing Company, California.

Harris, D.: 1996, *The Role of Argument in Higher Education for the Professions: Three Case Studies in Education, Management and Nursing*, paper presented at the British Educational Research Association Annual Conference, Lancaster University.

Kuhn, D.: 1991, *The Skills of Argument*, Cambridge University Press, Cambridge.

Kuhn, D.: 1992, 'Thinking as argument', *Harvard Educational Review* 62(2), 155–178.

Lipman, M.: 1991, *Thinking in Education*, Cambridge University Press, Cambridge.

Lipman, M.: 1993, *Thinking Children and Education*, Kendall/Hunt Publishing Company, Iowa.

Mann, E.: 1993, 'From the chalk-face: Thoughts of a reflective practitioner', *Curriculum* 14(1), 14–22.

Mitchell, S.: 1994, *The Teaching and Learning of Argument in Sixth Forms and Higher Education: Final Report*, The Leverhulme Trust/University of Hull.

Oléron, P.: 1993, *L'Argumentation* (third edition), Presses Universitaires de France, Paris.

Phelan, P. & Reynolds, P.: 1996, *Argument and Evidence: Critical Analysis for the Social Sciences*, Routledge, London.

Sargeant, J.: 1993, 'Gender and power: The meta-ethics of teaching argument in schools', *Curriculum* 14 (1), 6–13.

Trapp, R. & Schuetz, J. (eds.): 1990, *Perspectives on Argumentation: Essays in Honor of Wayne Brockriede*, Waveland Press, Illinois.

Weston, A.: 1992, *A Rulebook for Arguments*, Hackett Publishing Company, Indianapolis.

Wilkinson, A.: 1990, 'Argument as a primary act of mind', *English in Education* 24(1), 10–22.

Section 2

Knowledge About Language and the Language Learner

JEAN EMILE GOMBERT

METALINGUISTIC DEVELOPMENT IN FIRST-LANGUAGE ACQUISITION

At a very early age, the child is able to manipulate language appropriately, both in its comprehension and its production. Later comes the ability to reflect upon and deliberately control its use. The emergence of these metalinguistic abilities must be distinguished from that of ordinary verbal communication. The key questions concerning this topic are: What is metalinguistics? What knowledge do metalinguistic abilities require? Are they conscious activities? And how do they develop? (also see the review by Tunmer in Volume 2 and by Nicholson in this volume.)

EARLY DEVELOPMENT

The neologism *metalinguistics* emerged only a short time ago. Between 1950 and 1960, linguists employed this term to designate anything related to metalanguage, a language whose lexicon is composed of the entirety of words forming linguistic terminology (such as *syntax, semantics, phoneme*, as well as more common terms like *word, sentence, letter*, etc.).

In its initial linguistic sense, then, metalinguistics was concerned with linguistic activity which focuses on language. From this viewpoint, metalinguistic ability depends upon the capability of language to refer to itself. Nevertheless, in a functional perspective, which concentrates on the working of language as it is used by real speakers, this metalinguistic level of language, in which the language's signifiers become the signified, was granted a new status in the activity of language speakers (Benveniste, 1974). This perspective progressively generated the meaning of the term as it is actually used in psycholinguistics where it refers to the ability to distance ourselves from the normal usage of language, and thus to shift our attention from transmitted contents to the properties of language used to transmit them. This capacity is described by Cazden (1976) as «the ability to make language forms opaque and attend to them in and for themselves» (p. 603).

Following the ideas of Flavell (1976), many psychologists consider that metalinguistic capacities form an integral part of the general heading *metacognition* which '*refers to one's knowledge concerning one's own cognitive processes and products or anything related to them*' (p. 232). Thus, from the perspective of metacognition, the psycholinguistic meaning

L. van Lier and D. Corson (eds), Encyclopedia of Language and Education,
Volume 6: Knowledge about Language, 43–51.
© 1997 Kluwer Academic Publishers. Printed in the Netherlands.

of the term *metalinguistic* is broader than that which linguists give to the notion. From a linguistic viewpoint, metalinguistic covers anything which has to do with metalanguage. In other words, linguists identify the metalinguistic by examining verbal productions in order to find those linguistic features which indicate the existence of self-referential processes (the use of language to refer to itself). Psychologists, in contrast, analyze the subject's behavior (verbal or otherwise) to find elements which permit them to infer cognitive processes of conscious monitoring (*reflection upon* or *intentional control over*) of language objects, either as objects *per se* or in terms of the use to which they are put.

MAJOR CONTRIBUTIONS

Two books devoted to reviews of studies concerning metalinguistic development (Gombert, 1992; Tunmer, Pratt & Herriman, 1984) divided the field in subfields corresponding to different levels of linguistic analysis. In fact, metalinguistic activities and abilities may concern any aspect of language, whether phonological (in which case we speak of *metaphonological activities*), syntactic (*metasyntactic activities*), semantic (*metasemantic activities*) or pragmatic (*metapragmatic activities*).

On the whole, it is possible to consider that there is a general domain of metalinguistic knowledge. Within this, one category is central and this corresponds to knowledge of the nature of the linguistic information. It essentially comprises metaphonological knowledge, metasemantic knowledge and metasyntactic knowledge. Two other metalinguistic domains are less clear: Metapragmatic and metatextual domains.

Metapragmatic awareness corresponds to the subject's conscious awareness of the social rules of language (words and expressions which are suitable for use in particular situations, ways of speaking, ways of conducting a conversation, etc.) as they are reflected in his or her own explicit comments (Bates, 1976).

For a number of authors (for a review see Gombert, 1992), the field of metapragmatics includes awareness or knowledge both of the relationships between linguistic signs and the extralinguistic context *and* of the intralinguistic relationships between signs and their linguistic context. With reference to the pragmatics of language, this grouping is justified in that it concerns all the rules governing the entire set of relationships between signs and theirs users, which includes the relationship of utterances to the discourse in which they occur. Nevertheless, I think that we have to distinguish awareness of the relationship between language and its extralinguistic context from awareness of intralinguistic relations which I designated under the name *metatextual activities*. Thus, I drew a distinction between metapragmatic awareness of the relations which exist between the linguistic system and the context in which it is used and the metatextual operations involved in the intentional control of the ordering of utterances in larger linguistic units.

WORKS IN PROGRESS

The overview presented in 1984 by the Tunmer and Herriman paper is still current (in Tunmer, Pratt & Herriman, 1984: see the review by Tunmer in Volume 2). They contrasted three viewpoints concerning the relationship between metalinguistic development and language acquisition. These were the viewpoint of contemporaneity; the conception of metalinguistic awareness as reflecting, at the level of language, the acquisition of operational thought; and the affirmation of the simple effect of school education.

For Clark (1978), the first metalinguistic behavior would be contemporaneous with the emergence of language and constitute an intentional management component within it. From the very start of language acquisition, linguistic development would require children to become conscious of their own language errors (as well as their successes). In fact, formal errors, as well as pragmatic inadequacies, are no doubt self-corrected quasi-automatically when the productions of young speakers do not correspond to what they are trying to say or are not adapted to their context of utterance. Thus, this undeniable early language-monitoring behavior, which is dependent on nonexplicit feelings concerning the inadequacy of the production, does not seem to be of a metalinguistic nature.

For Van Kleeck (1982) it is the ability for decentration and the awareness of reversibility (characteristic of operational functioning in a Piagetian perspective) that, on the one hand, permit children to consider language both as a means of conveying meaning and as a separate object and, on the other, allow them to perform comparisons of meanings. Because of its excessive generality, this viewpoint alone is inadequate to a causal explanation of the development of metalinguistic awareness.

Several studies have shown that metalinguistic abilities seem to be essential in learning to read. As a matter of fact, learning to read is a formal linguistic task. In order to complete this task, the child needs to develop an explicit awareness of her own language structure which must be intentionally monitored.

In this domain, most researchers have emphasized the central importance of phonological skills in learning to read (cf. subsequent chapter). In fact, developmental models of reading postulated that, soon after the onset of learning to read, a stage of alphabetic reading dominated by the learning of the associations between graphemic components and phonemic components takes place (for instance, cf. Frith, 1985). In order to learn that graphemes represent phonemes, children must at least be able to break spoken words up into appropriate phonological segments. Thus, those learning to read should be aware of the phonemic structure of language, in order to become aware that each aural unit is represented by a grapheme.

This central role of phonemic awareness in learning to read is attested by the results of numerous studies submitting subjects from various chrono-logical and reading ages to various phonological analysis tasks (deletion, inversion, counting). In fact, phonemic awareness and learning to read interact together throughout development (for an extensive review, cf. Goswami & Bryant, 1990).

To a lesser extent, some data suggest that syntactic awareness also contributes to learning to read. Tunmer (1990) insisted on the fact that syntactic awareness could be essential in word recognition. Children could use their syntactic knowledge in order to extenuate phonological analysis mistakes when they read unfamiliar words or homographic words with more than one pronunciation (for example "*read*"). This author assumed that syntactic awareness contributes to reading in two ways. Firstly, it enhances children's recoding skills. Secondly, it facilitates the monitoring of comprehension, especially the processes of text integration (particularly when mistakes have been made in recoding). In fact several studies established the existence of significant correlations between syntactic tasks and reading skills, but these correlations were often higher between syntactic tasks and recoding skills than between syntactic tasks and comprehension skills. Nevertheless, it is possible that the difficulty in establishing the existence of a strong relationship between syntactic awareness and comprehension monitoring is linked to the fact that research principally focused on lexical access in reading, ignoring the development of comprehension skills (cf. Demont & Gombert, 1996).

On the whole, it is likely that both phonological and syntactic knowledge contribute simultaneously to learning to read and would therefore affect reading in complementary ways. Beyond the importance of metaphonology and metasyntax in beginning readers, it seems that metapragmatic and metatextual abilities are essential both at the later level of reading expertise and in the development of writing.

PROBLEMS AND DIFFICULTIES

It is generally agreed by psycholinguists that, like all other metacognitive activities, metalinguistic activities can only be deemed to acquire their "meta-activity" status if they are consciously performed by the subject. Therefore, it appears that the major problem faced by the psycholinguist who is interested in metalinguistic development is that of demonstrating the conscious character of mental activity. Traditionally, the subject's ability to provide an explicit verbal statement of the determining factors of his or her own behavior has been seen as evidence of consciousness. Unfortunately, this introspective approach is not always satisfactory. Indeed, even if on an initial analysis we can often qualify as "conscious" those cognitive processes which can be explained by the subject, it is clear that the failure to explain does not imply lack of consciousness. However, if lack of consciousness is difficult to establish in connection with spontaneous behavior, it remains possible to demonstrate its likelihood in experimental situations (see Gombert, 1992).

The fact that, generally, the ability for reflection and intentional self-monitoring is not fully developed in young children does not imply that their cognitive activities are not monitored. This issue was dealt with in 1983 by Karmiloff-Smith who explored '*a model which situates meta-processes as an essential component of acquisition, which continuously function at all levels of development, and do not merely occur as a late epiphenomenon*' (pp. 35–36). In fact, Karmiloff-Smith uses the term metaprocess in a broader sense, which leads her to distinguish between '*unconscious metaprocesses*' and other metaprocesses (which appear later on) available to conscious access and verbal statement (Karmiloff-Smith, 1986). It is the admission of so large a definition that has led a number of authors to postulate the existence of metalinguistic activity as early as age 2 (for a detailed review of this issue, see Gombert, 1992).

In fact, it seems that the term *metalinguistic* is used to designate dissimilar phenomena whose apparent similarity is due to an observation bias. In accordance with previous researchers, a distinction should be made between the skills manifested in spontaneous behavior (for example, the child's ability to automatically adapt discourse to the listener's age) on the one hand and, on the other, the abilities which are based on systematically-represented and intentionally-applied knowledge (for example, voluntary adapting of narratives to different audiences). It is more than a difference in degree that delimits these two sets of behavior, but rather a qualitative difference in cognitive activities themselves. Only the observer's adult-centeredness can, via a deforming assimilation process, prevent recognition of the specificity of the so-called *early metalinguistic* behaviors. For reasons of terminological clarity, therefore, the same expression must not be used to refer to different cases.

The concept *epilinguistic* created by the linguist Culioli (1968) has been used by several French-speaking linguists and psycholinguists, and seems to be perfectly adequate to refer to *unconscious metalinguistic* activities. The use of this term permits us to posit that a reflective, intentional character is inherent in strictly metalinguistic activity. We will therefore reserve the term *epilinguistic* for the designation of behavior which, although isomorphic to metalinguistic behavior, is not the result of the subject's conscious monitoring of his or her own linguistic processing.

If we call *epiprocesses* those *unconscious metaprocesses* which govern epilinguistic behavior, it could easily be agreed that they are at work in all linguistic behavior whose control level lies beyond the initial, purely associative response that often constitutes the child's first deictic utterances, greetings, or vocal games. However, epilinguistic behavior is the only kind of behavior in which the action of epiprocesses is manifest in the behavior itself. For that reason epilinguistic behavior may be similar to metalinguistic behavior.

FUTURE DIRECTIONS

From a developmental point of view, a twofold question arises concerning, on the one hand, the emergence of epiprocesses, and on the other, the question of how metalinguistic abilities are acquired.

Using Karmiloff-Smith's (1986) model for support, Gombert (1992, 1994) postulated that metalinguistic development is comprised of three successive phases. Each of the aspects of language is affected by meta-linguistic development in a manner independent of (and not necessarily contemporaneous with) the other aspects. Only the first two phases are virtually mandatory for all aspects, the occurrence of the third is strongly dependent upon nonsystematic contextual factors. The first phase corresponds to *the acquisition of first linguistic skills*, the second to *the acquisition of epilinguistic control*, and the third to *the acquisition of metalinguistic awareness*.

In all respects, the phase of the first linguistic skills is identical to the one described in Karmiloff-Smith's model. Basic linguistic skills are acquired via the model presented by adults in conjunction with negative and positive feedback which results in the rejection of incorrect productions and the reinforcement of correct ones. This leads to storage in memory of a multiplicity of uni-functional pairs wherein a correspondence is established between a given linguistic form and each of the pragmatic contexts in which it has continuously been positively reinforced. At the end of this phase, the child's usage of that particular linguistic form is similar to that of adults. This is one of the first processes of linguistic behavior automation.

The behavioral stability gained in this phase is then brought into question, due to an increase in the size and complexity of the adult models and the length of the child's own productions. This causes the reorganization process which is characteristic of the second phase. As in Karmiloff-Smith's model, that second phase (acquisition of epilinguistic control) corresponds to the organization in long term memory of the implicit knowledge accumulated during the first phase. It involves the substitution of multifunctional forms for the initial multitude of form-function pairs. However, Gombert's description of this phase differs from Karmiloff-Smith's on several points.

First, in Gombert's model the driving force of development is not only the inclination to control the internal organization of the knowledge acquired during phase 1, but also, owing to that organization, the need to interrelate that knowledge with other newly discovered knowledge about those same forms, or about other forms frequently associated with those currently being organized.

Second, for Gombert the extralinguistic context of children's linguistic processing, which is primarily a social context, plays a very important role during this second phase. The general process in operation during this phase is the internal articulation of implicit knowledge, which leads to a functional (i.e., unreflected) awareness of a system. Nevertheless, the building of usage rules for the linguistic form in question is determined by, and of significant interest to, the real and thus contextualized use of those forms.

For example, the early epilinguistic detection of agrammatical statements may be affected by two factors. First, the child may be alarmed by the dissonance of the utterance. This dissonance is not absolute, but relative, since it depends on the context of the utterance. The control process responsible for the detection is in part dependent upon the contexts previously encountered by the child, and in particular upon the contexts with which the current situation is functionally assimilated. The second potential factor has to do with the child's possible inability to understand the ill-formed utterance. This in effect is equivalent to the inability to locate a linguistic structure in memory that, in a context similar to the current context, activates a representation.

Thus, during this phase the child progressively acquires the ability to refer implicitly to a prototypical context by constructing a system of usage rules for each linguistic form currently implicated. This context, which corresponds to the common denominator of the most frequent and salient contexts in which that form actually occurred, may serve as a reference whenever the current context is unfamiliar. This elaboration of a stable pragmatic standard for each linguistic form is the main feature of this second phase of development. This stable state marks the end of the second phase, and provides subjects with a top-down component in the control they exert on their own linguistic processing.

Explicit awareness of the system of rules set up in this manner, i.e. the step up towards metalinguistic control, is not automatic. It can only be attained following a metacognitive effort that manifests itself only when necessary. Since epilinguistic control has become stable and efficient at handling daily verbal exchanges, new external prompting is necessary for awareness to set in. This explains why the transition to this third level of functioning does not always occur. As suggested in many studies, only those aspects of language that must be mastered in order to accomplish the required linguistic tasks will be mastered in a "meta" fashion (that is, consciously).

In fact, mastery of reading and writing requires conscious knowledge and intentional control of many aspects of language. In our society, then, it often plays the role of triggering the acquisition of metalinguistic competence.

Because conscious monitoring is a cognitively expensive operation, everything cannot be consciously mastered at the same time. The complexity of the systems to be acquired, their frequency in the language, and their usefulness to new, yet unresolved problems are at the origin of the differences found in the time of appearance of the corresponding metalinguistic skills. In other words, the various metalinguistic developments are non-contemporaneous.

Two interpretations of these differences are possible. For Karmiloff-Smith (see for instance Karmiloff Smith et al., 1993), metalinguistic awareness develops progressively over the early years of life. But, as different linguistic forms may be acquired at different rates, conscious attention to these forms and to their functions are likely to present a similar lack of contemporaneity. Another reason of theses differences may be found in Bialystok's (1991) analysis. She distinguished between two components of metalinguistic abilities: *The control of linguistic processing* which is the executive component responsible for directing attention when processing linguistic information; and *the analysis of linguistic knowledge* which is the skill component that is responsible for the structuring and explication of linguistic knowledge. Different tasks may place more or fewer demands on one or the other component. Further experiments are still necessary to investigate these two heuristic ways, which are not incompatible.

Université de Bourgogne
France

REFERENCES

Bates, E.: 1976, *Language and Context: The Acquisition of Pragmatics*, Academic Press, New York.

Benveniste, E.: 1974, *Problèmes de Linguistique Générale*, Vol. 2, Gallimard, Paris.

Bialystok, E. (ed.): 1991, *Language Processing in Bilingual Children*, Cambridge University Press, Cambridge.

Cazden, C.: 1976, 'Play with language and metalinguistic awareness: One dimension of language experience', in J.S. Bruner, A. Jolly & K. Sylva (eds.), *Plays: its Role in Development and Evolution*, Basic Books, New York, 603–618.

Clark, E.V.: 1978, 'Awareness of language: Some evidence from what children say and do', in A. Sinclair, R.J. Jarvella & W.J.M. Levelt (eds.), *The Child's Conception of Language*, Springer-Verlag, Berlin, 17–43.

Culioli, A.: 1968, 'La formalisation en linguistique', *Cahiers pour l'Analyse* 9, 106–117.

Demont, E. & Gombert, J.E.: 1996, 'Phonological awareness as a predictor of recoding skills and syntactic awareness as a predictor of comprehension skills', *British Journal of Educational Psychology* 66, 315–332.

Flavell, J.H.: 1976, 'Metacognitive aspects of problem solving', in B. Resnick (ed.), *The Nature of Intelligence*, Erlbaum, Hillsdale NJ, 127–146.

Frith, U.: 1985, 'Beneath the surface of developmental dyslexia', in K.E. Patterson, J.C. Marshall & M. Coltheart (eds.), *Surface Dyslexia: Cognitive and Neuropsychological Studies of Phonological Reading*, Lawrence Erlbaum, Hillsdale, NJ, 301–330.

Gombert, J.E.: 1992, *Metalinguistic Development*, University of Chicago Press, Chicago.

Gombert, J.E.: 1994, 'Development of meta-abilities and regulatory mechanisms in use of linguistic structures in children', in A. Vyt, H. Bloch & M.H. Bornstein (eds.), *Early Child Development in the French Tradition*, Lawrence Erlbaum Associates, Hillsdale NJ, 227–239.

Goswami, U.C. & Bryant, P.: 1990, *Phonological Skills and Learning to Read*, Lawrence Erlbaum, Hillsdale, NJ

Karmiloff-Smith, A.: 1983, 'A note on the concept of "metaprocedural processes" in linguistic and non-linguistic development', *Archives de Psychologie* 51, 35–40.

Karmiloff-Smith, A.: 1986, 'From meta-processes to conscious access: Evidence from metalinguistic and repair data', *Cognition* 23, 95–147.

Karmiloff-Smith, A., Johnson, H., Grant, J., Jones, M.C., Karmiloff, Y.N., Bartrip, J. & Cuckle, P.: 1993, 'From sentential to discourse functions: Detection and explanation of speech repairs by children and adults', *Discourse Processes* 16, 565–589.

Tunmer, W.E.: 1990, 'The role of language prediction skills in beginning reading', *New Zealand Journal of Educational Studies* 25, 95–114.

Tunmer, W.E., Pratt, C. & Herriman, M.L. (eds.): 1984, *Metalinguistic Awareness in Children: Theory, Research and Implications*, Springer-Verlag, Berlin.

Van Kleeck, A.: 1982, 'The emergence of linguistic awareness: A cognitive framework', *Merrill-Palmer Quarterly* 28, 237–265.

TOM NICHOLSON

PHONOLOGICAL AWARENESS AND LEARNING TO READ

Phonological awareness is part of a more general awareness of language, called metalinguistic awareness, which refers to the ability to think about the form of language as distinct from its content. A person who has meta-linguistic awareness knows that talk can be broken down into utterances which follow grammatical and pragmatic rules, that utterances can be broken into words, and that words can be broken into their component sounds (Tunmer & Bowey, 1984; see Tunmer's review in Volume 2). In Piagetian terms, metalinguistic awareness coincides with the emergence of concrete operational thinking, where the child is able to think about problems from two different perspectives.

Phonological awareness is a metalinguistic skill. The word "phonolog-ical is derived from ancient Greek ("phone" means "voice"; "logos" means "word"). It refers to the ability to reflect on and manipulate the sound components of spoken words. Some researchers distinguish phonological awareness and phonemic awareness. Phonemic awareness refers to a focus on the phoneme, but phonological awareness has a wider applicability (Share, 1995). It can refer to the syllabic structure of words (e.g., "cat-nap"), and to the onset-rhyme structure of the syllable (e.g., c-at). The onset is the beginning consonant(s) and the rime is the remainder of the syllable, including the vowel and optional consonants. Thus, the onset of "cat" is "c" and the rime is "-at".

Phonological awareness is the ability to think about the sounds of words separately from their spellings. Tests of phonological awareness usually involve looking at pictures of objects, or else listening to spoken words. The assessment of phonological awareness can range from tests of simple awareness (e.g., "What is the first sound in *cat*?"), through to tests of more complex awareness (e.g., "what are the sounds in *cat*?"). It seems that phonological awareness is something that emerges gradually in the child. To be aware of sounds in words, the child has to ignore the meaning of a word and focus on its form (Gough, Larson & Yopp, 1993). Thus, the child has to think about words in a different way, and this can be difficult. An illustration of this difficulty is when a 5-year-old is asked to say the sounds in *cat*, and she says "meow".

L. van Lier and D. Corson (eds), Encyclopedia of Language and Education,
Volume 6: Knowledge about Language, 53–61.
© 1997 Kluwer Academic Publishers. Printed in the Netherlands.

EARLY DEVELOPMENTS

Historically, teaching children about sounds in words dates back to the six-teenth century (see Thompson's review in Volume 2). However, research on phonological awareness and reading is much more recent (see Leong, 1991). Researchers in Russia in the 1960's were aware that preschool children lacked phonological awareness. Several Russian psychologists (e.g., Zhurova, 1973) were studying this problem. However, the work of these Russian researchers was not translated into English until the 1970's. In their writing it is clear that they were aware of the problem of phono-logical awareness and learning to read. Zaporozhets & Elkonin (1971) mentioned "glass theory" (p. 139). In this theory, children were not aware of the form of words. It was as if words were a glass through which the child looked at the world. They also noted that "the ability to analyze word sound composition is a very important precondition for the correct training in literacy" (p. 169). Elkonin (1973) described the written word as "a model of the spoken word – a model of the word's structure and its principle of construction" (p. 561).

While interesting work was being done in Moscow in the 1960's, United States researchers Alvin and Isabelle Liberman were also tackling the phonological awareness problem. Liberman, Cooper, Shankweiler and Studdert-Kennedy (1967) had published a paper in "Psychological Review" reporting results which showed that phonemes in words, though psychologically real in the sense that we think we can hear them separately, are in fact overlapping. The overlap from one sound to another made it impossible to isolate each sound separately. It was hypothesised that the listener had a special device or module that enabled him/her to recon-struct the phonological sound structure of words. Liberman, according to Bertelson & de Gelder (1991), may have been thinking of the relationship between phonological awareness and reading in a paper published in 1968, where Liberman wrote that if phonemes "are real they are not necessarily real at a high level of awareness. That is to say, it does not follow from anything I have said that the man in the street can tell you about phonemes, or that he can even tell you how many phonemes there are in particular uttererances." (cited in Bertelson & de Gelder, p. 394). According to Mann (1991), Isabelle Liberman in 1970 presented a paper in which she also linked phonological awareness with the task of learning to read. Much of her later research was also focused on this topic. This work, and the psycholinguistic rationale which underpinned it, is described in Liberman (1997).

Looking back, it seems that the Russian and United States researchers were both on the same path. They realized that the stumbling block in learning to read was the phoneme.

MAJOR CONTRIBUTIONS

Reviews of phonological awareness studies are in Brady & Shankweiler (1991), Sawyer & Fox (1991), Nicholson (1994), Nicholson (1996). The following studies are mentioned to give an historical overview, and to illustrate the international nature of much of the research.

Bruce (1964), in England, was one of the first researchers to publish work on children's knowledge of the sound structure of words. He assessed children's ability to delete and to substitute sounds in words (e.g., What word would be left if the "j" was taken off "jam"? What word would be left if the "k" was taken from the middle of "monkey"?). He tested 67 children, aged betweeen five and seven years, and found that it was not until children reached a mental age of seven years or beyond that they could easily deal with the task of deleting and substituting phonemes. Many children had difficulty with his phonological awareness test. For example, when asked to say what word would be left if the "s" were taken from the middle of "nest", one child said, "I can't actually do it. You see, I can't say the last letter without the middle."

I. Liberman, Shankweiler, Fischer & Carter (1974), in the United States, assessed the ability of 4-, 5- and 6-year-old children to tap the number of syllables (e.g., "ice-cream") or phonemes (e.g., "i-ce") in words. Liberman et al found that none of the 4-year-olds could do the phoneme task, though half could do the syllable task. Among the 5-year-olds, less than a fifth could do the phoneme task, though half could do the syllable task. Among the 6-year-olds, only 70% could do the phoneme task, while 90% could do the syllable task.

Bradley & Bryant (1978), in England, used a reading level match design to compare a group of 60 older children (average age 10 years) with a group of 30 younger children (average age 6 years). The younger children were slightly above-average readers for their age. The older readers were poor readers, who were reading at the same level as the younger readers. The intelligence scores of both groups were similar. What was interesting about the study was that older, poor readers were significantly worse than younger, average readers on a test of phonological awareness. The test involved picking one word out of four that did not follow the same phonological pattern (e.g., "weed", "peel", "need", "deed", where "peel" is the odd one out). The results suggested that phonological awareness difficulties could be responsible for reading difficulties.

Juel, Griffith & Gough (1986), in the United States, conducted a two year longitudinal study of the reading and writing progress of 129 children. They found that phonological awareness made a significant contribution to literacy development by facilitating the growth of letter-sound correspondence skills, which the researchers called "cipher knowledge". Juel (1988), in a follow up study of these children through fourth grade reported that children who became poor readers entered first grade with little or no phonemic awareness. In contrast, children who became good readers entered first grade with much higher levels of phonemic awareness.

According to Golinkoff (1978), it was not until American researchers heard of the work of the Russian researcher, Elkonin, that serious efforts were made to train phonological awareness skills. Elkonin's work was done in the 1960's. Elkonin (1971) reported research on the teaching of reading where preschoolers were trained to segment spoken words. The child would be given a card with a picture of an object, under which would be little boxes joined together, representing the number of sounds in the word (e.g., a picture of two "geese" would have, below the picture, four boxes, joined together to represent the sounds of the word – the Russian word for "geese" is "gusi"). The child would name the picture (e.g., "gusi"), then say the word sound by sound (e.g., "g-u-s-i"), at the same time placing a cardboard chip (different colour for consonants and vowels) in each box to represent each sound. This procedure was more effective than simply saying the word, or using chips alone. More than 8 out of 10 preschoolers (6-year-olds) had responded to the combination of saying the word, having the sound boxes available, and using the chips. Elkonin (1973) reported a classroom evaluation of this method. Children in kindergarten and first grade were able to learn how to analyse sounds in words in ten to twelve lessons. A difficulty with Elkonin's study, however, was that he did not give details of the results.

The first clear findings for phonological awareness training were published in *Nature* in 1983 by Oxford researchers, Bradley & Bryant. They conducted a training study in which 65 children were taught phonological awareness over a two year period. The children were 6-year-olds when the training began, and 8-year-olds when it finished. There were four training groups, each given different kinds of training: phonological awareness only, phonological awareness training combined with the use of letters of the alphabet, training that used the same materials for different purposes, i.e., to put pictures into categories, and no training at all. The results showed that the children who were trained in phonological awareness made gains, but that the children who made the clearest gains were those who received phonological awareness training along with the use of letters of the alphabet.

In another longitudinal study, Lundberg, Frost & Petersen (1988) trained 235 Danish preschoolers over an eight month period. The children received 160 phonological awareness lessons, including rhyme awareness. The researchers compared the progress of the trained children with a control group of 155 children who received no training. Lundberg et al. were able to produce significant gains in the phonological awareness skills of the trained children relative to the control children. They followed the children through their first two years of school, and found that the difference between the trained group and the control group increased from grades 1 to 2.

WORK IN PROGRESS

In regard to rhyme awareness, Bryant, Bradley, Maclean & Crossland (1989), in England, found that children's knowledge of traditional English nursery rhymes at three years of age strongly predicted their reading ability at six years of age. The predictive value of nursery rhymes held up even after taking account of factors such as intelligence and home background. Thus, it may be that the best place for teachers to start, in teaching phonological awareness, is with nursery rhymes. There are lots of playground rhymes that children learn informally, which teachers could make use of (e.g., "Inky, pinky, ponky, Daddy bought a donkey, Donkey died, daddy cried, Inky pinky ponky"). There are also jump-rope rhymes (e.g., "Cinderella, dressed in pink, Went downstairs to the kitchen sink, The kitchen sink was full of ink, How many mouthfuls did she drink? 1, 2, 3, 4, etc.) that can be a source of instructional material (Turner, Factor & Lowenstein, 1978). Layton, Deeny, Tall & Upton (1996), in England, reported that pre-reading children in nursery school (4-year-olds) responded better to rhyme activities (e.g., "What is wrong with Jack and Jill/Went up the road?") than to training involving word onsets. In the word onset training, children played the"tray" game, where they were shown a tray with items all beginning with the same sound, and were then asked which of several new items could go on the tray.

A difficulty with training of onsets is the concept of "beginning sound". Children often do not have a good sense of what "beginning" means. Hatcher (1994) used visual analogies to teach positional concepts such as "beginning" (e.g., an illustration showing several cars lined up at traffic lights, where the teacher would point to the car at the "beginning" of the line, and the car in the "middle" of the line, and the car at the "end" of the line). Such activities may make the teaching of onsets easier. Phil Gough (personal communication) has also suggested using the "I spy" game to teach preschoolers about beginning sounds: "I spy with my little eye, something beginning with f" (where the first phoneme is said, not the letter name of the thing that is spied).

Castle, Riach & Nicholson (1994) carried out two training studies to find out whether children who were receiving whole language instruction would benefit from the addition of phonological awareness instruction. The children in the two studies were 5-year-olds, mostly from middle-class backgrounds, in their first year of school. One study looked at spelling; the other at both spelling and reading. Each study included a group of children who were trained in phonological awareness and a matched control group. Children receiving phonological awareness training engaged in activities which focused specifically on phonemes, such as slowed pronunciation of words (e.g., "mmmm-ou-sss"), segmenting of the initial phoneme (e.g., What is the first sound in *fish*? "bbbbb-bear"), rhyme (e.g., "Which pictures rhyme?" – show pictures of *log*, *dog* and *sun*), phoneme deletion (e.g., "Say *cat* without the *c*"), phoneme substitution (e.g., "what would *cat* say if it started with *b* instead of *k*), and phonemic segmentation (e.g., using the Elkonin (1973) method, where the child places counters in square boxes below the picture of an object, one counter for each sound in the word). In the first training study, results showed that phonological awareness training produced significant gains in spelling of single words. In the second training study, results showed that the phonological awareness training led to significant gains in spelling of dictated sentences and in reading of pseudowords. A similar pattern of results was obtained with five-year-old children from low-income backgrounds (Nicholson, 1996), though the Castle et al. (1994) gains were more fragile than those obtained with middle class children.These results suggested that the inclusion of phonological awareness training at school entry can give children a better start in learning to read and spell within a whole language programme.

The above studies are only a sample of the many training studies that have been carried out in a number of different countries (for a more detailed review, see Nicholson, 1997). The weight of evidence from these international studies indicates that, in many parts of the world, children who enter school with low levels of phonological awareness will benefit from specific instruction in phonological awareness skills.

PROBLEMS, DIFFICULTIES AND FUTURE DIRECTIONS

Although many studies have shown that phonological awareness training can improve children's reading and spelling, a problem with much of the research is that phonological training has also been accompanied by reading instruction, which makes it difficult to know whether it is the phonological awareness training itself that has made the difference, or some interaction of reading instruction with the training. It appears that the interaction is important. Bradley & Bryant (1983) and Hatcher, Hulme & Ellis (1994) have reported that phonological awareness training alone is not as effective as the combination of phonological training with the teaching of letter-sound correspondences. This raises the question, is phonological awareness a prerequisite to learning to read, or is it a result of learning to read? Ehri (1995) has briefly reviewed the controversy on this topic. Her thinking is that learning to read teaches children phonological awareness. She has argued that children become more consciously aware of the phonological structure of words when they see speech represented in written form. The invisible nature of phonemes is made visible in print. Further, Read (1978) has made the point that the appearance of phonological awareness in children at about the same time they are taught to read in school is "highly suspicious" (p. 73). However, research such as that carried out by Lundberg et al. (1988) and Juel (1988) supports the alternative view, that phonological awareness is necessary in order to learn to read. At the present time, most researchers accept that some phonological awareness is necessary in order to learn to read, but that reading instruction can facilitate the development of more sophisticated levels of phonological awareness (Stanovich, 1986).

Another problem with phonological awareness instruction is that it does not fit comfortably with a whole language approach to reading, in that it has the appearance of "skills and drills", which are frowned on by whole language teachers. One solution is to combine phonological awareness instruction with reading instruction, which is more in line with the holistic nature of whole language. Another solution is to introduce phonological awareness teaching before children start formal schooling. This would have the advantage that children would already have phonological awareness when their formal reading instruction began, rather than having to confront the more complex task of acquiring phonological awareness and the alphabet at the same time.

Also problematic for phonological awareness instruction is knowing what level of phonological awareness to aim for. Is it enough to teach rhyme awareness, which is a very simple level of phonological awareness? Should we aim for the ability to isolate the beginning sounds of words? A child may be told that the letter *c* has a *k* sound, yet this will not be of use unless the child also knows that *k* is a sound that occurs in spoken words (e.g., there is a *k* in *cat*). Or perhaps we have to aim for complete segmentation ability (e.g., where the child can explicitly segment the sounds in *cat*). With full segmentation skill, it would be easier for the child to infer the alphabetic principle, that written words represent the phonological structure of spoken words (Gough, Larson & Yopp, 1993).

Future research on phonological awareness will need to sort out how to teach more advanced phonological segmentation skills easily and enjoyably, so that all children achieve the best possible start in learning to read. Researchers in this exciting field have already made considerable progress, but there are still some interesting puzzles to solve.

University of Auckland
New Zealand

REFERENCES

Bertelson, P. & de Gelder, B.: 1993, 'The emergence of phonological awareness: Comparative approaches', in I.G. Mattingly & M. Studdert-Kennedy (eds.), *Modularity and the Motor Theory of Speech Perception*, Lawrence Erlbaum, Hillsdale New Jersey, 393–412.

Bradley, L. & Bryant, P.E.: 1978, 'Difficulties in auditory organisation as a possible cause of reading backwardness', *Nature* 271, 746–747.

Bradley, L. & Bryant, P.E.: 1983, 'Categorizing sounds and learning to read – A causal connection, *Nature* 301, 419–421.

Brady, S.A. & Shankweiler, D.P (eds.): 1991, *Phonological Processes in Literacy*, Lawrence Erlbaum, Hillsdale New Jersey.

Bruce, D.J.: 1964, 'The analysis of word sounds by young children', *British Journal of Educational Psychology* 34, 158–170.

Bryant, P., Bradley, L., Maclean, M. & Crossland, J.: 1989, 'Nursery rhymes, phonological skills and reading', *Journal of Child Language* 16, 407–428.

Castle, J.M., Riach, J. & Nicholson, T.: 1994, 'Getting off to a better start in reading and spelling: The effects of phonemic awareness instruction within a whole language program', *Journal of Educational Psychology* 86, 350–359.

Ehri, L.C.: 1996, 'Researching how children learn to read: Controversies in science are not like controversies in practice', in G.G. Brannigan (ed.), *The Enlightened Educator*, McGraw-Hill, New York, 179–206.

Elkonin, D.B.: 1971, 'Development of speech', in A.V. Zaporozhets & D.B. Elkonin (eds.), *The Psychology of Preschool Children*, MIT Press, Cambridge Massachusetts, 111–185.

Elkonin, D.B.: 1973, 'USSR', in J. Downing (ed.) *Comparative Reading: Cross-National Studies of Behavior and Processes in Reading and Writing*, Macmillan, New York, 551–580.

Golinkoff, R.M.: 1978 'Phonemic awareness skills and reading achievement', in F.B. Murray (ed.) *The Acquisition of Reading: Cognitive, Linguistic and Perceptual Prerequisites*, University Park Press, Baltimore, Maryland, 23–41.

Gough, P.B., Larson, K. & Yopp, H.: 1993, *The Structure of Phonemic Awareness*, paper presented to the International Society for the Study of Behavioral Development, Recife, Brazil.

Hatcher, P.: 1994, *Sound Linkage: An Integrated Programme for Overcoming Reading Difficulties*, Whurr, London.

Hatcher, P.J., Hulme, C. & Ellis, A.W.: 1994, 'Ameliorating early reading failure by integrating the teaching of reading and phonological skills: The phonological linkage hypothesis', *Child Development* 65, 41–57.

Juel, C.: 1988, 'Learning to read and write: A longitudinal study of 54 children from first through fourth grades', *Journal of Educational Psychology* 80, 437–447.

Juel, C., Griffith, P.L. & Gough, P.B.: 1986, 'Acquisition of literacy: A longitudinal study of children in first and second grade', *Journal of Educational Psychology* 78, 243–255.

Layton, L., Deeny, K., Tall, G. & Upton, G.: 1996, 'Researching and promoting phonological awareness in the nursery class', *Journal of Research in Reading* 19, 1–13.

Leong, C.K.: 1991, 'From phonemic awareness to phonological processing to language access in children developing reading proficiency', in D.J. Sawyer & B.J. Fox (eds.), *Phonological Awareness in Reading*, Springer-Verlag, New York, 217–254.

Liberman, A.M.: 1997, 'When theories of speech meet the real world', *Applied Psycholinguistics*.

Liberman, A.M., Cooper, F.S., Shankweiler, D.P. & Studdert-Kennedy, M.: 1967, 'Perception of the speech code', *Psychological Review* 74, 431–461.

Liberman, I., Shankweiler, D., Fischer, W.F. & Carter, B.: 1974, 'Explicit syllable and phoneme segmentation in the young child', *Journal of Experimental Child Psychology* 18, 201–212.

Lundberg, I., Frost, J. & Petersen, O.P.: 1988, 'Effects of an extensive program for stimulating phonological awareness in preschool children', *Reading Research Quarterly* 23, 267–284.

Mann, V.: 1991, 'Phonological awareness and early reading ability: One perspective', in D.J. Sawyer & B.J. Fox (eds.), *Phonological Awareness in Reading*, Springer-Verlag, New York, 191–216.

Nicholson, T.: 1997, 'Closing the gap on reading failure: Social background, phonemic awareness and learning to read', in B.A. Blachman (ed.), *Foundations of Reading Acquisition and Dyslexia: Implications for Early Intervention*, Lawrence Erlbaum, Mahwah New Jersey.

Nicholson, T.: 1994, *At the Cutting Edge: Recent Research on Learning to Read and Spell*, New Zealand Council for Educational Research, Wellington.

Nicholson, T.: 1996, *The Struggletown Project*, unpublished manuscript, School of Education, University of Auckland, Auckland, New Zealand.

Read, C.: 1978, 'Children's awareness of language, with emphasis on sound systems', in A. Sinclair, R.J. Jarvella & W.J. Levelt (eds.), *The Child's Conception of Language*, Springer-Verlag, Berlin Germany, 65–82.

Sawyer, D.J. & Fox, B.J. (eds.): 1991, *Phonological Awareness in Reading*, Springer-Verlag, New York, 191–216.

Share, D.L.: 1995, 'Phonological recoding and self-teaching: Sine qua non of reading acquisition', *Cognition* 55, 151–218.

Stanovich, K.E.: 1986, 'Matthew effects in reading: some consequences of individual differences in the acquisition of literacy', *Reading Research Quarterly* 21, 360–407.

Tunmer, W.E. & Bowey, J.: 1984, 'Metalinguistic awareness and reading acquisition', in W.E. Tunmer, C. Pratt & M.L. Herriman (eds.), *Metalinguistic Awareness in Children*, Springer-Verlag, Berlin Germany, 144–168.

Turner, I., Factor, J. & Lowenstein, W.: 1978, *Cinderella dressed in yella*, Heinemann, Richmond, Victoria, Australia.

Zaporozhets, A.V. & Elkonin, D.B. (eds.): 1971, *The Psychology of Pre-School Children*, MIT Press, Cambridge, Massachusetts.

Zhurova, L.Y.: 1973, 'The development of analysis of words into their sounds by preschool children', in C.A. Ferguson & D.I. Slobin (eds.), *Studies of Child Language Development*, Holt, Rinehart, & Winston, New York, 141–154.

DOMINIEK SANDRA

MORPHOLOGICAL AWARENESS AND THE SECOND LANGUAGE LEARNER

The pervasiveness of morphological structure in the lexicon of many languages suggests that language communities, which are "responsible" for creating a lexicon, find it more helpful to have morphemes as the constituents of words than not to have them. Quite probably, morphemes serve an important function in the process of verbal communication. As in any other form of communication, correct meaning transmission is central to this process and any factor obscuring this should be avoided. The use of polymorphemic words is one way to help achieve this goal of communicative efficiency. Expressing a novel concept in terms of familiar morphemes probably makes it easier for listeners to arrive at the new meaning than using an entirely novel phonological form. For instance, one has the strong intuition that the small animal that jumps around in the grass is better referred to with the name *grasshopper* than with a name like *clanck* (although the latter would be equally good as a linguistic sign). Quite likely the presence of a morphological make-up contributes to the ultimate goal of communicative success.

If morphological structure has a beneficial effect on the process of understanding new words, it might also affect the nature of a word's representation in the mental lexicon. It seems plausible that language users' perception of a word's morphosemantic structure results in a mental representation that is easy to retrieve on subsequent occasions. The present contribution deals with exactly this issue in the context of second language (L2) learning. What is the role of morphology in learning L2 vocabulary? Language awareness will be an important factor in the discussion. L2 learners, being older than children acquiring their first language, may be expected to have reached a level of language awareness which allows them to apply metalinguistic skills to the task of language learning (see also Corson, 1995). Morphological structure is one linguistic domain where such awareness can play a role, which could lead to beneficial effects in learning certain parts of the L2 vocabulary. As few studies have directly addressed the issue at hand, we will also have to look beyond the L2 domain into research on the mental lexicon for L1.

L. van Lier and D. Corson (eds), Encyclopedia of Language and Education,
Volume 6: Knowledge about Language, 63–71.
© *1997 Kluwer Academic Publishers. Printed in the Netherlands.*

EARLY DEVELOPMENTS

In the early seventies a number of psycholinguists became interested in the question whether morphemes are salient units in native speakers' perception of (written) words presented out of linguistic context (Gibson & Guinet, 1971; Murrell & Morton, 1974; Osgood & Hoosain, 1974). Word perception, as the term is used here, does not refer to a mental construct that the language user is aware of (i.e. the perceiver does not have to be aware of the salient units in the perceived word) but to information that is retrieved from memory by automatized perceptual processes eluding awareness. Nonetheless, the issue is important for the present topic, for if words are perceived in terms of their morphemes this would suggest that the latter are representational units in the mental lexicon, i.e. that language users treat them as the building-blocks of words. If this is the 'natural' thing to do, one might argue that it would also help when learning L2 vocabulary.

In the studies of word perception referred to above, brief flashes of words were presented in a tachistoscope (a device for presenting stimuli with millisecond accuracy) and adult subjects were asked to report what they had seen. Murrell & Morton (1974) found that prior study of an item like *car* (the so called prime) in a memory task facilitated the perception of this same morpheme in a tachistoscopically presented word like *cars* (the so called target), which was morphologically related to the prime. Such facilitation was absent when the target was only formally related to the prime (e.g., *car – card*). On the basis of this pattern of findings the authors proposed that the units functioning as entries to the mental lexicon correspond to morphemes.

The relevance of these early findings to the present topic lies at an inferential level. If morphemic representations are present in the native language mental lexicon, learners of a second language might benefit by building their L2 mental lexicon after the native model. This suggests a learning strategy in which novel polymorphemic words are learnt by relating them to their constituent morphemes (if these are familiar to the learner).

MAJOR CONTRIBUTIONS

In this section I will present the major findings concerning the involvement of morphology at the level of the native language mental lexicon and also report on studies that directly aimed at the role of morphology in an L2 context.

Taft & Forster (1975, 1976) published a set of experimental findings that would determine psycholinguistic research on morphology for the next two decades. On the basis of their results they concluded that a single morpheme constitutes the access code to a polymorphemic word in the mental lexicon. In the case of derivations this would be the morpheme that remains after all affixes have been removed (e.g., *happy* in *unhappily*), in the case of compounds it would be the first constituent of the word (e.g., *sun* in *sunshine*). Taft and Forster collected their data in lexical decision experiments, where subjects have to decide whether individually presented letter strings are words in their language or non-words (e.g., *mish*) – i.e. lexical decision requires subjects to consult their mental lexicon – and have to make these decisions under time pressure. The result that is probably most often referred to in the literature is the finding that nonword stems like *trieve* (from *retrieve*), i.e. stems that require an affix, delay reaction times in a lexical decision task, whereas items like *pertoire* (from *repertoire*), i.e. non-morphemic strings with the same degree of orthographic similarity to a real word, do not. According to Taft and Forster this finding indicates that bound stems have a representation in the mental lexicon (suggesting a 'yes' response whereas 'no' is the correct answer), and more particularly serve as the access representation to the word (i.e. comparable to the function of a dictionary entry). Subsequent research by Taft and many other researchers was generally designed with this Taft and Forster model in mind. Although not all results confirmed the model, many findings revealed the importance of morphology at the level of the mental lexicon.

Experiments of the Taft and Forster type tap into knowledge that language users are not consciously aware of. The nature of our mental representations eludes conscious awareness, and this is true for words just as well as for syntactic rules. Even if patterns of lexical organization might suggest learning strategies in school situations – in the present case, morpheme-based learning strategies – it needs to be demonstrated that learners are consciously aware of these relationships and can use them to their advantage in learning situations. A number of experimental studies have addressed this issue.

Freyd & Baron (1982) demonstrated that superior 5th-grade students (about 11 years old), who ranked as exceptionally good students and fast vocabulary learners, made active use of derivational rules whereas ordinary 8th-grade students (about 14 years old) did not. In a vocabulary test, where subjects had to provide definitions for both simple and suffix-derived words, the former group had a greater tendency to analyze the derived words into root and suffix (e.g. *impurity = to be impure*). In a paired associate learning task, where all pairs consisted of a nonsense word followed by an English word (e.g. *skaf-steal*) and half of the pairs were morphologically related to another pair in the list (e.g. *skaffist-thief*), the 5th-grade fast vocabulary learners benefited from the derivational relationships whereas the older 8th-grade subjects did not.

Freyd and Baron's data show that children who are especially good at learning vocabulary have a stronger awareness of morphological relations than slower, though older learners and benefit from this in lexical learning tasks. As a matter of fact, their quick perception of lexical relationships (in this case: morphosemantic relationships) probably explains why they are fast vocabulary learners in the first place. Essentially, the study demonstrates that language awareness and its concomitant metalinguistic skills, which require an abstract attitude with respect to language, determine vocabulary learning rate. The higher a student's level of language awareness the more advantaged he appears to be in lexical learning.

Even though Freyd and Baron's research did not address the issue of learning words in a second language, it seems legitimate to draw some inferences from their paired-associate learning task. Indeed, the first members of the pairs, being nonsense words, are comparable to the novel forms that L2 learners have to learn. Furthermore, the second members of the pairs, i.e. words from the native language, call to mind the presentation format of the translation method that is so often used in L2 teaching. Thus considered, Freyd and Baron's finding in the paired associate learning task suggests that efficient L2 learners might capitalize on derivational relationships.

In some of my own research (Sandra, 1988) I studied the use of morphological relationships by L2 learners directly. Dutch-speaking 17-year old subjects studying English as a foreign language received a list of derived words (type *clearing*) and a list of monomorphemic words (type *ordeal*), the English words being followed by their Dutch translation. One group of subjects received additional information on the morphological composition of each derived word and its semantic motivation (e.g. *clearing*: place in the wood where there are no trees, hence where it is clear), whereas another group received no such information. In a translation test (Dutch into English) higher recall scores were obtained for the derived words than for the monomorphemic ones. The morphosemantic comments which one of the subject groups received did not affect this difference. In other words, learners became spontaneously aware of the morphological relationship between the derived words and their stem. One of the error types was particularly informative on the nature of the learning process involved. Errors of the type *lighting* for *clearing* occurred relatively often. This not only suggests that subjects perceived the morpheme *clear* in *clearing* but also that they encoded its semantic features and used these as a retrieval cue, which sometimes caused lexical intrusion errors at the time of recall (choosing *light* instead of *clear*). Error data like these demonstrate quite clearly that language awareness, i.e. the metalinguistic manipulation of morphological structure, was involved in subjects' learning process.

WORK IN PROGRESS

It has become clear from the foregoing that the topic of morphological awareness in L2 learning has not been widely studied in the international literature. Whereas the domain of morphology has been very popular in research on first language acquisition and the native mental lexicon, it has been largely neglected in the context of learning a second language. It is quite telling that an exhaustive search through the last five years of the social sciences citation index on CD-ROM – using "morph" as a (very broad) search term – did not bring up a single study where the role of morphological awareness was investigated in an L2 learning environment.

Some years ago I ran a couple of follow-up experiments on my previous study (Sandra, 1993). As mentioned above, the earlier study had shown that learners tag the semantic property that is lexicalized by the stem (i.e. the presence of a lot of light) and use this property at the time of recall (hence the *lighting/clearing* substitution errors). What apparently gets stored in memory is the semantic motivation for the morphological relationship. This property of the memorization technique suggested further experiments. If perception of the morphosemantic relationship was central to the effect, the use of semantically non-transparent derivations should make it more difficult for learners to make successful use of the technique.

In an experiment with computer-paced item presentation the stem-based encoding technique was studied with semantically less transparent items. Nonsense combinations of an existing stem and suffix were made and presented with a short description of the item's meaning (e.g., *tandeling* = tooth + suffix; E. tax collector). Subjects in the experimental condition received comments that explicated the morphosemantic relationship (e.g., 'bites off' pieces of people's income), whereas those in the control condition did not (all subjects were first year undergraduates). On average, experimental subjects needed fewer presentations of the derived words before they could produce them than control subjects. This shows that morphosemantic comments for semantically less transparent derived words are helpful in memory encoding and subsequent recall. Somewhat surprisingly, the effect was absent in a later final recall test. Possibly, this recall test was administered too soon after the learning phase, making it difficult to detect differences in memory decay between the two learning conditions. There was indeed only a short distraction task between the learning phase (criterion: no remaining errors) and the recall task. The item list also contained a number of less opaque items, which may have encouraged control subjects to actively look for morphosemantic relationships, which would have obliterated differences between the two conditions on a final recall test (although not necessarily on the required presentation frequency during learning).

Interestingly, the notion of semantic transparency has also recently attracted the attention of researchers investigating the role of morphology at the level of the native mental lexicon. Marslen-Wilson, Tyler, Waksler & Older (1994) explicitly state that semantic transparency is one of the factors that must be taken into account when studying the mental representation of polymorphemic words (see also Sandra (1990) and Zwitserlood (1994) for similar points of view in the area of compound words). In their study of derived words Marslen-Wilson et al. used the so-called immediate cross-modal priming technique, where a visual stimulus is presented immediately upon the disappearance of an auditory stimulus and subjects have to decide as quickly as possible whether the visual stimulus is a word or a non-word (lexical decision). They observed that subjects made faster lexical decisions to a word like *govern* when the preceding auditory stimulus was a word like *government* than when it was a non-related word. This facilitation effect was absent for auditory-visual pairs like *department – depart*. Pretest data on the words' semantic transparency (i.e. ratings on a 7-point scale) had indicated that *government* type words and *department* type words belonged to two distinct categories in subjects' perception: semantically transparent and semantically opaque items respectively. On the basis of this experimental outcome Marslen-Wilson et al. concluded that semantically transparent suffix-derived words are represented as stem + suffix (*govern* + *ment*), whereas semantically opaque suffix-derived words are stored as if they were monomorphemic (*department*).

It is important to emphasise that in Marslen-Wilson et al.'s study semantic transparency is not defined in linguistic terms but as a function of subjects' perception of the semantic relationship between the derived words and their stems. The fact that, linguistically speaking, a linguistic entity is a morpheme does not necessarily mean that language users also perceive it as such in a particular word of the language. We are dealing here with 'a cognitive, or psycholinguistic, concept of the morpheme, developmentally definable for each [language user] in terms of its synchronic semantic interpretability' (Marslen-Wilson et al., 1994, p. 31).

Other researchers too have defended the claim that the lexical representation of morphologically complex words cannot be studied without considering the (synchronic) semantic relationship to their constituent morphemes. In a recent paper Schreuder & Baayen (1995) set out from the claim that 'the role of morphology is essentially one of computing (new) meaning' (p. 132). In their model semantically transparent and opaque words develop different kinds of representations in the mental lexicon. Note that this view essentially amounts to the view presented at the beginning of this paper: the very existence of morphologically complex words at all and their persistence across the lexicons of various languages results from the function of morphology in communicative situations, which is meaning computation.

PROBLEMS AND DIFFICULTIES

As has been mentioned earlier, few studies have directly addressed the question whether the task of vocabulary learning is facilitated by L2 learners' metalinguistic awareness of morphological relationships (and, if so, what the underlying mechanisms are). At this stage, the scarce data have to be supplemented by evidence bearing on the lexical representation of polymorphemic words in the native language. This is quite problematic, even if it may seem intuitively plausible that L2 learners use the same principles of lexical representation in L2 as in their L1. Indeed, one should keep in mind that L1 and L2 learners usually differ in age and, consequently, in a number of age-related cognitive abilities such as metalinguistic awareness.

There are several sources of evidence that language awareness plays a larger role in L2 learning than in L1 acquisition. For instance, morphological awareness has been shown to increase with age (Derwing & Baker, 1979, 1986). Whereas young children's judgments of morphological relatedness are primarily guided by the words' phonetic similarity, adult language users consider both phonetic and semantic overlap. In addition to this age effect, language awareness may involve other factors. For instance, Freyd and Baron's finding that fast vocabulary learners are more aware of the morphosemantic structure of words than average learners (while being younger) reveals such a factor (general or verbal intelligence?). There have also been explicit demonstrations that L2 learners transfer their own L1 vocabulary knowledge to the task of L2 vocabulary learning. For instance, Hancin-Bhatt & Nagy (1994) have shown that low-frequency Latinate words in English are more transparent to Spanish-speaking learners than to other L2 learners because the Spanish counterparts of these words occur frequently in the language (e.g. E. *infirm* versus Sp. *enfermo*). In other words, there are reasons to believe that L2 learners differ along a number of important dimensions from young children acquiring their native lexicon (see Corson, 1995, for more discussion of the concept of language awareness). These differences make it difficult to draw inferences from research on the L1 mental lexicon with respect to the learning and representation of L2 vocabulary.

Yet, at the same time it cannot be denied that there is an encouraging parallelism between the results from experimental studies on the L1 lexicon and the findings in experiments on L2 vocabulary learning. Both lines of research have revealed the language user's sensitivity to the semantic transparency of polymorphemic words when representing these items in memory (compare Marslen-Wilson et al.'s results for the L1 mental lexicon to Sandra's findings for L2 vocabulary learning). Possibly, this parallelism results from the use of adult subjects in both areas of research. Indeed, as psycholinguistic research on representational issues concerning the L1 mental lexicon does not address language acquisition but the "steady state" of the representational system, only adult subjects (usually university undergraduates) are studied. Now, even if the initial acquisition of words in L1 may be relatively unaffected by factors of language awareness (*in casu:* morphological awareness), the eventual representation of words in the adult's mental lexicon may still be affected by such factors, i.e. representations in the mental lexicon may change with developing language awareness. For instance, the representation of polymorphemic words may depend on the adult language user's perception of morphosemantic structure. It seems an interesting hypothesis – although thus far it is not more than a hypothesis – that the morpheme-based encoding technique for semantically transparent derivations that I witnessed in vocabulary learning experiments (Sandra, 1988, 1993) hinges on the same encoding process that is applied to the L1 vocabulary and that results in morphologically segmented lexical representations (Marslen-Wilson et al., 1994).

FUTURE DIRECTIONS

Clearly, more work is needed on the kind of metalinguistic strategies that L2 learners bring to the task of vocabulary learning. As far as the role of morphological awareness is concerned, little is known at the present point in time. Three issues are important for future research on this topic: (i) How does morphological awareness interact with semantic transparency?, (ii) How does morphological awareness interact with learner variables (age, rate of vocabulary learning)? and (iii) Under which circumstances (as defined by, for instance, learner and word characteristics) do L2 learners benefit from explicitly provided relationships between polymorphemic words and their constituent morphemes?

University of Antwerp
Belgium

REFERENCES

Corson, D.: 1995, *Using English words*, Kluwer Academic Publishers, Dordrecht.
Derwing, B.L. & Baker, W.J.: 1979, 'Recent research on the acquisition of English morphology', in P. Fletcher & M. Garman (eds.), *Language Acquisition: Studies in First Language Development*, Cambridge University Press.
Derwing, B.L. & Baker, W.J.: 1986, 'Assessing morphological development', in P. Fletcher & M. Garman (eds.), *Language Acquisition: Studies in First Language Development* (second edition), Cambridge University Press.
Freyd, P. & Baron, J.: 1982, 'Individual differences in acquisition of derivational morphology', *Journal of Verbal Learning and Verbal Behavior* 21, 282–295.
Gibson, E. & Guinet, L.: 1971, 'Perception of inflections in brief visual presentations of words', *Journal of Verbal Learning and Verbal Behavior* 10, 182–189.
Hancin-Bhatt, B. & Nagy, W.: 1994, 'Lexical transfer and second language morphological development', *Applied Psycholinguistics* 15, 289–310.

Henderson, L.: 1985, 'Toward a psychology of morphemes', in A.W. Ellis (ed.), *Progress in the Psychology of Language* (Vol. 1), Lawrence Erlbaum, Hove.

Marslen-Wilson, W., Tyler, L., Waksler, R. & Older, L.: 1994, 'Morphology and meaning in the English mental lexicon', *Psychological Review* 101, 3–33.

Murrell, G. & Morton, J.: 1974, 'Word recognition and morphemic structure', *Journal of Experimental Psychology* 102, 963–968.

Osgood, C. & Hoosain, R.: 1974, 'Salience of the word as a unit in the perception of language', *Perception and Psychophysics* 15, 168–192.

Sandra, D.: 1988, 'Is morphology used to encode derivations when learning a foreign language?', *ITL Review of Applied Linguistics* 79/80, 1–23.

Sandra, D.: 1990, 'On the representation and processing of compound words: Automatic access to constituent morphemes does not occur', *Quarterly Journal of Experimental Psychology* 42A, 529–567.

Sandra, D.: 1993, 'The use of lexical morphology as a natural mnemonic aid in learning foreign language vocabulary', in J. Chapelle & M.-T. Claes (eds.), *Proceedings of the First International Congress on Memory and Memorization in Acquiring and Learning Languages*, CLL, Louvain-la-Neuve, 263–294.

Schreuder, R. & Baayen, H.: 1995, 'Modeling morphological processing', in L.B. Feldman (ed.), *Morphological Aspects of Language Processing*, Lawrence Erlbaum, Hove, 131–154.

Taft, M. & Forster, K.: 1975, 'Lexical storage and retrieval of prefixed words', *Journal of Verbal Learning and Verbal Behavior* 14, 638–647.

Taft, M. & Forster, K.: 1976, 'Lexical storage and retrieval of prefixed words', *Journal of Verbal Learning and Verbal Behavior* 15, 607–620.

Zwitserlood, P.: 1994, 'The Role of semantic transparency in the processing and representation of Dutch compounds', *Language and Cognitive Processes* 9, 341–368.

SABINE JONES

LANGUAGE AWARENESS AND LEARNING STYLES

The interest in individual differences in perception led to research into cognitive learning styles in the 1950s and 60s. The aim of this review is to show the background to the early developments in cognitive style theory and to point out how the concept has changed today. From an early emphasis on cognition, more recently attempts have been made to develop more integrated learning styles which encapsulate the multidimensional nature of the learning process. It has become an educational aim to make learners aware of their own learning styles, i.e. to make the processes underlying language learning explicit in order to enable them to gain some control over their learning procedures. Factors involved in raising learners' awareness are presented and difficulties are pointed out (also see the reviews by Gardner and by Hamayan in Volume 4).

EARLY DEVELOPMENTS

In the 1950s research into cognitive learning styles emanated from the New Look Movement, a loose confederation of perception psychologists who were critical of the then dominant approaches to perception which neglected the point of view of the person who does the perceiving (Witkin & Goodenough, 1982, p. 1). It was, for example, the early behaviourist position that language learning was an external not an internal phenomenon, the emphasis being on the importance of input; learning was a process of habit formation through repetition and reinforcement. In sharp contrast, nativistic theorising, exemplified most notably by Chomsky, assumed that the way our perceptual systems organise language acquisition is innately given and everybody therefore follows a uniform pattern. A different line of research investigated individual differences in perception, which were then used as points of departure for research into cognitive learning styles.

The educational interest in individual learner differences found support from psychological theory and neurological evidence in the 1950s and 60s. Cantril & Livingston (1963) suggest that the term *transaction* more appropriately describes a psychological event than does the term interaction, in that it emphasises 'the contribution the perceiving individual makes in shaping his own perceptions' (p. 6). From neurological evidence Cantril and Livingston present the picture of a 'central transactional core' (p. 7) in the central nervous system which exerts a constant modulating influence

L. van Lier and D. Corson (eds), Encyclopedia of Language and Education,
Volume 6: Knowledge about Language, 73–84.
© 1997 Kluwer Academic Publishers. Printed in the Netherlands.

on sensory input as well as on motor output. The view that the individual actively participates in the learning process is at the core of transactional theory of learning.

Further support for this comes from personality theory. Kelly (1955) asserts that the whole of the individual's psychological processes are thought of as arising directly from his personal constructs, i.e. from the ways in which he interprets as well as from the ways in which he anticipates events. Ames (1953) addressed the question as to the origin of our perceptual constancies. In his theory of *transactional functionalism* he tried to show that our fundamental perceptions are learnt reactions based on our interactions and transactions with the environment, they are 'pragmatic truths', which means that they work for us in practice. This functional point of view also seems to partly explain why people have different learning styles – because the procedures were found expedient in the past.

MAJOR CONTRIBUTIONS

An interest in individual differences in processing information led to the theory of *cognitive learning styles* which was widely researched during the 1960s and early 1970s. (Vernon 1973; Witkin et al., 1977; Claxton & Ralston, 1978; Entwistle, 1981; Witkin & Goodenough, 1982). According to Witkin and his colleagues, who did the most extensive research into this area, cognitive learning styles reflect systematic differences in the way individuals tend to approach learning and problem-solving. The emphasis is placed on 'how' the individual processes information and not on 'what' or 'how much' is processed. Witkin et al. (1977) describe them as follows:

Cognitive styles are concerned with the form rather than the content of cognitive activity. They refer to individual differences in how we perceive, think, solve problems, learn, relate to others, etc. The definition of cognitive styles is thus cast in process terms (p. 15).

The concept of cognitive style is not limited to cognition in the narrow sense. Witkin & Goodenough (1982) describe it more in holistic terms:

It is a pervasive dimension of individual functioning, showing itself in the perceptual, intellectual, personality, and social domains, and connected in its formation with the development of the organism as a whole (p. 57).

The two probably most extensively investigated cognitive learning styles are *field-dependence – field-independence* (Witkin et al., 1977; Witkin & Goodenough, 1982). Very briefly summarised, a field-independent person tends to approach situations in an analytical way, separating elements from their background, whereas a field-dependent person tends to see the whole rather than the parts and approaches situations in a global way. The two style dimensions can be assessed by the Group Embedded Figures Test (Oltman et al., 1971), a self-diagnostic test which enables students to identify their own learning style preferences.

Cognitive learning styles are not exclusive categories, they are rather individual tendencies, they are labels representing more of one and less of the other aspect. Furthermore, cognitive learning styles are a relatively stable factor, they have been shown to remain consistent over a period of many years. However, as Witkin et al. (1977) point out, although they are 'stable over time', 'this does not imply that they are unchangeable' (p. 15).

The term *learning style* has emerged more recently as a more common term or as a replacement term for cognitive learning style. One main difference between the two concepts is that, whilst cognitive style is a bipolar dimension, learning style models are multidimensional rather than bipolar and encompass a range of variables including many of a non-cognitive nature.

Learning styles are normally assessed by means of questionnaires, self-diagnostic tests or problem-solving tasks (for description of test-instruments see Murray-Harvey, 1994). Here follow some examples of cognitive/learning style models which have been found significant for language learning: cognitive complexity-simplicity (Bieri, 1961); toler-ance for unrealistic experiences (Klein, Gardner, & Schlesinger, 1962); impulsive-reflective (Kagan, 1965); holist-serialist (Pask, 1976); deep-level – surface-level processing (Marton & Säljö, 1976); field-dependent – field-independent (Witkin et al., 1977); visual-auditory-hands-on styles (Reid, 1987). Multidimensional or integrated models of learning styles are: The Myers-Briggs Type Indicator (MBTI) (Myers & Briggs, 1967), which consists of 4 scales: extraversion-introversion, sensation-intuition, thinking-feeling and judging-perceiving; and the Kolb Model (Kolb, 1984), a self-report Learning Style Inventory (LSI) which assesses the following individual dimensions: abstract-concrete and active-reflective.

Generally a difference is drawn between learning style and *learning strategy*. Style is considered to be a fairly fixed characteristic of an indi-vidual, 'a superordinate construct which is involved in many cognitive operations' (Vernon, 1973, p. 141), while strategies are more specific actions which apply to specific learning tasks; they are tools in the acqui-sition or learning of a language. Making students aware of their learning styles therefore needs to be complemented by instructional strategies which make effective use of the different styles (Birckbichler & Omaggio, 1978; Oxford, 1990 and see the review by Oxford in Volume 4).

Present Position on Learning Styles

Riding & Cheema (1991) undertook a literature search which 'revealed over 30 labels referred to as cognitive/learning styles' (p. 196). An obvious conclusion is that there is now a need for clarification and systematisation. Curry (1983) and Riding & Cheema (1991) argue that one of the root causes preventing significant progress in the application of cognitive/learning styles to training and education is the bewildering confusion of definitions surrounding learning style conceptualisations and the concomitant wide variation in scale or scope of behaviour claimed to be predicted by learning style models.

Riding & Cheema (1991) made an attempt at economising while at the same time capturing the main personality dimensions. They found that an analysis of a multitude of cognitive/learning styles suggested that they may be grouped into two principal cognitive styles and a number of learning strategies. These were labelled the wholist-analytic style and verbaliser-imager style (p. 196). These two styles may be thought of as independent of one another, and they can be assessed using the Cognitive Styles Analysis which is a computer presented test.

A further attempt at capturing the main personality dimensions was made by Miller (1991). Miller's personality typology is composed of cognitive, affective and conative dimensions, and he defines main types in terms of the analytic-holistic and objective-subjective dimensions, assuming further that each of these main types exhibits stable and unstable variants (p. 227).

Curry (1983) attempted to systematise the number of assessment instruments. He proposed that all cognitive/learning style measures may be grouped into three main types or 'strata resembling layers of an onion' (in Riding & Cheema, p. 195); in this 'onion model' learning style measures are organised in that they range from the most easily influenced level of measurement in the outermost layer to measurements of relatively permanent personality dimensions in the third innermost layer.

Some Research Findings

Oxford & Anderson (1995) in their state of the art article on *crosscultural* views of learning styles present ample evidence that learning styles have a strong cultural component and that our cognitive development is determined by the demands of the environment in which we grew up. Cultural differences also affect the kind of style assessment one should choose. In a class with Hispanic or Arabic students, for example, a personal interview or whole-class discussion about styles might be considered both useful and entertaining, but to a Japanese or Korean student the same process might be daunting (Oxford & Anderson, 1995, p. 212).

Learning styles are found to have a developmental aspect. For western societies, field independence/dependence, for example, follows a developmental curve. Children become increasingly field-independent until about the age of 15. Field-independence then stabilises until approximately age 30 when it gradually begins to decrease (Witkin & Goodenough, 1982). In addition, with regard to gender difference, in western societies consistent differences between men and women have been found: men tend to be slightly more field-independent than women (Witkin & Goodenough, 1982).

WORK IN PROGRESS

Over the last 10 years educational practitioners as well as theorists have combined their interest in individual differences with ways of making learners aware of their personal learning styles and strategies. This coincided with a related trend towards independent learning and the autonomous learner. *Awareness* has come under investigation under various labels, such as consciousness, metacognition, interlanguage, introspection or implicit/explicit learning (Sorace, 1985; Munsell, Rauen, & Kinjo, 1988; Schmidt, 1990; Matsumoto, 1993; Ellis, 1995; see also Ellis, this volume). In spite of the lack of any unifying theory, some issues are presented in the following which are involved in making learners aware of their learning processes.

Consciousness

Schmidt (1990) distinguishes several senses of the term consciousness: consciousness as awareness, consciousness as intention and consciousness as knowledge (p. 131). There are degrees or levels of consciousness as awareness, they are: level 1: perception, level 2: noticing or focal awareness and level 3: understanding (p. 132).

Various researchers hold that attention (or focal awareness) to input is necessary for input to become intake, which is only then available for further mental processing (e.g. Schmidt, 1990). The basic finding, that memory requires attention and awareness, was established early within the information processing model. It was found that unattended material makes it into short term memory, but since there is no opportunity to selectively attend and notice, it cannot be processed into long term memory (Schmidt, 1990, p. 141). Craik & Lockhart (1972) found similarly that only stimuli which receive full attention, and undergo a greater degree of semantic or cognitive analysis, yield a deeper encoding of the event and a longer-lasting memory trace. Craik & Tulving (1975) concluded from their experiments that the durability of a memory trace depended mostly on the 'mental activity' (p. 292) of the learner on the item. Simon (1994) goes one step further in linking a wide range of phenomena regarding attention; he sees components of cognition, motivation and emotion acting together in regulating behaviour, with attention being the principal link between them.

Other studies focus on understanding as necessary for processing input. Ausubel (1971) found that only meaningfully learnt material is stored and thus retrievable. Learning experiences are not meaningful 'unless they are built on a foundation of clearly understood concepts and principles, and unless the constituent operations are themselves meaningful' (p. 198).

There is no consensus on the role of consciousness in second/foreign language learning. Some people seem to benefit from conscious analysis, others seem to benefit little; this suggests there may exist a continuum between conscious and unconscious processes. Factors relating to either end of the continuum may include the following: they may relate to cultural background; Pohl (1994), for example, found great resistance to processes of inquiry and introspection inherent in language awareness tasks he employed among Hungarian trainee teachers. He concludes that these methods were inappropriate to 'the socio-educational context in which learners and teachers operate' (p. 158). Developmental factors may also play a role with regard to the degree of conscious/unconscious behaviour: Ceci & Howe (1982) report a number of experiments in support of the hypothesis that the major change from child to adult consciousness is a shift from a passive mode that includes an open awareness of the environment, to a more controlled mode that includes the strategic allocation of attention. The age range during which this shift takes place approximates to the sensitive period for language acquisition (Schmidt, 1990, p. 145). A further factor involved in conscious or unconscious information processing may relate to different learning styles: at one end of the continuum Schmeck (1983) places ' "deep-elaborative learners" (those who "think" while they study', and at the other end ' "shallow-reiterative learners" (those who rely on sheer repetition)' (p. 271).

Implicit/Explicit Learning

Language awareness means making explicit and conscious the students' intuitive use of learning procedures, drawing, of course, on the current state of knowledge in these matters. Reber (1993) describes implicit learning as 'a process that takes place largely outside of consciousness' (p. 133), whereas explicit learning is a more conscious operation. Implicit and explicit learning are, however, not completely separate and independent processes; 'they should properly be viewed as interactive components or cooperative processes' (Reber, 1993, p. 23). In evolutionary terms, processes such as implicit learning, which operate independently of consciousness, are more primitive and basic than those that are dependent on conscious control, and therefore, according to Reber, implicit cognitive processes tend to be more 'robust and resilient', and 'we should expect to find fewer individual differences between people when implicit processes are in use than when explicit processes are' (p. 7).

Explicit knowledge has a role in that it not only helps the learner to understand language, that is to establish connections between meaning and form; but it has also an additional role in that it can feed back on acquisition, that is it can serve as a functional stimulus to the acquisition process.

Process and Procedural Knowledge

In Schmidt's (1990) concept of 'consciousness as knowledge' (see above) a distinction is made between declarative knowledge (knowledge of facts) and procedural knowledge (knowledge 'how'). Procedural knowledge varies along a continuum from controlled to automatic (p. 134). Recent interlanguage studies describe procedural knowledge as being responsible for access to the internalised knowledge and therefore for the ability to perform on the basis of it; procedural knowledge is in fact considered itself to be a second kind of competence (Sorace, 1985, p. 239). The best strategy users, according to Sorace, are 'those who, in addition to their adequate metalinguistic knowledge, have also developed adequate procedural knowledge' (p. 251). It would be wrong to see process and content as a dichotomy, it is rather the case that they interrelate. When we emphasise process, Parker & Rubin (1966) argue, 'knowledge becomes the vehicle rather than the destination' (p. 2), and process becomes 'the life-blood of content' (p. 4). Processes seem to integrate the knowledge system itself and maintain it as a bounded organisation, they are adjustive processes across boundaries.

Bialystok & Sharwood Smith (1985) are of the view that the processes which underlie first- and second-language acquisition are the same; adult learners have further resources at their disposal to facilitate the process, 'but the process itself does not change' (p. 104). Also, there is no dichotomy of learning vs communication strategies – the functions overlap. Bialystok & Sharwood Smith conclude that 'if the categories of learning and communication are abandoned, then what is left is simply a repertoire of strategies from which learners select under various conditions' (p. 113).

According to Parker & Rubin (1966), 'every process, whatever its character, necessarily must have a construct – an underlying scheme which provides order and direction' (p. 2). The cognitive learning style approach provides an underlying scheme or framework which gives some order and direction to our learning processes; the principles it offers shed light on and give some meaning to the nature of process. Making students aware of their learning styles and of the strategies they employ is one way of providing them with guidelines and criteria which can make their learning more meaningful to them and which gives them some direction when they reflect about their learning.

Introspective Methods

Cohen & Hosenfeld (1981) were among the first researchers to argue for the usefulness of self-observation of mental processes by L2 learners, emphasising that the learners themselves have important insights and intuitions into the internal processing involved in language use and learning. Today increasing attention is being paid to metacognitive strategies learners employ, that is to strategies which involve thinking about the learning process, as well as planning, monitoring and evaluating it, and the methodology of verbal reporting has again come to the fore. Matsumoto (1993) investigates 4 major introspective methods used in second language research, which are thinking-aloud, questionnaires, interviews, diary-keeping, and she concludes that introspective verbal reports will continue to 'provide us with useful information concerning the inner workings of the mind unobtainable from extrospective observational studies alone' (p. 51). However, mentalistic approaches enjoy a modified support. Some argue that conscious awareness is limited to the products of mental processes and the processes themselves are beyond the reach of introspection.

PROBLEMS AND DIFFICULTIES

Dealing with Style Conflicts

Pask's (1976) research shows that 'if you impose on learners the strategy which does not correspond to their "type", they do not learn properly and do not retain what they have learnt' (p. 132). However, as various studies on cognitive styles indicate (e.g. Witkin, 1977, pp. 28, 33), teachers are equally influenced and guided in their teaching by their cognitive styles, in that they show different patterns of teaching behaviour.

One way of overcoming what Oxford & Lavine (1992) call 'style wars in the classroom', is to match learning and teaching styles. It was found that if the teaching strategy is matched to the student's learning style, 'the student will learn more quickly and retain the information for longer' (Pask, 1976, p. 132); and teacher-student match in terms of cognitive style also makes for greater interpersonal attraction than mismatch (Witkin, 1977, p. 33). However, philosophical and pragmatic questions have been raised as to the wisdom of this. Arguments used against matching are that a diversification of student learning styles may better allow students to meet the demands of academic teaching methods and assignments (Reid, 1987, p. 101), and that students need to develop the compensation techniques needed for situations in which style conflicts exist – for instance in the business world (Oxford & Lavine, 1992, p. 42).

Is Versatility a Desirable Educational Goal?

Versatility, or the ability to adapt flexibly to life's demands, is a common theme in conceptions of the optimal personality. Furthermore, driven by the information explosion, or the knowledge explosion, our expectations about what students should learn have changed; not only has the capacity to develop lifelong learning skills become a necessity, our increasing knowledge about the nature of learning points inevitably to the interest in individualised learning and to the creation of customized learning environments that accommodate the diverse learning styles of our students. Witkin et al. (1977) write:

For the educator, the development of greater diversity in behaviors within individuals seems as important an objective as the recognition and the utilization of diversity among individuals (p. 53).

There are claims of success in such endeavours (e.g. Kolb, 1984, p. 206), but Miller (1991) has his reservations. The more stylistically 'specialised' an individual, he argues, the more difficult will it be to encourage versatility. This is because specialisation serves a defensive function in protecting the individual from anxiety. Extremely specialised students should be left alone, secure within the confines of their dominant mode, and attempts should rather be made to adjust teaching to suit these styles, but not to change them. It follows that 'versatility is a reasonable goal for those who are already predisposed to it' (Miller, p. 235). Ethical questions are also raised by attempts to modify styles. Separating out relatively flexible students for special treatment smacks of elitism and would be controversial (Miller, p. 236).

Solutions suggested

- A more practicable solution lies in sensitising teachers and students to the complexity of reciprocal interaction in the classroom and in equipping students with some specific tools, i.e. strategies, for handling those interactions.
- Strategy training, integrated into regular classroom activities rather than offered as a separate how-to-learn course has been documented, for example, by Oxford (1990).
- Oxford & Lavine (1992) suggest a change in the way style conflicts are viewed: we could present style differences in a positive light.
- The role of the teacher will be seen in a new light: teachers need to sharpen their skills as diagnosticians and also as strategists; they need to become aware of diverse learner styles and characteristics and of the likely impact of their own teaching strategies on learners with different styles. This has implications for teacher training.

- Claxton & Ralston (1978) draw attention to institutional characteristics which may influence the use of alternative modes of instruction, such as investigating students' learning styles; the atmosphere of the institution toward educational change would be one such influencing factor (p. 39).

FUTURE DIRECTIONS

Riding & Cheema (1991) highlighted the bewildering confusion of definitions surrounding learning style conceptualisations, and this view is reflected in much of the research literature. It would further our understanding of learning styles if they were incorporated into a theory, such as for example, the systems theory presented by Grinker (1967). Learning style, as a process and a superordinate construct, obviously plays a different role in the personality system than does a learning strategy which is easily changed. The holistic approach to learning, according to which everything is interrelated can easily lead to a totally relativistic position with regard to learning styles – unless they are presented in a theoretical framework with a hierarchic structure.

Miller (1991) points out that many well-established learning styles reflect a cognitive emphasis. Although this is being remedied in the integrated models of learning styles, it is true that the conative (or motivational) dimension has been neglected in style dimensions – and this is also the case with regard to strategies. A new interest in conation is, however, noticeable.

There are some references to a developmental pattern for metalinguistic abilities (e.g. Sorace, 1985, p. 248); the relationship between a development in declarative and a development in procedural knowledge is, however, not clear. One of the values of Kolb's experiential learning model is that it takes into account the developmental pattern of learning throughout life. Kolb suggests that people go through three growth processes: acquisition, specialisation, and integration (in Claxton & Ralston, 1978, p. 30). The data from empirical research into learning styles have so far not been related to maturational stages.

There is some experimental evidence as well as a fair amount of support from educational theory for making students aware of their own learning processes (i.e. styles and strategies); and some advantages of this have been presented. So far, very little has been published which sees language awareness in a more critical light and which points at possible disadvantages of raising awareness.

University of Ulster at Coleraine
Northern Ireland

REFERENCES

Ames, A. Jr.,: 1953, 'Reconsideration of the origin and nature of perception', in S. Ratner (ed.), *Vision and Action*, Rutgers University Press, New Brunswick, N.J.

Ausubel, D.P.: 1971, 'Reception learning and the rote-meaningful dimension', in E. Stones (ed.), *Readings in Educational Psychology* (2nd edn), Methuen & Co., London.

Bialystok, E. & Sharwood Smith, M.: 1985, 'Interlanguage is not a state of mind: An evaluation of the construct for second-language acquisition', *Applied Linguistics* 6(2), 101–117.

Bieri, J.: 1961, 'Complexity-simplicity as a personality variable in cognitive and preferential behavior', in D.W. Fiske & S.R. Maddi (eds.), *Functions of Varied Experience*, Dorsey Press, Homewood, IL.

Birckbichler, D.W. & Omaggio, A.C.: 1978, 'Diagnosing and responding to individual learner needs', *Modern Language Journal* 62, 336–344.

Cantril, H. & Livingston, W.K.: 1963, 'The concept of transaction in psychology and neurology', *Journal of Individual Psychology* XIX, 3–16.

Ceci, S. & Howe, M.: 1982, 'Metamemory and effects of intending, attending, and intending to attend', in G. Underwood (ed.), *Aspects of Consciousness*, vol. 3, Academic Press, London.

Claxton, C.S. & Ralston, Y.: 1978, *Learning Styles: Their Impact on Teaching and Administration* (Research Report No 10), American Association for Higher Education, Washington, DC.

Cohen, A.D. & Hosenfeld, C.: 1981, 'Some uses of mentalistic data in second language research', *Language Learning* 31(2).

Craik, F.I.M. & Lockhart, R.S.: 1972, 'Levels of processing: A framework for memory research', *Journal of Verbal Learning and Verbal Behavior* 11, 671–684.

Craik, F.I.M. & Tulving, E.: 1975, 'Depth processing and the retention of words in episodic memory', *Journal of Experimental Psychology: General* 104(3), 268–294.

Curry, L.: 1983, 'An organization of learning styles theory and constructs', *ERIC Document* 235: 185.

Ellis, N.C.: 1995, 'Consciousness in second language acquisition: A review of field studies and laboratory experiments', *Language Awareness* 4(3), 123–146.

Entwistle, N.: 1981, *Styles of Learning and Teaching. An Integrated Outline of Educational Psychology for Students, Teachers, and Lecturers*, John Wiley & Sons, Chichester.

Grinker, R.R. (ed.): 1967, *Toward a Unified Theory of Human Behaviour. An Introduction to General Systems Theory*, Basic Books, Inc., New York.

Kagan, J.:1965, 'Reflection impulsivity and reading ability in primary grade children', *Child Development* 36, 609–628.

Kelly, G.A.: 1955, *The Psychology of Personal Constructs*, Norton, New York.

Klein, G.C, Gardner, R.W. & Schlesinger, H.J.: 1962, 'Tolerance for unrealistic experiences: A study of the generality of cognitive controls', *British Journal of Psychology* 53, 41–55.

Kolb, D.A.: 1984, *Experiential Learning. Experience as the Source of Learning and Development*, Prentice-Hall, Englewood Cliffs, N.J.

Marton, F. & Säljö, R.: 1976, 'On qualitative differences in learning: I – Outcome and process', *British Journal of Educational Psychology* 46, 4–11.

Matsumoto, K.: 1993, 'Verbal-Report data and introspective methods in second language research: State of the art', *RELC Journal* 24(1), 32–60.

Miller, A.: 1991, 'Personality types, learning styles and educational goals', *Educational Psychology* 11(3), 217–238.

Munsell, P.E., Rauen, M.G. & Kinjo, M.: 1988, 'Review essay. Language learning and the brain: A comprehensive survey recent conclusions', *Language Learning* 38(2), 261–278.

Murray-Harvey, R.: 1994, 'Learning styles and approaches learning: Distinguishing between concepts and instruments', *British Journal of Educational Psychology* 64, 373–388.

Myers, I. & Briggs, K.: 1967, *The Myers-Briggs Type Indicator*, Educational Testing Service, Princeton.

Oltman, P.K., Raskin, E. & Witkin, H.A.: 1971, *Group Embedded Figures Test*, Consulting Psychologists Press, Palo Alto.

Oxford, R.L.: 1990, *Language Learning Strategies. What Every Teacher Should Know*, Heinle & Heinle Publ., Boston, Mass.

Oxford, R.L. & Lavine, R.Z.: 1992, 'Teacher-student style wars in the language classroom: Research insights and suggestions', *ADFL Bulletin* 23, 38–45.

Oxford, R.L. & Anderson, N.J.: 1995, 'A crosscultural view of learning styles' state of the art article', *Language Teaching* 28, 201–215.

Parker, J.C. & Rubin, L.J.: 1966, *Process as Content. Curriculum Design and the Application of Knowledge*, Rand McNally College Publishing Company, Chicago/Ill.

Pask, G.: 1976, 'Styles and strategies of learning', *British Journal of Educational Psychology* 46, 128–148.

Pohl, J.-U.: 1994, 'The process side of language awareness: A Hungarian case study', *Language Awareness* 3(3&4), 151–160.

Reber, A.S.: 1993, *Implicit Learning and Tacit Knowledge. An Essay on the Cognitive Unconscious*, Oxford University Press, New York.

Reid, J.: 1987, 'The learning style preferences of ESL students', *TESOL Quarterly* 21(1), 87–111.

Riding, R.J. & Cheema, I.: 1991, 'Cognitive styles – an overview and integration', *Educational Psychology* 11(3), 193–215.

Schmeck, R.R.: 1983, 'Learning styles of college students', in R.D. Dillon & R.R. Schmeck (eds.), *Individual Differences in Cognition*, vol.1, Academic Press, New York, 233–279.

Schmidt, R.: 1990, 'The role of consciousness in second language learning', *Applied Linguistics* 11, 129–158.

Simon, H.A.: 1994, 'The bottleneck of attention: Connecting thought with motivation', in W.D. Spaulding (ed.), *Integrative Views of Motivation, Cognition, and Emotion*, vol. 41 of the Nebraska Symposium on Motivation, University of Nebraska Press, Lincoln and London, 1–21.

Sorace, A.: 1985, 'Metalinguistic knowledge and language use in acquisition-poor environments', *Applied Linguistics* 6(3), 239–254.

Vernon, P.E.: 1973, 'Multivariate approaches to the study of cognitive styles', in J.R. Royce (ed.), *Multivariate Analysis and Psychological Theory*, Academic Press, London, 125–141.

Witkin, H.A., Moore, C.A., Goodenough, D.R. & Cox, P.W.: 1977, 'Field-dependent and field-independent cognitive styles and their educational implications', *Review of Educational Research* 47, 1–64.

Witkin. H.A. & Goodenough, D.R.: 1982, (1st edn 1981), *Cognitive Styles: Essence and Origins. Field Dependence and Field Independence* (Psychological Issues, Monograph 51), International Universities Press, New York.

Section 3

Knowledge About Language, the Curriculum, and the Classroom

KENNETH S. GOODMAN

WHOLE LANGUAGE: THE WHOLE STORY

Whole language has often been represented, particularly in the popular press, as a method of teaching reading that contrasts with phonics, which is also represented as a method of teaching reading. It has also been equated with literature-based reading instruction and with a laissez-faire approach to written language development. It is none of those and much more than any of them. Whole language has emerged among teachers as a term for an inclusive pedagogy, a philosophy of curriculum and teaching, which puts language at the center of learning. It is whole in the sense that language is treated as an integral whole and it is whole in the sense that language is viewed as only existing in the context of its purposeful and functional use – integrated in literacy events and speech acts that are authentic within cultural practices. Whole language teachers, at all levels, build on the existing strengths of the learners, developing literacy in the context of using literacy to learn. The term has come also to be an umbrella that subsumes process writing, integrated curriculum, use of literature in reading instruction, writing across the curriculum, inquiry and problem solving curricula and the use of theme cycles, and invented spelling and punctuation.

EARLY DEVELOPMENTS

About 1978 the term, whole language, emerged from its incidental use to describe aspects of teaching, learning and curriculum to become a name for a pedagogy, a belief system and a movement among teachers. Incidental use of the term occurred much earlier than that in the continuing struggle to move away from a test and textbook technology based in behavioristic views of learning and in views of teaching as administering this technology in an atomistic sequence of skill lessons. The term whole language began to be used by teachers in Canada to describe themselves and their belief systems and to differentiate their holistic pedagogy from the part-to-whole skill sequence based in behavioral psychology and incorporated in American tests and text books, particularly the basal readers (reading schemes) that Canadian teachers were rejecting.

The history of whole language in each of the English speaking countries is somewhat different. But in every case the emergence of whole language depended on two separate but related factors. First is the development of a base of well educated and highly professional teachers. And second is

L. van Lier and D. Corson (eds), Encyclopedia of Language and Education,
Volume 6: Knowledge about Language, 87–97.
© *1997 Kluwer Academic Publishers. Printed in the Netherlands.*

the integration of a knowledge base from interdisciplinary sources. What differentiates whole language from other prior movements in fundamentally changing education is that it is led by empowered and knowledgeable teachers: its strength is in a grassroots movement that changes classroom practice from within. Professional teachers are basing what they do on what they know.

In Canada, the term and the concepts it represents spread from teacher to teacher, school to school, local authority to local authority, and province to province. By the late 80's most school policies and practice incorporated at least some aspects of whole language. The growth of whole language in Canada, as in the United States, has been school based with teacher education and researchers following rather than leading the way.

New Zealand took the calm and sane path to change possible in a small country with a single unified educational system. Starting in the thirties, New Zealand built a child-centered system of education based in Dewey's progressive philosophy (NZ Department of Education, 1985). This philosophical base provided a basis for absorbing useful new insights from research and theory. They developed holistic materials in the form of school journals, reading magazines published at several levels several times a year in which local authors provided a range of relevant fiction and non-fiction. They also commissioned local authors to write "little books", single story paperbacks for use in early literacy instruction. Don Holdaway pioneered shared reading of big books, much enlarged versions of predictable published books, in beginning reading instruction (Holdaway, 1970). Emphasis in the New Zealand schools was on empowered teachers supported by informed advisors. New Zealand became, as demonstrated in international studies, the most literate nation in the world. Recently, another small country, Finland, has rivaled New Zealand for that distinction (Elley, 1992).

Australia has had still another history. After World War II, they began to draw on carefully selected European and North American sources to support their curriculum building and their increasingly professional teachers. They sent many of their educational leaders abroad to earn higher degrees, people like Garth Boomer who were selective in bringing back research and theory which they felt could be integrated into dynamic reforms in Australian literacy education (Boomer, G., 1985) Like the United States, each Australian state has a separate and autonomous school system. But the central government, with Garth Boomer in a leading role, influenced teachers through wide-spread staff development. Brian Cambourne led in building a distinctive Australian whole language curriculum (Cambourne, 1989). New Zealand and Australia developed models for staff development that were based on intensive "courses" with local staff developers educated to pass on the ideas and innovations to other teachers. Virtually every Australian teacher experienced the ELIC

(Early Literacy In-Service Course) which was based on a similar course developed in New Zealand. Marie Clay's Reading Recovery, a program for supporting less successful young readers is also based on this model of educating a group of educators who can in turn educate others (Clay, M., 1972). (See the review by Clay in Volume 2.)

Britain's movement toward whole language was also school based, but two important reports, the Plowden report and the Bullock Report, A Language for Life, legitimatized the changes already taking place (DES, 1975). The latter was also influential in most of the other English speaking countries. Jimmy Britton, Harold Rosen (Britton et al., 1975) and Margaret Meek Spencer (Meek, 1988) and the London Institute of Education helped to disseminate whole language concepts through the Role of Language in Education course which many British teachers took. A key role was also played by the Centre for Primary Language Education, in the former Inner London Education Authority, led by Moira McKenzie and subsequently by Myra Barrs (1988).

In the United States, teachers quickly picked up the term whole language from their Canadian counterparts to describe their own shift away from skill-drill, teach-test views. But their transitions were strewn with barriers such as mandated text books, tests, and evaluation procedures. Principals and administrators were often less knowledgeable than the teachers and threatened by their knowledge and enthusiasm for change. So, whereas teachers in other English speaking countries found the transitions relatively easy, American teachers had to struggle to achieve change. Still the movement passed from teacher to teacher and picked up momentum. School, district, and state policies and policy documents began to shift as teachers carried their own understandings and commitment to whole language into meetings, school committees, and teacher conferences.

By 1987, when the California Department of Education released its new English Language Arts Framework (1987), whole language had become the agenda in American education particularly in grades Kindergarten to three, those called in the United States primary. The California framework did not use the term whole language and was broadly eclectic, but it included many of the innovations whole language classroom teachers had themselves introduced. Among these was the use of trade books, real children's literature, in place of the sequential and highly controlling basals. Another was an emphasis on writing at all levels integrating development of spelling, handwriting (penmanship) and punctuation into functional writing. Even more important, since California is so huge a market for text publishers, when California announced it would only consider texts for adoption that fit the framework, publishers rushed to produce programs they called literature based. Test publishers began collaborating with states in developing more process-centered and holistic tests moving away from multiple choice, norm-referenced formats. Teachers were greatly encouraged that they had brought changes in the two aspects of education deemed by pessimists to be virtually immutable; texts and tests were in fact changing.

As a term, whole language has been in most common use in North America. But it has profited from strong international interactions. Publishers in New Zealand and Australia for several years have sold more materials in North America than in their own countries. There was a period when American whole language research and theory was better known among Australian, New Zealand and British teachers than among American teachers. Whole language has international roots as well. Antecedents include the 19th century movements led by Herbart, Froebel, Pestalozzi, Horace Mann, and Bronson Alcott, and carried into the 20th century by John Dewey. It draws on the progressive education of Dewey (1949), Kilpatrick (1918), Counts, and Childs and of great curriculum innovators in the United States like Lucy Spragg Mitchell (1950) and her colleagues in the Bureau of Educational Experimentation and Bank Street College. It expands on the developers of integrated curriculum in social studies like Hilda Taba (1980)). It builds also on the British developments of the integrated day and language across the curriculum (Martin, N. et al., 1976).

SCIENTIFIC AND HUMANISTIC BASES FOR WHOLE LANGUAGE

Whole language surely extends the humanistic traditions in education of Rousseau, Comenius and the 19th century reformers mentioned above. In this view, children are viewed as essentially good, eager and able to learn. Education is viewed as an expansion of natural development. Children are to be cherished and loved. Inquiry and problem solving are key aspects of education capitalizing on the universal thirst for knowledge among children and young people. As Dewey said, education is life, not the preparation for life; children learn by doing. Schools adjust to the learners, building on their strengths rather than requiring learners to adjust to an unyielding and inflexible school. Whole language is thus a democratic pedagogy that emphasizes empowered and self-directed learners with empowered teachers.

Scientific Foundations of Whole Language

Whole language, however, is also based in science. In this it brings together scientific understandings of language, learning, teaching, curriculum and community. It draws on the functional linguistics of Halliday, viewing language as a social semiotic and recognizing that language learning is, as Halliday puts it learning how to mean (1978). Language is seen as both personal and social and so language learning is viewed as developing through a dialectic in which personal invention and social convention shape personal and social language and move the language learner toward the conventions of the language community. Eventually these processes also lead to learner's control over written language and the genres and literacy practices of the community.

Whole language bases its view of learning on the psychogenesis of Piaget (1969), the social constructionism and mediation of Vygotsky (1978) and the cognitive views of Bruner (1983). And it builds on the holistic views of Kurt Lewin (1951) and gestalt psychology. It recognizes the unique role that language plays in human learning. In humans, language is the medium of thought, of learning and communication. So language must be central to school curriculum and learning as well. Like the emerging discursive psychology, whole language views learners as individuals who are always embedded in different sociocultural discourses. Corson, in explaining the central focus of discursive psychology, says: "... so each individual stands at a unique intersection of discourses and relationships: a 'position' embedded in historical, political, cultural, social, and interpersonal contexts ..." (Corson, 1995). In whole language, language development and its use are not removed from the sociocultural contexts that students bring with them to school. Neither are language or knowledge development in school separated from each other, divided usefully into separate disciplines, or arranged in skill hierarchies.

Whole language teachers have reinvented teaching, rejecting the role of the teacher as a technician transmitting knowledge through a technology of texts and tests. Whole language teachers are advocates for learners. They are mediators of learning. They are liberators who free learners of artificial floors, ceilings, and other barriers. They are kid-watchers observing learners with a professional eye and knowing what to do at the right time with the right learner. They are curriculum directors in their classrooms organizing experiences through theme cycles and inquiries building what the learners need to learn on the base of what they know. They are initiators inviting the participation of learners in developmentally appropriate experiences.

The curriculum in whole language classrooms starts where the learners are, to quote Dewey again. It uses inquiry and problem solving involving the learners in choosing what they will study and how they will go about the study. In this, whole language draws on the old progressive traditions of curriculum and new traditions that come of new rationales for integrating language and learning. Language is learned best in its use and therefore the language and literacy curriculum is integrated with the science, social studies and mathematics and humanities curriculum.

And whole language recognizes the importance of the classroom as a social community with strong links to the community the learners come from. Literature groups meet to discuss books the pupils have chosen to read. Committees take responsibility, jointly, for planning research on aspects of inquiries. The classroom itself is a democratic community in which governance is shared and the pupils take much of the responsibility for the on-going operations.

READING AND WRITING IN THE WHOLE LANGUAGE CLASSROOM

Whole language bases literacy instruction on a transactional psycho-sociolinguistic view of written language processes. Writing is seen as a process of expression of meaning and reading is viewed as a process of meaning construction. So learning to read is learning to make sense of text – to construct meaning. Learners build strategies for sampling and selecting from print, making inferences and predictions, confirming or disconfirming their predictions and correcting as they need to do so. Proficient readers are both effective and efficient. They are effective in getting to meaning and they are efficient in using the least amount of time, energy and input to get to meaning. This view builds on Ken Goodman's miscue research which examined, in great depth, the oral reading of readers of varying ages, language backgrounds and levels of proficiency (Goodman, 1996) (also see the review by K. Goodman in Volume 2). Whole language views of written language also are built on Frank Smith's synthesis of a wide range of research in psychology and psycholinguistics (Smith, 1988).

In building literacy, whole language uses a rich body of research on early literacy development. Emilia Ferreiro (1982) and a group of Piagetian researchers who began their original research in Argentina have studied literacy development from a psychogenetic perspective. Other researchers on early literacy development are Yetta Goodman (Goodman, 1991), Jerome Harste (1984), and Anne Haas Dyson (1989). Literacy instruction in whole language also draws on the writing research of Donald Graves (1983) and of Yetta Goodman and her associates (Goodman & Wilde, 1992).

Whole Language Literacy Instruction

Development of whole language literacy practices is very dynamic. Much of the dynamics is due to highly effective teachers networking with other teachers in small groups, at conferences and through their writing. Teachers are conducting research in their classrooms and sharing their successes and setbacks with other teachers as well as researchers and teacher educators. And part of the dynamics comes from the achievements of pupils at all ages responding to the possibilities for productive learning that their whole language teachers are creating.

Teachers and others are finding the capabilities and achievements of pupils far exceed what they have traditionally been expected and permitted to do. They can write earlier and more effectively, read earlier and more widely, and use literacy in inquiries and problem solving in ways that weren't considered possible. Nancy Atwell (1987), Linda Rief (1995), Regie Routman (1991), Wendy Hood (1989), Tom Romano (1995), Debra Goodman (1991) are a few of the teacher researchers who have been writing about how they use time and space in classrooms, how they support learners in taking ownership of their learning, how they integrate the social goals of the community with the personal goals of the learners in building relevant curriculum, and how they use authentic materials and experiences to replace the textbooks and canned curricula that have dominated education.

MAJOR ACHIEVEMENTS

Whole language and the associated movements it brings together have accomplished some remarkable changes in education at the end of the millennium:

- It has brought about a golden age of literature for children and young adults. In English speaking countries, and now in the rest of the world, there has been an explosion of the publishing, sales, and readership of books specifically written for young people. Circulation of books in children's rooms of public libraries has also increased dramatically. At the same time, the quality and range of topics covered in books for young people have also been increasing. Results from the 1994 National Assessment of Educational Progress in the United States reported almost half of fourth graders read at home for fun almost every day and that two out of three 4th grade pupils read 3 or more books a month (Campbell, 1996).
- More students are getting to read books of their own choosing silently in school almost every day.
- Students at all levels are writing more and they are having more choice in what they write.
- Dramatic shifts are taking place in the form and content of reading texts and tests.
- Assessments have shifted away from multiple choice to more authentic assessments and even to self-assessments and teacher con-structed assessments.
- Teachers have reinvented teaching and redesigned their classrooms and curricula.

PROBLEMS AND DIFFICULTIES

But whole language has also been a focal point in the attacks on public education. These attacks unite powerful forces attempting to discredit and privatize public education. Conservatives within and without education vigorously oppose some or all of the innovations that whole language represents. In England, a conservative government focused on the teaching of reading and language. Newspapers and cabinet ministers berated schools for their handling of phonics, grammar, and non-standard English. Similar attacks have taken place in Canada, New Zealand and Australia. In Britain, since the term, whole language, was not widely known by the British public, the critics used the term 'the real books approach' instead of whole language as a label for what they were attacking.

In the United States, following a sharp conservative swing in the 1994 elections, whole language became the target of right wing groups who blamed whole language for declining test scores. When the 1994 national assessment (Campbell, 1996) showed California's means near the bottom of the states that participated (14 chose not to do so), politicians and the press created a scenario that reading was declining in California children and that was because of the shift toward whole language.

Actually, the full reports of the 1994 NAEP study, not released until mid 1996, do not show any evidence that use of whole language is involved in low California means on the test. Whole language is not in fact mentioned in the reports or the questionnaires used with pupils or teachers. But several aspects of whole language show very positive effects on test performance. A notable shift away from basal readers (reading schemes) to trade books (real books rather than text books) and to mixed use of basals and trade books is reported by teachers. Teachers using trade books only had pupils with higher mean scores than those using basals only, with teachers using mixed materials in the middle (Campbell, 1996).

Other aspects of whole language showing positive results were providing time in school for pupils to read silently and allowing pupils to choose the books they read in school. Almost half of all fourth graders reported having time almost daily to choose their own books and to read.

Furthermore, almost half of all fourth grade pupils in the NAEP testing reported that they read almost every day at home for fun. Whole language teachers can claim with some justification that that's because of the experiences with books and authors that are characteristic of whole language classrooms.

More likely factors in California's low performance are the high pupil teacher ratios, higher by far than any other state, and a long term de-emphasis in California on professional education of teachers. California is currently attempting to reduce class size in kindergarten through third grade.

In England, with a much more centralized governmental system it was possible to mandate change nationally and even to abolish local school authorities, such as the Inner London Education Authority. In the United States with school structures varying from state to state and each of the thousands of school systems largely in control of its own decision making, the focus has been on discrediting whole language and public education in the press and on state legislatures and school boards mandating explicit change. Far-right groups have taken control of some local school boards through electing their own candidates dedicated to reversing the changes. In both countries the press has played a role in creating a sense of crisis which requires a quick return to "basics".

FUTURE DIRECTIONS

Because whole language classrooms are dynamic and place high value on innovation they will continue to inspire all manner of research on language, literacy, learning, teaching and curriculum. Much of this research will be collaborative with teams of school based and university based researchers. As whole language spreads beyond the English speaking world, research also will expand its reach. There is strong interest in whole language in Latin America, Asia, Oceania and Europe and beginnings in Africa. A key in developing nations is finding the means of bringing the knowledge and concepts needed to change school practice to minimally educated teachers working with minimal resources in overcrowded classrooms.

Terms in education tend to be worn down by attack or worn out by overuse. That may be the fate of whole language as a term. But the changes in curriculum, teaching and learning that whole language represents have been so pervasive in educational practice that they will not easily be rolled back. As teachers become professionals even in developing nations and as these professionals put the knowledge whole language represents to work in the cause of educating all learners in democratic classrooms for informed citizenship in democratic societies, whole language concepts will become central to education at all levels.

University of Arizona
USA

REFERENCES

Atwell, N.: 1987, *In the Middle*, Heinemann, Portsmouth, NH.
Barrs, M., Ellis S., Hester H. & Thomas A.: 1988, *The Primary Language Record*, Heinemann, Portsmouth, NH.
Boomer, G.: 1985, *Fair Dinkum Teaching and Learning: Reflections on Literacy and Power*, Boynton Cook, Upper Montclair, NJ.

Britton, J., Burgess, T., Martin, N., McLeod, A. & Rosen, H.: 1975, *The Development of Writing Abilities*, Macmillan Education Ltd., London.

Bruner, J.: 1983, In Search of Mind, Harper & Row, New York.

Cambourne, B.: 1989, *The Whole Story*, Ashton-Scholastic, Sidney.

Campbell, J.R. et al.: 1996, *NAEP 1994 Reading Report Card for the Nation and States*, Office of Educational Research and Improvement, US Department of Education, Washington DC.

Clay, M., 1972: *Reading: The Patterning of Complex Behavior*, Heinemann Educational Books, Auckland, New Zealand.

Committee on English Language Arts Curriculum Framework: 1987, *English-Language Arts Framework*, State Department of Education, Sacramento, California.

Corson, D.: 1995. *Using English Words*, Kluwer, Dordrecht.

Department of Education and Science (DES): 1975, *A language for life*, Her Majesty's Stationery Office, London.

Dewey, J. & Bentley, L.: 1949, *Knowing and the Known*, Beacon, Boston.

Dyson, A H.: 1989, *Multiple Worlds of Child Writers: Friends Learning to Write*, Teachers College Press, New York.

Elley, W.: 1992, *How in the World Do Students Read*, International Association for the Evaluation of Educational Achievement, The Hague.

Ferreiro, E. & Teberosky A.: 1982, *Literacy Before Schooling*, Trans. Karen Goodman, Heinemann, Portsmouth, NH.

Goodman, D. & Curry, T.K.: 1991, 'Teaching in the real world', in Y. Goodman, W. Hood & K. Goodman (eds.), *Organizing for Whole Language*, Heinemann, Portsmouth, NH.

Goodman, K.: 1986, *What's Whole in Whole Language*, Scholastic TAB, Richmond Hill, Ontario.

Goodman, K.: 1996, *Ken Goodman on Reading*, Scholastic TAB, Richmond Hill, Ontario.

Goodman, Y. (ed.): 1991, *How Children Construct Literacy*, International Reading Association, Newark, DE.

Goodman, Y.M. & Wilde, S. (eds.): 1992, *Literacy Events in a Community of Young Writers*, Teachers College Press, New York.

Graves, D.: 1983, *Writing: Teachers and Children at Work*, Heinemann, Portsmouth, NH.

Halliday, M.A.K.: 1978, *Language as a Social Semiotic: The Social Interpretation of Language and Meaning*, University Park Press, Baltimore, MD.

Harste, J., Burke, C. & Woodward, V.: 1984, *Language Stories and Literacy Lessons*, Heinemann, Exeter, NH.

Holdaway, D.: 1979, *The Foundations of Literacy*, Ashton-Scholastic, Sydney, Australia.

Hood, W.: 1989, 'If the teacher comes over, pretend it's a telescope!', in K. Goodman, Y. Goodman & W. Hood (eds), *The Whole Language Evaluation Book*, Heinemann, Portsmouth, NH, 27–45.

Kilpatrick, W.H.: 1918, 'The project method', *The Teachers College Record* 19, 319–335.

Lewin, K.: 1951, *Field Theory in Social Science: Selecting Theoretical Papers*, Harper, New York.

Martin, N. et al.: 1976, *Writing and Learning Across the Curriculum*, Schools Council Writing Across the Curriculum Project, Ward Lock, London.

Meek, M.: 1988, *How Texts Teach What Students Learn*, Thimble Press, Avonset, Bath.

Mitchell, L.S.: 1950, *Our Children and Our Schools*, Simon & Schuster, New York.

New Zealand Department of Education: 1985, *Reading in Junior Classes*, Wellington, New Zealand.

Piaget, J. & Imhelder, B.: 1969, *The Psychology of the Child*, Basic Books, New York.

Rief, L.: 1992, *Seeking Diversity: Language Arts with Adolescents*, Heinemann, Portsmouth, NH.

Romano, T.: 1995, *Writing with Passion: Life Stories, Multiple Genres*, Boynton/Cook, Portsmouth, NH.
Routman, R.: 1991, *Invitations: Changing as Teachers and Learners K-12*, Heinemann, Portsmouth, NH.
Ruddell, R., Ruddell, M.R. & Singer, H. (eds.): 1994, *Theoretical Models and Processes of Reading*, 4th edn., International Reading Association, Newark, DE.
Smith, F.: 1988, *Understanding Reading*, 4th edn., Erlbaum, Hillsdale, NJ.
Taba, H.: 1950, *Elementary Curriculum in Intergroup Relations*, American Council on Education, Washington, DC.
Vygotsky, L.: 1978, 'Mind in society', in M. Cole, E. Scribner, V. Steiner & E. Souberman (eds.), Harvard University Press, Cambrige, MA.
Weber, L.: 1971, *The English Infant School and Informal Education*, Prentice Hall, Englewood Cliffs, NJ.

ANTHONY J. DEFAZIO

LANGUAGE AWARENESS AT THE INTERNATIONAL HIGH SCHOOL

Friedlander (1991) estimates that over 5 million immigrant students will have entered public schools in the United States by the end of the decade. These students who speak over 150 languages are concentrated in urban centers such as Los Angeles and New York City. In 1996 there were over 180,000 students in New York City who identified English as their second language. These students are alternatively described in the literature as new learners of English, linguistically diverse, language minority or limited English proficient. (I will use the terms interchangeably.)

Various models have been offered to meet the educational challenges of this population. One model for the education of language minority students is The International High School at LaGuardia Community College in New York City. Founded in 1985, it offers new learners of English a four-year comprehensive high school where they can satisfy state-mandated subject matter requirements while they learn English.

MAJOR CONTRIBUTIONS

Programs offered to language minority students include submersion in the dominant language with little or no support for the new learner of English; English as a second language programs; content-based English as a second language which teaches English through academic content; bilingual structured immersion; and transitional bilingual programs (Ginsburg, 1992; Clair, 1994). Friedlander (1991) describes newcomer programs which offer academic and social support as students learn English. Many of these programs concentrate on English language development with the goal of mainstreaming new English language learners into English only programs after a specified time.

Effective programs for language minority students share certain characteristics. Almost all of them insist on seeing the student's first language as a resource rather than a liability (Hakuta, 1990; Garcia, 1991; Auerbach, 1993). Hakuta (1990) surveys research in second language acquisition and concludes that those involved with new learners of English should see the complementary nature of the first and second languages and should value the student's first language as a resource to be developed. Garcia (1991) notes that effective programs for language minority students do not

L. van Lier and D. Corson (eds), Encyclopedia of Language and Education,
Volume 6: Knowledge about Language, 99–107.
© 1997 Kluwer Academic Publishers. Printed in the Netherlands.

pressure students to move to English but allow students to move gradually from the first language to English. Krashen (1991) also stresses the importance of first language maintenance. Cummins & Sayers (1995) argue that the exclusion of students' culture and language from the school and a curriculum that does not address the realities of linguistically diverse students almost guarantee student failure. Besides the importance attributed to first language, other characteristics of effective programs include student/student interaction in collaborative learning environments; thematic organization of materials to be learned; a transition from native language literacy to English learning without pressure to do so; high expectations for student achievement, and parental involvement (Garcia, 1991; Berman, Minicucci, McLaughlin, Nelson & Woodworth, 1995).

THE INTERNATIONAL HIGH SCHOOL: INNOVATION AND IMPLEMENTATION

The International High School is a collaborative effort of the New York City Board of Education and the City University of New York. Its students come from over sixty countries and speak over fifty different languages. Entering students score in the lowest quarter on tests of English proficiency, yet more than ninety percent of them graduate within four years and move on to institutes of post secondary education (Bush, 1992; Jacobson, 1995). There are currently three International High schools in different boroughs of New York City. (Unless otherwise noted, this essay concentrates on the original International High School founded in 1985.) These three schools, sharing a common vision, student body, and educational philosophy, formed the International Schools Partnership in 1995.

The mission statement of the International High Schools specifies their approach to the education of language minority students. It stresses the importance of language as key to learning and maintains that small groups of heterogeneous students and faculty working together is the best way to encourage academic and personal development. Career education is built into the curriculum to encourage students to explore career options and to motivate students to continue language learning. The rationale for language awareness at the International High School stems from the following beliefs:

- Limited English proficient students require the ability to understand, speak, read, and write English to realize their full potential within an English-speaking society.
- In an increasingly interdependent world, fluency in a language other than English must be viewed as a resource for the student, the school, and the society.
- Language skills are most effectively learned in context and emerge most naturally in experiential, language rich, interdisciplinary study.

- Individuals learn best from each other in heterogeneous, collaborative groupings. Learning is facilitated when collaboration exists between the school and the larger community.
- Assessment must support individual growth as well as offer a variety of opportunities for students and faculty to demonstrate what they know and what they can do.
- When teachers actively participate in school governance, the most effective instruction takes place (The International Schools Partnership, 1996).

The International High School has been at the center of many initiatives involved in reorganizing the ways schools and students work together. It was one of the first schools in New York City which was allowed to choose and develop its own personnel procedures. Prior to this, teachers were assigned by a central agency to various schools throughout the city on a seniority basis. The International High School developed and implemented a process by which teachers select other teachers to work within a school and developed procedures to guide teachers working together to support and evaluate each other. These personnel procedures have been adopted as a city-wide model and approved for system-wide use (Partnership, 1996, pp. 15–17).

The school itself has undergone shifts in the way it delivers instruction to new learners of English. Earlier on, the school was organized into the standard academic departments often found in high schools in the United States: English, English as a second language, mathematics, social studies, the natural and physical sciences. Classes ran for thirty-five minutes instead of the usual forty-five minutes associated with high school programs to allow students to take more subjects. Even within this standard model, classes were often thematically linked and team-taught by a pair of teachers. Over the past several years, however, the school has reorganized itself into six interdisciplinary teams, each team responsible for developing at least two interdisciplinary programs. Each linked program runs for 13 weeks, with the group of teachers in the program responsible for overseeing a group of approximately 75 students. Such linked programs are often cited as beneficial for students (Sizer, 1984). The diversity of these programs can be seen by an abbreviated listing of the school's interdisciplinary offerings and the core subjects students are credited with when they finish a program:

- Origins, Growth, and Structure (chemistry, mathematics, linguistics, art).
- Motion (physics, mathematics, literature, physical education).
- American Reality (native language arts, human development, career education).

Students are required to take a minimum of eight out of the twelve interdisciplinary programs during their tenure at the International High School. A student's remaining program is comprised of intensive one-month courses taken between the fall and spring semesters.

Reorganizing the curriculum has necessitated rethinking assessment of students. Students at the International High School undergo portfolio assessment where they demonstrate their academic, linguistic and social proficiencies. Traditional testing is eschewed because it is often unfair and counterproductive to linguistically diverse populations who often know much more than they may be able to articulate in English. Portfolio assessment encourages retention, higher-level cognitive skills, development of internal standards, creativity and variety in solving problems. (Partnership, 1996). Students undergo these assessments informally during the course of a semester and more formally at the end. Students also present a master portfolio as they prepare to graduate. Students meet with peer and faculty examiners; they present the result of their work in humanities and math/science/technology, and are certified as either proficient or not. These public forums where students demonstrate what they have learned make the school a 'workplace where the processes and the products of individual and collaborative student work are at the center of the enterprise ... ' (Darling-Hammond, Ancess & Falk, 1995, p. 166).

LANGUAGE AWARENESS

Carter (1990) identifies language awareness as the capacity to reflect on linguistic matters rather than amassing discrete grammatical information. Van Lier (1996) notes that although schools conduct their business through language, it receives scant attention even though language across the curriculum may 'well be the single most important policy issue in the schools today' (p. 6). The study of language as a tool for thinking, for organizing information, for dealing with social relations is one of the themes of language awareness which could be a focus of schooling (van Lier, 1995). Postman (1995) concurs, arguing that the study of language could be one of the organizing principles used to connect various parts of the curriculum. Carter (1990) offers several reasons why language awareness is crucial for both teachers and students: for teachers, knowledge about language can expand the ability to incorporate language-rich activities into a class; it can help teachers understand students' language difficulties; it can equip them to deal with questions of register, dialect, and grammar within the school and larger community; it can unlock relationships between language and learning. For students, developing language awareness can mean more reflective as well as analytical approaches to learning about language plus new knowledge about the relationship between language and power. Such teaching, however, should not be based on transmission models but focus instead on inquiry and analysis of language data (van Lier, 1992).

Language study is central at The International High Schools. The centrality of human language to learning and development is fundamental to its educational program. Students use both English and their native language for all phases of learning and assessment (Sylvan, 1994). An analysis of several interdisciplinary programs will demonstrate how language functions both as a medium of instruction and an object of analysis at the International High School.

Motion/visibility. Students study physics, math, literature and physical education in these two programs and complete two extensive portfolios in which they comment on their development and knowledge in areas related to the subjects they are studying. They also write intensive and extensive self evaluations as well as evaluate the work of other students in the class. Students often write in their native language, sometimes partially in their native language and partially in English. The sanctioning of language choices students make is crucial to their success. While sanctioning these choices, the *lingua franca* of the class remains English since there are often as many as fifteen different languages represented in a class. To aid them in translation in languages they may not know, teachers often ask other students for help or seek help from the community at large.

A recent development has been to extend the assessment program to involve a student's parents or guardian. Teachers in the program began asking students to write letters home (Slater, 1996) in the student's native language to describe the interdisciplinary program the student was involved with, to explain what they were learning, and explain the portfolio/grading process. Students who complained that they did not remember enough of their native language to write a letter home were advised to seek help from their parents or guardian. Parents were encouraged to respond to the letters in either the native language or English. If the parents wrote back in a language the classroom teacher could not read, students were asked to write an English translation. The letter writing campaign helped instantiate several aspects of the school's language philosophy: the importance of the native language; the need for the parent/guardian and school to work together regardless of language; the development and importance of bi- and multilingualism; language respect. Students who may know more English than their parents are often asked to be the translators and interpreters for them; this letter writing campaign helped shift the locus of language control to parents who could become the tutors for their children in their native language.

American dream. Students formally explore their native language, human development, and career education in this interdisciplinary program. In the native language component, students spend at least half their school day doing academic reading and writing in their native language. Resources include abundant native language materials that teachers, students, and parents purchased for the school. Students produce both native language and English language magazines and articles; their writing is read by teachers and students proficient in the native language. If no one on staff is proficient in the language, teachers go into the community to find volunteers willing to spend time reading and commenting on the students' work. Students often comment that they had not realized how much of their native language they had forgotten.

Origins/growth/structures. In this program students study linguistics, chemistry, biology, mathematics, global studies, and art. There are two major student language portfolios in this grouping of classes: an autobiography/biography and a series of works based on comparative linguistics. In the autobiography segment, students spend several weeks researching and writing about their lives in either English, their native language, or both. They are asked to write about their grandparents and their parents and thus to engage in a dialogue with them about their lives before coming to the United States. They do family trees, time lines of their lives, and project themselves into the future to imagine what their lives will be like. Students also research the cultural and intellectual histories of the places where they were born.

In the biography project, students choose to write about the life of another student in the class. The student may or may not speak the same language as the interviewee, and the language of the text can be either the native language or English. Students discuss their interviewees' lives before coming to the United States and their lives now. Students write their own questions and conduct their interviews. Once again students who write in a language unfamiliar to the teacher will have their work translated into English by a peer or choose instead to present a summary of the biography in English. Harris & Savitzsky (1988) present similar examples of personal stories written by their students in the Afro-Caribbean Language and Literacy Project in Great Britain. The goals of the British project are similar to those of the International High Schools: to promote the maximum level of students' performance in standard English while valuing the native language.

Another project focuses directly on linguistics. Students learn what it means when a linguist says that all language is rule-governed. They use a series of teacher-constructed activities to establish rules of syntax in English and then determine syntactic rules in their native languages. Students work in same-language groups when they are researching structures for native languages they share or they may be working in heterogeneous language groups when they are researching more general questions. There is some but not an inordinate amount of information transmitted through lecturing. Early activities ask students to use semantic maps to determine what language is and what they think all languages share. Later activities focus on inductive approaches to lexical categories, to question formation, embedded sentences, concord. Students determine how such structures function in English and then determine how they work in their individual languages. Once they reach consensus, they write essays for a comparative linguistics book which they assemble throughout the semester. Chapters vary from term to term, but often include the following:

- What is language? What do all languages share?
- How do sounds in English compare with sounds in my native language?
- How does the syntax of English compare with the syntax of my native language?
- How are questions formed?

Students learn about phrase structure rules in English and build three-dimensional models of sentences in their native languages and English. These mobiles give students a tangible sense of how the languages in the world operate, what they have in common, and how they differ. Students also – through their work with the International Phonetic Alphabet – get to practice the sounds in each others' language, to write cartoon strips in phonetics, to practice riddles and tongue twisters in the languages represented by the class. The students' linguistics books culminate with a community research project in which students apply their learning to some question or problem in the school or larger community. Past projects have included students' analyses of sentence patterns used by their teachers as well as a school-wide assessment of what teachers, administrators, and students know about language and linguistics. Most recently students have been interviewing members of their communities about bilingual education, dialect, and language prejudice, analyzing the results, and presenting them as the last chapter in their linguistics book. An additional project asks students to write multilingual children's books on some aspect of language/linguistics, results ranging from "The Monster that Ate Polish Words," and "How the Chinese Got Language," to an abecedarium for elementary school students. Similar language awareness projects are underway in many British schools. Burrell (1991) and the ILEA Afro-Caribbean Language and Literacy Project (1990) provide extensive shorter term activities on similar topics designed to promote knowledge about language. Bain, Fitzgerald & Taylor (1992) describe several case studies of language awareness projects which have been undertaken by teachers in Great Britain.

FUTURE DIRECTIONS

Two areas of research are in progress. One is increasing the level of language awareness of other colleagues in New York City public schools.

This involves not only disseminating information about the centrality of language education, but also the importance of bringing language minority students into the schools. One such initiative currently being undertaken is the Small Schools Language Forum, an International Schools Partnership dissemination project. A specific area the Language Forum is dealing with is demonstrating how monolingual teachers can work with multilingual classes.

A second area of research is the need to establish more sophisticated computer network links so our students can communicate in their native languages and English with others. This becomes most acute when a student is the only person in the school who speaks a particular language. Being on-line would allow that student to access other people who speak his/her language, diminish the student's linguistic isolation, and provide correspondents for the student to communicate with.

International High School
New York, USA

REFERENCES

Auerbach, E.: 1993, 'Reexamining English only in the ESL classroom', *TESOL Quarterly* 27, 9–20.
Bain, R., Fitzgerald B. & Taylor, M.: 1992, *Looking into Language*, Hodder & Stoughton, London.
Berman, P., Minicucci, C., McLaughlin, B., Nelson, B. & Woodworth, K.: 1995, *School Reform and Student Diversity*, National Clearinghouse for Bilingual Education, Washington.
Burrell, K.: 1991, *Knowledge About Language*, Thomas Nelson & Sons Ltd., Walton on Thames.
Bush, T.: 1992, 'International High School: Six years new', *College ESL* 2, 23–28.
Carter, R. (ed.): 1990, *Knowledge about Language and the Curriculum*, Hodder & Stoughton, London.
Clair, N.: 1994, 'Informed choices: Articulating assumptions behind programs for language minority students', *ERIC/CLL Newst Bulletin* 18(1), 5–8.
Cummins, J. & Sayers, D.: 1995, *Brave New Schools*, St. Martin's Press, New York.
Darling-Hammond, L., Ancess, J. & Falk, B.: 1995, *Authentic Assessment in Action*, Teachers College Press, New York.
Friedlander, M.: 1991, *The Newcomer Program: Helping Immigrant Students Succeed in U.S. Schools*, National Clearinghouse for Bilingual Education, Washington.
Garcia, E.: 1991, *Education of Linguistically and Culturally Diverse Students*, National Center for Research on Cultural Diversity and Second Language Learning, Santa Cruz, CA.
Ginsburg, A.L.: 1992, 'Improving bilingual education programs through evaluation', in *Proceeding of the Second National Research Symposium on Limited English Proficient Student Issues*, United States Department of Education, Office of Bilingual and Minority Language Affairs, Washington, 31–42.
Hakuta, K. 1990. *Bilingualism and Bilingual Education: A Research Perspective*, National Clearinghouse for Bilingual Education, Washington.

Harris, R. & Savitzky, F.(eds.): 1988, *My Personal Language History*, New Beacon Books Ltd., London.

ILEA Afro-Caribbean Language and Literacy Project in Further and Adult Education: 1990, *Language and Power*, Harcourt Brace, Jovanovich Ltd., London.

International Schools Partnership: 1995–96, *Network Portfolio for Annual Review and Planning*, Ms. International High School.

Jacobson, D.: 1995, 'Human resource innovation in an alternative high school', *IEE Brief* 11, 1–4.

Krashen, S.: 1991, *Bilingual Education: A Focus on Current Research*, National Clearinghouse for Bilingual Education, Washington.

Postman, N.: 1995, *The End of Education*, Knopf, New York.

Sizer, T.R. 1984. *Horace's Compromise*, Houghton Mifflin, Boston.

Slater, M.: 1996, 'Letters to and from home: Bilingual progress reports', Ms, International High School.

Sylvan, C.E.: 1994, 'Assessment in a multilingual school: The International High School', *The Educational Forum* 59, 74–80.

van Lier, L.: 1992, 'Not the nine o'clock linguistics class: Investigating contingency grammar', *Language Awareness* 1, 91–108.

van Lier, L.: 1995, *Introducing Language Awareness*, Penguin Books, London.

ROD ELLIS

EXPLICIT KNOWLEDGE AND SECOND LANGUAGE PEDAGOGY

The terms **implicit** and **explicit knowledge** refer respectively to 'knowledge of language' and 'knowledge about language'. It is important to distinguish implicit/explicit *learning* and implicit/explicit *knowledge*; the latter refers to a product – the knowledge that exists in the mind of the learner – whereas the former refers to a process – how L2 knowledge is internalized. There is considerable controversy surrounding the implicit/explicit learning distinction relating to the problem of 'consciousness' (see McLaughlin, 1990). Whereas it is difficult – perhaps impossible – to ascertain reliably whether a learning process takes place consciously or not, it is possible to determine whether learners' knowledge of a grammatical structure is conscious or not by comparing what they say about it with what they actually do with it in spontaneous language use. The focus of this review is second language (L2) knowledge, not learning (see reviews in Volume 4).

EARLY DEVELOPMENTS

A survey of the literature on **implicit knowledge** reveals considerable definitional discrepancies (compare, for instance, Bialystok's (1990) description with Reber's (1989)). The following is an attempt to provide a broad characterization of implicit knowledge.

According to Bialystok (1990), implicit L2 knowledge is typically manifest in some form of naturally occurring language behavior (e.g. conversation) and cannot easily be accessed separately from this behavior. It is 'unanalyzed'. Similarly, Mathews et al. (1989) argue that implicit knowledge takes the form of compilations of memories of past experiences rather than of an integrated model that reflects analytical cognition (i.e. it is 'memory-based' rather than 'rule-based'). Both Bialystok and Mathews et al. also characterize implicit knowledge as easily accessible.

Reber (1989) suggests that implicit L2 knowledge is 'veridical' but 'partial'. That is, it reflects with considerable accuracy the environmental stimulus from which it was derived but it typically fails, at least initially, to incorporate all the invariances present in the stimulus. In contrast to Bialystok and Mathews et al, he claims that implicit knowledge is, in

L. van Lier and D. Corson (eds), Encyclopedia of Language and Education,
Volume 6: Knowledge about Language, 109–118.
© *1997 Kluwer Academic Publishers. Printed in the Netherlands.*

part, abstract and structured. That is, it can deal with 'different symbol sets' (i.e. different input) to those from which it was derived. According to this view, then, implicit knowledge is rule-based. Evidence for this comes from studies such as Berko's (1958) which demonstrate language learners' ability to apply 'rules' they have internalized to new language contexts. Not all implicit knowledge is abstract and structured, however. Reber (1989) acknowledges that it can take the form of 'a rather concrete, instantiated memorial system' (e.g. routines, formulas and discrete items).

A further point of some importance is that implicit knowledge is amenable to conscious examination, although often only with considerable difficulty. In this way, it can serve as a basis for the construction of explicit knowledge (as is the case with linguists who rely on their intuitions as data).

Explicit knowledge, broadly defined as 'knowledge about the L2' can be broken down into **analyzed knowledge** and **metalanguage**. **Analyzed knowledge** refers to that knowledge about L2 items and structures of which the learner is aware but not necessarily conscious. According to Bialystok (1994) analyzed knowledge is derived from implicit knowledge. **Metalanguage**, 'the language used to analyze or describe a language' (Richards, Platt & Weber, 1985), on the other hand is learnt through instruction or observation. Analyzed knowledge can exist quite independently of whether the learner has acquired the technical language with which to articulate it, although, fairly obviously, it is likely to be more precise, clearer, and better-structured if the learner has access to metalingual terms to talk about it.

Analyzed knowledge typically manifests itself in some form of problem-solving activity that calls for learners to pay focal attention to the choice of linguistic forms (as in a cloze task or grammaticality judgement task). Analyzed knowledge can also manifest itself intermittently in naturally occurring language behavior. Bialystok (1990) and others have argued that certain types of language tasks (e.g. those calling for disembedded language use and the manipulation of complex formal schemata) require access to *analyzed* linguistic knowledge. However, because this kind of knowledge cannot be accessed easily and rapidly, it is typically only used when there is opportunity for deliberate language planning (i.e. monitoring).

Explicit knowledge is frequently fragmentary and anomalous (Sorace, 1985; Green & Hecht, 1992); that is, it often constitutes an inaccurate or incomplete representation of implicit knowledge. Like implicit knowledge, though, explicit knowledge consists of both knowledge of the formal properties of the language being learned (e.g. how the passive is constructed in English) and of form-function mappings (e.g. the use of the passive to place the grammatical object in topic position in a sentence). Because explicit knowledge is amenable to study through conscious, intentional reflection, it can easily be re-analyzed. Learners are constantly refining their analyzed knowledge.

Metalanguage can consist of technical (e.g. 'the most typical semantic role of a subject is agentive' – Quirk & Greenbaum, 1973) or semi-technical terminology (e.g. the subject typically tells us who does an action). Research has shown that L2 learners vary enormously in the amount of metalanguage they learn (Green & Hecht, 1992).

MAJOR CONTRIBUTIONS

In an attempt to relate the work on implicit and explicit knowledge to language pedagogy, Ellis (1993, 1994) has developed a weak-interface model of L2 acquisition. This hypothesizes that explicit knowledge of L2 items and structures may but usually does not convert directly into implicit L2 knowledge. This position is grounded in research which indicates that learners do not bypass developmental sequences, which are assumed to reflect implicit knowledge, even when they are able to practice using their explicit knowledge of target structures (Pienemann, 1984; Spada & Lightbown, 1993).

Ellis' weak-interface model, unlike Krashen's Monitor Model (see Krashen, 1982), allows for explicit knowledge to convert into implicit knowledge. This can occur in two major ways. First, it may prove possible for non-developmental features (Pienemann (1984) calls them 'variational features') to be acquired via explicit knowledge. However it is currently not clear which features are developmental and variational or how they can be independently established. Second, formal instruction may help learners achieve mastery over grammatical features that they have partially acquired (i.e. features they know but cannot use accurately). This is by no means a minor role, especially as grammar teaching is often directed at improving accuracy rather than teaching new features.

Ellis' model also allows for implicit L2 knowledge to convert into explicit L2 knowledge (cf. Bialystok's (1978) Model of L2 Learning). The process by which this occurs is self-reflection. Like linguists, L2 learners reflect on their implicit knowledge, thereby 'analyzing' it. This is important for the kinds of consciousness-raising tasks discussed below, as these require that at least some of the learners have access to implicit knowledge of the targeted features.

The main thrust of Ellis' model, however, rests in the claim that explicit L2 knowledge functions as a facilitator of implicit L2 knowledge. This occurs in three possible ways. First, it helps learners to *notice* linguistic properties of the input that otherwise might not be noticed. That is, it can assist in the process of input-enhancement (Sharwood Smith, 1993). Input is processed by means of top-down strategies designed to derive the message-content with maximum efficiency by utilizing context cues in conjunction with bottom-up strategies where the learner attends to and attempts to decode specific L2 items and structures. However, as Schmidt (1990), has argued, bottom-up processing is necessary for acquisition to take place (i.e. no noticing, no acquisition). Learners with explicit knowledge of a specific feature are likely to be better able to engage in bottom-up processing. In other words, explicit knowledge helps learners obtain **intake** (i.e. to process grammatical information for short term and maybe medium term memory).

Second, intake is also enhanced when learners are able to compare what they have noticed in the input with what they currently produce (or might produce) in their own output. This kind of cognitive comparison is hypothesized to help learners identify what it is that they still need to learn. It can serve two functions; it can help learners notice the gap (Schmidt & Frota, 1986) between the input and their own output and it can provide them with evidence that an existing hypothesis regarding a target language structure is the correct one. In other words, as Swain (1995) suggests, cognitive comparisons can serve as a mechanism for disconfirming or confirming hypotheses in implicit knowledge.

Third, as Krashen (1982) has argued, explicit knowledge can be used to monitor output from implicit knowledge, either before the output is uttered or after. Monitoring can also assist acquisition. For example, it can help the conversion of implicit knowledge into explicit knowledge. Monitored output also constitutes 'auto-input' which can be used for acquisition.

It is not easy, however, to demonstrate that explicit L2 knowledge facilitates the acquisition of implicit L2 knowledge in these ways. Fotos (1993) provides evidence to suggest that learners who have been equipped with explicit L2 knowledge of a specific grammatical feature do indeed notice it in subsequent input to a greater extent than those who have not. However, Fotos' study does not examine whether this noticing contributes to subsequent implicit knowledge. There is, however, some indirect evidence in support of this claim. In general, learners who receive formal instruction (grammar teaching) achieve higher levels of grammatical proficiency than those who do not (Long, 1983). If, as has been claimed, explicit instruction frequently does not contribute *directly* to the acquisition of implicit L2 knowledge, an explanation for the faster rate of learning seen in instructed learners may lie in the *indirect* contribution of explicit L2 knowledge, as described above.

WORK IN PROGRESS

The model introduced above provides a basis for addressing a number of key questions relating to the role of formal instruction in L2 acquisition. Future research will need to address these.

1. Is it possible to teach items and structures for implicit L2 knowledge?

2. Are there any grounds for teaching learners explicit knowledge of L2 items and structures?
3. Assuming explicit knowledge is useful, is it necessary to teach meta-lingual knowledge or is it sufficient to raise learners' awareness of linguistic properties?
4. How should explicit knowledge be taught?
5. What can teachers do to help learners make effective use of their explicit knowledge in processing L2 input?
6. What can teachers do to help learners make effective use of their explicit knowledge in processing L2 output?

Questions (1) and (2) concern whether grammar should be taught and, if it should, what type of grammatical knowledge should be the pedagogical target. The model introduced above suggests that it is possible to teach items and structures directly for implicit knowledge but only if the sequence of instruction matches the sequence by which this kind of knowledge is internalized. Despite Pienemann, Johnston & Brindley's (1988) proposals for achieving this match, it is not clear that this is a practical course of action (see Long, 1985). The model suggests, however, that there are clear grounds for teaching explicit knowledge of L2 items. It is assumed that this type of knowledge is 'teachable', as it is not subject to the developmental constraints that govern implicit L2 knowledge, although it may well prove subject to constraints of a non-developmental kind (e.g. the complexity of information required to formulate an explicit rule).

Question (3) addresses an important issue about which little is currently known. Research by Alderson, Clapham & Steel (1995) suggests that metalingual knowledge is not related to general language proficiency. It may be, therefore, that it is explicit knowledge as awareness rather than as metalanguage which is important. Question (4) concerns the pedagogical options available for developing explicit L2 knowledge. (5) concerns the pedagogical options available for helping learners use their explicit knowledge to notice target language features in the input and to carry out cognitive comparisons. (6) concerns the pedagogical options for helping learners to use their explicit knowledge to construct output (e.g. by monitoring). The following section provides a pedagogic account of some of the major options available for developing explicit knowledge.

DIRECTIONS FOR LANGUAGE PEDAGOGY

One obvious way of imparting explicit knowledge is by direct explanation – of the kind used in the grammar-translation method, for example. Fotos & Ellis (1991) found that in the case of Japanese college students, who had considerable experience of this kind of formal instruction, direct explanation was very effective. There are, however, sound educational reasons for not pursuing such an approach. It is based on a transmission-model of education and, as such, does not actively engage the learners in taking responsibility for their own learning. An alternative to direct explanation is to devise some kind of task to help learners develop explicit L2 knowledge for themselves (i.e. a consciousness-raising (CR) task). Fotos and Ellis found that this, too, was quite successful, even though the learners had little prior experience of it. One major advantage of this discovery approach is that it provides opportunities for learners to interact in the target language while learning about it. Grammar becomes both the object of learning and a topic for discussion.

A CR task of the kinds used by Fotos and Ellis can be defined as follows:

> A CR task is a pedagogic activity where the learners are provided with L2 *data* in some form and required to perform some *operation* on or with it, the purpose of which is to arrive at an explicit understanding of some linguistic property or properties of the target language.

It can be argued that all grammar activities can serve to raise awareness – even a pattern drill. However, a defining characteristic of a CR task is that it is not intended to elicit learner production and is not designed to lead directly to correct use of the target feature in spontaneous language use. Instead the aim is to construct a conscious representation of the target feature and to this end any production of the feature will be strictly limited and incidental.

Two broad types of CR task can be identified – **inductive** and **deductive**. This distinction is common in language pedagogy, where it is traditionally used to distinguish the pattern-practice associated with audiolingualism from the rule-giving approach associated with the grammar-translation or cognitive-code methods. In terms of CR tasks, it has a rather different denotation. In an inductive CR task, learners are supplied with L2 data and are required to induce an explicit representation of a target language structure. In a deductive CR task, learners are supplied with a description of a target language structure and are required to utilize this description by applying it to L2 data.

Inductive tasks raise the question of where learners are to obtain the information to derive explicit knowledge. There are two possibilities. First, some learners may already have implicit knowledge of the property in question, as discussed earlier. The task serves as a device to help them analyze this knowledge. Second, the data may be structured in such a way that learners are able to discover the underlying regularity for themselves. These two possibilities are not mutually exclusive.

In deductive tasks there are a number of options relating to how the descriptive information about the target structure is provided. One concerns the manner of presentation. The information can be supplied verbally or non-verbally (for example, by means of a diagram) or in both ways. A second option concerns whether the information provided is non-contrastive (i.e. concerns only the target language) or contrastive (i.e. concerns both the target language and the learners' first language). In a third option, the information supplied can be complete and accurate (in relation to the data supplied) or partial in some way. In the case of partial information, the learner is required to discover its limitations and to develop a more complete/accurate account of the structure in question.

Irrespective of whether a CR task is inductive or deductive, it will consist of (1) data of some kind and (2) some required operation to be performed on the data. It follows that the range of options for devising CR tasks can be described by specifying the different types of data and the various operations that can be performed on them.

Data options include the following:

1. Authentic vs. contrived (i.e. whether the data consist of text prepared by native speakers for other native speakers for some purpose other than language teaching).
2. Oral vs. written (i.e. whether the data represent spoken language or written language). Spoken language data can be made available to the learner in the form of a recording, or, more likely, by means of a transcription.
3. Discrete sentences vs. continuous text (i.e. whether the data consist of a series of disconnected sentences or continuous discourse).
4. Well-formed vs. deviant (i.e. whether the data conform to the norms of the target variety or whether they include deviations from these norms, as, for example, in grammaticality judgement tasks).
5. Gap vs. non-gap (i.e. whether the data are distributed among the learners in such a way that the information contained in the data has to be shared or whether each learner has access to all the data).

The types of operations that can be performed on the data include the following:

1. Identification (i.e. the learners are invited to identify incidences of a specific feature in the data by, for example, underlining it).
2. Judgement (i.e. the learners are invited to judge the correctness of appropriateness of features in the data).
3. Completion (i.e. the learners are invited to complete a text, for example, by filling in blanks as in a cloze passage or by selecting from choices supplied).
4. Modification (i.e. the learners are invited to modify a text in some way, for example, by replacing one item with another item, by reordering elements in the text, by inserting some additional item into the text, or by rewriting part of it).
5. Sorting (i.e. the learners are invited to classify specific items present in the data by sorting them into defined categories).

6. Matching (i.e. the learners are invited to match parts of the data according to some defined principle).
7. Rule provision (i.e. in the case of inductive tasks learners may or may not be asked to give a 'rule' to account for the phenomena they have investigated; the rule can be presented verbally or non-verbally – see above).

There are, of course, other options of a more general methodological nature. A task can be performed individually by the learners, in small group work or in lock-step with the whole class. It can be performed in the L2 or in the learners' first language. It can be accomplished orally or in writing. It can be conducted 'straight' or in the form of a game, involving a competitive element e.g. learners could be invited to engage in an auction where the objects on sale are 'correct and incorrect sentences').

PROBLEMS AND DIFFICULTIES

An approach to grammar teaching based on tasks designed to help learners construct explicit knowledge may not be appropriate for all learners. They may not be appropriate for beginner learners as they will have very limited implicit L2 knowledge to draw on and will need to complete the tasks through the medium of their L1. Younger L2 learners may find the conscious study of language unattractive, although it may be possible to devise tasks in the format of games that are more appealing. Learners of the 'data-gathering' kind (Hatch, 1974) may also resist tasks that are essentially 'rule-forming' in nature. Also, as a study by Reber, Walkenfield & Hernstadt (1991) indicates, learners may differ in their ability to engage in explicit learning tasks according to their general intelligence. In contrast, Reber et al. suggest that implicit learning 'operates largely independently of intelligence' (p. 894). It may be, therefore, that consciousness-raising is not for every learner.

FUTURE DIRECTIONS

The list of options for designing and teaching CR tasks constitute 'provisional specifications', which teachers will need to investigate in the context of their own classrooms. In addition, teachers will need to discover what kinds of learners CR tasks are best suited to.

It is not envisaged that CR tasks directed at teaching explicit knowledge should constitute the entire content or even the major part of a language program. If used, CR tasks will need to be used in conjunction with tasks which have no specific linguistic focus and are, instead, designed to cater for the acquisition of implicit knowledge. One of the challenges facing language pedagogy is to determine the balance and relationship between teaching directed at implicit knowledge and that directed at explicit knowledge.

Temple University
USA

REFERENCES

Alderson, C., Clapham, C. & Steel, D.: 1995, *Metalinguistic Knowledge, Language Aptitude and Language Proficiency*, mimeograph, University of Lancaster.

Berko, J.: 1958, 'The child's learning of English morphology', *Word* 14, 150–177.

Bialystok, E.: 1978, 'A theoretical model of second language learning', *Language Learning* 28, 69–84.

Bialystok, E.: 1990, 'The competence of processing: Classifying theories of second language acquisition', *TESOL Quarterly* 24, 635–648.

Bialystok, E.: 1994, 'Representation and ways of knowing: Three issues in second language acquisition', in N. Ellis (ed.), *Implicit and Explicit Learning of Languages*, Academic Press, London, 549–569.

Ellis, R.: 1993, 'Second language acquisition and the structural syllabus', *TESOL Quarterly* 27, 91–113.

Ellis, R.: 1994, 'A theory of instructed second language acquisition', in N. Ellis (ed.), *Implicit and Explicit Learning of Languages*, Academic Press, London, 79–114.

Fotos, S.: 1993, 'Consciousness-raising and noticing through focus on form: Grammar task performance versus formal instruction', *Applied Linguistics* 14(4).

Fotos, S. & Ellis, R.: 1991, 'Communicating about grammar: A task-based approach', *TESOL Quarterly* 25, 605–628.

Green, P & Hecht, K: 1992, 'Implicit and explicit grammar: An empirical study', *Applied Linguistics* 13, 168–184.

Hatch, E.: 1974, 'Second language learning – universals?' *Working Papers on Bilingualism* 3, 1–17.

Krashen, S.: 1982, *Principles and Practice in Second Language Acquisition*, Pergamon, Oxford.

Long, M.: 1983, 'Does second language instruction make a difference? A review of the research', *TESOL Quarterly* 17, 359–382.

Long, M.: 1985, 'A role for instruction in second language acquisition: Task-based language teaching', in K. Hyltenstam & M. Pienemann (eds.), *Modelling and Assessing Second Language Acquisition, Multilingual Matters*, Clevedon, Avon, 77–99.

Mathews, R., Buss, R., Stanley. W., Blanchard-Fields, F., Cho, J., & Druhan, B. 1989, 'Role of implicit and explicit processes in learning from examples: A synergistic effect', *Journal of Experimental Psychology: Learning, Memory, and Cognition* 15, 1083–1100.

McLaughlin, B.: 1990, ' "conscious" vs. "unconscious" learning', *TESOL Quarterly* 24, 617–634.

Pienemann, M.: 1984, 'Psychological constraints on the teachability of languages', *Studies in Second Language Acquisition* 6, 186–214.

Pienemann, M., Johnston, M. & Brindley: 1988, 'Constructing an acquisition-based procedure for assessing second language acquisition', *Studies in Second Language Acquisition* 10, 217–243.

Quirk, R. & Greenbaum, S.: 1973, *A University Grammar of English*, Longman, London.

Reber, A.: 1989, 'Implicit learning and tacit knowledge', *Journal of Experimental Psychology: General* 118, 219–235.

Reber, A., Walkenfield, F. & Hernstadt, R: 1991, 'Implicit and explicit learning: Individual
    differences and IQ', *Journal of Experimental Psychology: Learning, Memory, and
    Cognition 17*, 888–896.
Richards, J. Platt, J. & Weber, H.: 1985, *Longman Dictionary of Applied Linguistics*,
    Longman, London.
Schmidt, R.: 1990, 'The role of consciousness in second language learning', *Applied
    Linguistics 11*, 129–158.
Schmidt, E. & Frota, S.: 1986, 'Developing basic conversational ability in a second
    language: A case-study of an adult learner', in R. Day (ed.), *Talking to Learning*,
    Newbury House, Rowley, MA, 237–326.
Sharwood-Smith, M.: 1993, 'Input enhancement in instructed SLA: Theoretical bases',
    Studies in Second Language Acquisition 15, 165–179.
Sorace, A.: 1985, 'Metalinguistic knowledge and language use in acquisition-poor envi-
    ronments', *Applied Linguistics 6*, 239–254.
Spada, N. & Lightbown, P.: 1993, 'Instruction and the development of L2 questions',
    Studies in Second Language Acquisition 15, 205–224.
Swain, M.: 1995, 'Three functions of output in second language learning', in G. Cook &
    B. Seidlhofer (eds.), *Principle and Practice in Applied Linguistics: Studies in Honour
    of H.G. Widdowson*, Oxford University Press, 125–144.

PATRICK ZABALBEASCOA

LANGUAGE AWARENESS AND TRANSLATION

Translation may appear to be a straightforward matter of rendering the meaning of a message in a different language from the one it was originally produced in, but in actual fact it is a highly complex type of human communication which involves a considerable number of linguistic and extralinguistic variables. Both common-sense and prescriptive accounts have shown their limitations and contradictions; so too have single tier models, some of which are the result of studies from within a discipline that is somehow related to one or more aspects of translation but not to all. Indeed there are quite a few dimensions to translation and an almost open-ended number of variables. The various dimensions include linguistic and semiotic variables, sociocultural practices and beliefs, historical contexts, stylistic standards and publishing policies, technological means and know-how, educational policies and institutions, the cognitive and psychological dimensions of individual translators and their readers, and the working conditions imposed by their clients or employers. Awareness of such a large number of variables has become a fundamental ingredient of Translation Studies, and a particularly relevant concept in research aimed at improving our understanding of translator competence and the social dimension of translation, including the role and image of translators in society. This has become possible largely due to a theoretical shift away from producing prescriptive guidelines – for practitioners and critics to follow – in an endeavour to establish translation as the object of an empirical science related to the human and social sciences.

In this review I will primarily discuss translation pedagogy, as practiced in translator training, but I will also review briefly some pertinent aspects of pedagogical translation, as an aid to the teaching and learning of foreign languages. It is important to distinguish one type of practice from the other.

Apart from the problem that there are almost as many definitions of translation as specialized publications there is also one major ambiguity. In the collocation 'translation and interpretation', the first element refers to written texts and the second to simultaneous, or consecutive, oral rendering of oral discourse in another language. However, in this review, and in most modern studies, the term 'translation' is used to refer both to oral and written modes of discourse unless otherwise stated. Both are seen as varieties of interlingual, intercultural communication with a common

L. van Lier and D. Corson (eds), Encyclopedia of Language and Education, Volume 6: Knowledge about Language, 119–130.
© 1997 Kluwer Academic Publishers. Printed in the Netherlands.

ground that is well worth exploring. Of course, there are also some very important differences, e.g. the interpreter must have additional oral skills and frequently has to interpret a text as it unfolds when a written version is not provided beforehand and there is hardly any maneuverabilty to go back and make corrections. From a researcher's point of view, written translation is much easier to study since there are thousands of readily available written translations: this is certainly not the case for recordings or transcriptions of interpreters' output.

EARLY DEVELOPMENTS

Pedagogical translation in the foreign language classroom tends to bring to mind the traditional grammar-translation method, originally designed for teaching classical Greek and Latin all over Europe and later on applied to the teaching of modern languages. Possibly an imperfect method even for teaching dead languages, it soon had to face some very strong arguments against its use in modern language teaching and in favour of alternative approaches. In the specialized literature the heyday of this method is usually depicted as the 'Dark Ages' of language teaching. Almost all subsequent methods were some form of reaction against it, especially its translational component. Out of the ashes of the shortcomings of the traditional grammar translation method grew a number of teaching theories and methods based on the principle of "no mother tongue", such as the Direct Method, Audiolingualism and early communicative approaches. Translation had seemingly been banned from foreign language teaching and learning forever.

Translator training programmes and Translation Studies have not fared much better than pedagogical translation. The debate is still alive as to whether translation is a natural or an acquired skill. It has often been said and written that if you cannot write then you should translate, and if you cannot translate then you should teach translation or theorize about it. Translation has been viewed with suspicion and mistrust by many people. In fact it still is and will be, probably for a long time to come. It has often been regarded as a minor skill, both intellectually and professionally, and even as a theoretical impossibility leading to inevitable betrayal and misrepresentation giving rise to texts and linguistic forms of expression that can apparently only be evaluated in negative terms. Consequently, the study of translational phenomena has also suffered. Even within the field it is very popular, for example, to study errors that translators make as an almost exclusive approach of investigation and evaluation. Certain dichotomies (namely, the process vs. the product, literal vs. free renderings, objectivity vs. subjectivity) and myths (the theoretical impossibility of truly satisfactory translations, translation as a necessary evil, translation as betrayal, etc.) seem to have straightjacketed any real academic progress towards gaining further insight into the nature of translation. Lawrence Venuti (1995) is an exception to the general trend and denounces this state of affairs quite vigorously. He shows clearly that, in the English-speaking world particularly, though certainly not exclusively, the best translator is considered to be the one who provides the readers, or listeners, in the case of an interpreter, with the illusion that s/he does not exist, and that they are actually reading or listening to the original author/speaker. This social attitude towards translation has profound implications on the production of translations and shows the importance of their social dimension. Frequently, translations are not presented as such, especially in the press and in advertising, and many translators are forced into anonymity, so that the end-users of translations are very frequently completely unaware of the precise nature of text they are being presented with and they are certainly not aware of who the translator was or in what circumstances the translation was produced.

Yet so many people feel quite comfortable talking about translators and their work, usually to remark that they would much rather live in a world where there were no translations at all because they are all so bad and hardly ever do credit to the original. For example, a lot of people have been reported to have said that they enjoy a book less once they are aware that it is a translation. Some people are even unaware that the Bible was not originally written in English. According to Venuti there is a considerable lack of awareness due to the reduced number of translations in the U.S. and the U.K., and partly due to the way in which translations are produced to create the illusion of transparency. He says that what is so remarkable is that the illusory effect conceals the numerous conditions under which the translation is made, starting with the translator's crucial intervention in the foreign text. The more fluent the translation, the more invisible the translator, and, presumably, the more visible the writer or meaning of the foreign text.

The reasons that Venuti gives to justify his concept of invisiblity, and the need to denounce it, can be summarized as follows:
- fluency as the basic standard of acceptability;
- the authority of "plain styles" in English-language writing;
- an individualistic conception of authorship, whereby translation is defined as second-order representation and the illusion of authorial presence;
- translators receive minimal recognition for their work: no mention in reviews, book covers, advertisements, etc.;
- the existence of an ambiguous unfavourable legal status of translation copyright law and actual contractual arrangements; the translator's authorship is never given full recognition.

This creates a contradictory situation where certain communities and individuals often demand very high standards for their translations but at the same time are not willing to give translators a high intellectual or professional status. The general opinion that translating is a necessary evil and the fact that it is often a marginal aspect of text production is instrumental in keeping down the quality of many translations and the social and professional status of translators and interpreters.

MAJOR CONTRIBUTIONS

Currently, some applied linguists defend a return of translation to the language classroom, along with the necessary precautions. Among them, Alan Duff (1995) argues that translation practice can be used as a resource for the promotion of language learning and as such many activities and exercises can be used to develop language awareness, without always necessarily proceeding to the final stage of producing a polished version. The drawbacks of the grammar-translation method can be overcome first by realising the difference between translation pedagogy and pedagogical translation, and between translator competence and linguistic competence; and second, by integrating a variety of translation activities with other parts of an eclectic, essentially communicative methodology that is sensitive to learners' needs and abilities. After its period of banishment (e.g. during the late 1970s and early 1980s almost every language academy in Spain advertised teachers that were native) pedagogical translation is gradually but slowly coming back to EFL. Specific examples can be found in an increasing number of EFL textbooks, although none of them reflect a wholehearted commitment to Duff's proposal. Further research into how to make the best use of translating activities still needs to be carried out. For example, Duff argues for an active role of translation in the classroom, but so far translation, when mentioned at all, seems to be restricted to such areas as the teacher's guide or self-study workbooks but not the main student's book (e.g. Swan & Walter, 1984; Doff, 1991).

One of the main factors of foreign language learning is the influence of the mother tongue. Translating is one way of helping the learner to control mother-tongue interference by being more aware of its nature. Translating is also very useful in helping learners to become more aware of their own language and understand that it is not more 'natural' or more logical than any other language, but simply a different system. Group discussion about translations appearing in various types of publications or done by students is a very natural way of introducing the topic of language into a class's conversations. Translation exercises can also show differences in structural patterns and pragmatic strategies between languages as well as the close relationship between language and culture. Duff (1995) stresses the fact that language competence is a two-way system. Most foreign language users need to be able to communicate both ways: into and from the foreign language, and translation is ideally suited for practice in communicating back into the mother tongue.

Translation as an object of study is, obviously, closely linked to language; however, it is more open to debate whether translation can best be dealt with as a branch of linguistics or literature studies. In 1972 James Holmes (1988) claimed that translation deserves a discipline of its own, and he even proposed a name for it: Translation Studies. Contrary to his stated desire, the name he proposed and argued for so well was not picked up by many scholars; consequently Translation Studies has often been used to refer exclusively to Holmes' followers within the discipline, and among these are some of the most influential translation scholars of our time, notably Gideon Toury, Jose Lambert and Theo Hermans. Like Venuti, although from a completely different angle, Holmes was also reacting against approaches to translation that took too much for granted. Translation cannot be fully and satisfactorily explained by any single branch of linguistics, not even contrastive linguistics, because the basis of translation is not so much language as a system, or even two language systems; its natural basis is the understanding of texts as they are produced, received and interpreted within different systems at a given time, (language systems, literary systems, political systems, market systems, educational systems, legal systems, communication systems, etc.). Of course, any narrow understanding of the scope of linguistics (e.g. including only morphology, syntax and lexical semantics) cannot offer a satisfactory working model of translation. It is also true, though, that linguistics has been consistently broadening its own horizons to such an extent that it has blurred the lines that used to distinguish it from pragmatics, semiotics and, to some degree, many other social and human sciences (e.g. with the growth of branches such as sociolinguistics, critical linguistics and psycholinguistics), as well as the relationship that mathematical, computational and corpus-based linguistics have with the so-called 'hard' sciences. So, as it grows and develops, linguistics is better equipped to provide help in gaining further insight into translation and related phenomena, the study of which, due to the number and complex relationship of all of the intervening factors, can benefit from every branch of linguistics. The academic situation has also improved by the narrowing of the divide between linguistic and literary models of textual analysis.

In Holmes' agenda, as stated in 'The Name and Nature of Translation Studies', 1972 (Holmes, 1988), translation can be the object of an independent albeit interdisciplinary field of study that can be divided into "pure" studies that would produce descriptive and theoretical models and case studies, on the one hand, and applied translation studies, on the other, involving translation criticism, translating aids (anything specifically designed to be helpful during the process) and translator training. Furthermore, Toury (1995) stresses the necessary ties between the two branches. On the other hand, what Holmes envisaged as a discipline with two main branches is seen rather differently by many linguists and even some translation theorists. For example, relevance theory advocate Ernst Gutt (1991) is convinced that one branch, the pure studies (in particular its theoretical component), is unnecessary since theoretical linguistic models or schools make them redundant. As for the other branch, applied translation studies, it tends to be seen as 'belonging' to applied linguistics. Regardless of whether translation studies should belong to linguistics or literary studies, or even become entirely independent, it is quite clear that it can develop more rapidly and fruitfully by benefiting from the insights, discoveries and models that come from linguistics, literary studies, communication theories, pragmatics, semiotics, and all of the other human and social sciences, combined with questions that arise directly from observation of translational phenomena. It is also important to see the difference between two equally legitimate approaches. In one, translation can be regarded as an aspect of language phenomena and can therefore be studied within linguistics; in the other, the nature of language and interlingual communication can be seen as part (albeit a fundamental part) of the multidimensional nature of translation to be studied within Translation Studies. In other words, a better understanding of translation can help towards a better understanding of language and vice versa.

Below is a brief account of the nature of Translation Studies and its organic structure as envisaged by Holmes (1972) and later commented on by Toury (1995).

1. 'PURE' studies, as opposed to 'applied', aimed at improving our understanding of the nature of translations, translational phenomena and the influence of related factors:

   (a) THEORETICAL (models, classifications, explanations, definitions, predictions, abstraction) broken down into:

      (i) a GENERAL theory of translation that would try to establish regularities of behaviour and formulate a series of coherent 'laws' which would state the inherent relations between all the variables found to be relevant to translation;

      (ii) PARTIAL theories that would provide a basis for the general theory (i.e. models, statements, etc. with a restricted number of variables or restricted in scope) such as any combination of the following:
         • medium restricted (such as limiting scope to human or machine processes)
         • area restricted (only certain language pairs or cultures)
         • rank restricted (only certain lexical, morphological, syntactic or textual levels)
         • text-type restricted (only certain genres or text-types)

- time restricted (only certain historical periods)
- problem restricted (only certain translation problems, i.e. the translation of wordplay, the translation of metaphors, etc.).

(b) DESCRIPTIVE (as opposed, not only to theoretical, but also to speculative and prescriptive approaches) that could also be subdivided into partial studies, as above, with the following three interdependent fields:

   (i) PRODUCT oriented, focusing on the nature of the texts that are the result of the translating process;

  (ii) PROCESS oriented, focusing on how translations are produced, what stages, means and processes are involved;

 (iii) FUNCTION oriented, focusing on how translations are received and interpreted, and their systemic position.

2. APPLIED studies, using insights, theoretical models and/or hypotheses, and/or experimental or descriptive studies to develop ways of assisting or training translators and translation critics, and indirect means of influencing translators:

(a) translator TRAINING (teaching methodologies for translation pedagogy);

(b) translation AIDS (e.g. computer-assisted translation programs, context-sensitive, possibly single-purpose, handbooks and reference materials);

(c) translation CRITICISM (e.g. evaluative and prescriptive models).

WORK IN PROGRESS

Translator 'competence' usually refers to the compendium of qualities required to be a good, competent translator. Only relatively recently have scholars in the field realized the importance of distinguishing ideal, desired, competence from the actual qualities and skills that real-world translators (human or electronic) display in their output or during the process, as well as their actual potential. Traditionally, common sense seemed to dictate that the obvious requirements of any self-respecting translator included a perfect knowledge of two languages, a moral sense of loyalty, objectivity and empathy, a knowledge of the subject-matter and the skills expected of a good writer. In the 1980s and 1990s the centre of the field has gradually but steadily begun to shift from speculative and normative approaches over to descriptive and empirical studies, ranging from neurolinguistic studies to surveys on translators' working conditions and legal status.

Experimental studies in translation are very recent, but are perceived as a necessary branch of the new discipline of translation studies. Interest in the cognitive dimension of translation and the translator's thought processes have led some researchers to experiment with the so-called think aloud protocols and other methods of observation of the translator at work. However, machine translation and computer-assisted translation systems are the areas where most money has been spent on experimental studies, involving industries and public institutions. It is becoming clearer that machine-related translation systems and purely human translation have a lot to learn from each other. Another important area for investigation is in developing translator-training methodologies and course profiles.

Since the 1950s the number of institutions offering formal training in translation has grown quite remarkably in tune with the growth of international relations and institutions, especially the U.N. and the European Common Market and, later on, the European Community. Teaching experience and studies carried out mostly in Training Schools and Universities have shown that there is no simple formula that can be applied universally when it comes to translating or translator training. Rather, the improvement of translator competence requires gaining relevant knowledge about specific aspects of certain areas, including languages, subject-matters, discourse- and text-types, reference sources and translator's aids (thus suggesting the need for specialization among translators) and, also, raising the trainee's awareness of the large number of variables or factors that can impinge on a given translation (e.g. communicative, linguistic, cultural, textual, contextual, professional, economic, ideological, stylistic, academic, technological) and the wide range of potentially useful strategies and solutions. For example, a model of translation, such as the one proposed by Theo Hermans (1985), based on the concept of norms that are variable and can account for translational phenomena, implies that translator competence would be greatly enhanced by a sensitivity, or better still, an awareness of the presence and importance of a potentially different set of norms for each new assignment.

The arrival of discourse analysis and text-linguistics models of translation (e.g. Delisle, 1988; Hatim & Mason, 1990; de Beaugrande & Dressler, 1981), and even corpus linguistics (e.g. Baker et al., 1993), have been very influential in the way trainees – and researchers – are now made aware of the number and range of factors that need to be taken into account in text analysis for the purpose of translation. Other contributions to translation pedagogy have come from Christiane Nord's (1991) functional model of translation, a development of Hans Vermeer's (1986) 'Skopos theory', where the functions and skopos, or uses, are variable, and, more importantly, determine the nature of the final product; and also Hewson & Martin's (1991) proposal of a variational approach to translation teaching and training. In all of these models special emphasis is laid on the importance of shaping a translation to fit in with its context (by complying with the strongest norms) and imbue it with the strong sense of purpose that most successful real-life translations tend to have. Daniel Gile (1995) and Paul Kussmaul (1995) have made their contribution by answering the demand for ways to design curricula for trainee translators and interpreters. Finally, the early and mid 1990s have witnessed a boom in the number of published coursebooks for trainee translators (e.g. Bell, 1991; Nord, 1991; Baker, 1992; Delisle, 1993), most of which make an effort not to oversimplify the factors involved in the process of producing a foreign-language version of a source text, one that will justify its existence by responding to the reasons why a new version was deemed necessary, or desirable. Spain, for example, is quite an interesting case study because: (1) there has been a spectacular increase in the number of universities that offer a degree in translating and interpreting (from 3 to 15 between 1990 and 1995); (2) there are four official languages in different stages of development and social acceptance; (3) there is a high level of language awareness and translation awareness among the people, so language and translation are a part of many political party policies.

PROBLEMS AND DIFFICULTIES

Possibly the most serious problem that has always faced translation is its professional, academic and social status, along with the abovementioned misconceptions and mistrust. Translation is certainly not a profession where a single person makes all the decisions and goes through all the stages of the process, so, each one of the participants (source text writers, translators, readers, publishers and any others) can affect the final result. Because of the transparency ('invisibility') of translation in many countries, most people are not aware of the important role it has played in the shaping of their societies, languages and literary systems. In this respect, books like Delisle & Woodsworth (1996) do an important job of illustrating just how important translation is and has always been in our daily lives. Translators have contributed towards the emergence and development of alphabets, national languages and literatures, and the spread of knowledge, power, religions and cultural values.

There is an enormous amount of work still to be done in almost every branch and area of Translation Studies, be it empirical, descriptive, theoretical or applied. Holmes's proposal included a division of labour where work would be carried out in restricted areas, according to language pairs, historical parameters, human or machine translation, oral or written, certain problems in translation, etc., all of which would eventually contribute to a general theory of translation. The complexity of the factors involved in translating have only become more evident through research into machine translation. One of the consequences of the realization that high-quality fully-automatic translation is still a long-term project has been to help promote the concept and the products of machine-aided human translation which requires interaction between the human translator and computer tools. Such tools are varied and range from communications systems to information management and expert systems. In any case, the findings of work done in both computer-assisted translation and fully automatic translation also provide us with highly relevant information regarding the nature of translation and the factors involved.

Nowadays, staff translators are highly qualified professionals, very often with a university degree in their speciality, a knowledge of three or four languages, and a set of skills that enable them to adapt very quickly to other editing and writing jobs. New technologies have had a great impact on the profession and an increasing number of translators are familiar with a wide range of computer and communications applications. The social and professional standing of translators varies considerably. A translator who is just beginning can hope to move up the promotional ladder within a company or institution. A translator's role as a 'teamplayer' also varies considerably depending on the speciality and the working environment. Depending on factors such as the country, the moment, the genre, and other writing activities a translator can range between becoming well-known and remaining absolutely anonymous.

FUTURE DIRECTIONS

Translation Studies is a new discipline and still has a long way to go. More and more scholars are embarking on the new field and bringing with them a variety of new perspectives. Its interdisciplinary nature means that at different times new breakthroughs in other sciences will promote new approaches from different angles. Thus, there is growing interest at the present time in the ideological and sociological aspects of translation, partly due to the arrival of critical linguistics, gender studies, and literary models of deconstruction and postmodernism among others. Awareness of translation and its effects is part of sociolinguistics and sociological and semiotic studies focused on bilingual and multilingual societies. On an economic and technological level there is renewed interest and faith in the possibilities of both fully automatic translation and computer-assisted translation, partly due to the development of corpus linguistics and computer technology and the fact that the demand for computerized translation products is still intact if not stronger. Despite the undeniable importance of translation in many areas and aspects of human communication and social intercourse it has not yet caught many foreign language teachers' interest as much as other proposed methods or teaching aids, such as role-play or the use of videorecordings. However, research into translation pedagogy will continue to develop, no doubt driven by the existence of so many university degrees and postgraduate programmes. If the boom in international conferences and journals that deal with translation over the last ten years has any continuity, this may also be instrumental in bringing many studies out of their isolation and do away with the traditional ignorance that scholars have shown of the contributions of colleagues from other countries.

Universitat Pompeu Fabra
Spain

REFERENCES

Baker, M.: 1992, *In Other Words*, Routledge, London.
Baker, M., Francis, G. & Tognini-Bonelli, E.: 1993, *Text and Technology in Honour of John Sinclair*, John Benjamins, Philadelphia.
Beaugrande, R. de & Dressler, W.: 1981, *Introduction to Text Linguistics*, Longman, London.
Bell, R: 1991, *Translation and Translating*, Longman, Harlow, England.
Delisle, J: 1988, *Translation: An Interpretive Approach*, University of Ottawa Press, Ottawa.
Delisle, J.: 1993, *La traduction raisonée*, University of Ottawa, Ottawa.
Delisle, J. & Woodsworth, J. (eds.): 1995, *Translators Through History*, John Benjamins Unesco Editions, Philadelphia.
Doff, A.: 1991, *Language in Use*, Cambridge University Press, Cambridge.
Duff, A.: 1989, *Translation*, Oxford University Press, Oxford.
Gile, D.: 1995, *Basic Concepts and Models for Interpreter and Translator Training*, John Benjamins, Amsterdam.
Gutt, E.: 1991, *Translation and Relevance*, Cognition and Context, Basil Blackwell, Oxford.
Hatim, B. & Mason, I.: 1990, *Discourse and the Translator*, Longman, Harlow, England.
Hermans, T. (ed.): 1985, *The Manipulation of Literature Studies in Literary Translation*, Croom Helm, London.
Hewson, L. & Martin, J.: 1991, *Redefining Translation. The Variational Approach*, Routledge, London.
Holmes, J.: 1972, 'The name and nature of translation studies', in J. Holmes (ed.), *Translated! Papers on Literary Translation and Translation Studies*, Rodopi, Amsterdam, 1988, 67–80.
Kiraly, D.: 1995, *Pathways to Translation*, The Kent State University Press, Kent, Ohio.
Kussmaul, P: 1995, *Training the Translator*, John Benjamins, Amsterdam.
Lefevere, A.: 1992, *Translating, Rewriting, and the Manipulation of Literary Fame*, Routledge, London.
Neubert, A. & Schreve, G.: 1992, *Translation as Text*, The Kent State University Press, Ohio.
Nord, C.: 1991, *Text Analysis in Translation*, Rodopi, Amsterdam.
Swan, M. & Walter, C.: 1984, *The Cambridge English Course 1*, Cambridge University Press, Cambridge.
Tirkkonen-Condit, S. (ed.): 1991, *Empirical Research in Translation and Intercultural Studies Selected Papers of the TRANSIF Seminar*, Savonlinna, 1988, Gunter Narr, Tübingen.
Toury, G.: 1995, *Descriptive Translation Studies and Beyond*, John Benjamins, Amsterdam.
Venuti, L.: 1995, *The Translator's Invisibility*, Routledge, London and New York.

130   PATRICK ZABALBEASCOA

Vermeer, H.: 1986, *Voraussetzungen für eine Translationstheorie: Einige Kapitel Kultur- und Sprachtheorie*, Selbstverlag Heidelberg.
Zabalbeascoa, P.: 1995, 'Levels of prescriptiveness in translation', in I. Mason & C. Pagnoulle (eds.), *Cross Words. Issues and Debates in Literary and Non-Literary Translating*, Liège: L3-Liège Language and Literature (University of Liège), 41–49.

SOPHIA PAPAEFTHYMIOU-LYTRA

AWARENESS AND LANGUAGE SWITCH IN SECOND/FOREIGN LANGUAGE LEARNING CONTEXTS

In this paper I will discuss the interplay of *awareness* and *language switch* in second/foreign language (S/FL) learning contexts with particular reference to self-learning FL situations, FL classroom environments as well as SL learning settings. In particular, I will report research concerning the factors that lead to awareness and language switch and I will discuss the functions that they serve as learning parameters in these language learning contexts.

The research about awareness and language switch in FL self-learning contexts has been carried out in the context of a project funded by the European Union. The project concerns the production of intermediate multi-media self-learning materials for adults in Greek, Spanish and German. Three institutions, the Universities of Athens and Barcelona and the Goethe Institute in Munich, have been involved in the project.

EARLY DEVELOPMENTS

Language switch as a marked or unmarked characteristic of the conversation of bilingual and multilingual speakers has received a lot of attention. Language switch was initially considered a structurally unified phenomenon whose significance derived from a universal pattern of relationships between form, function and context (Heller, 1988; Gumperz, 1971). Eventually it was seen as a resource for indexing situationally salient aspects of context in the speakers' attempts to accomplish their interaction goals. Merritt et al. (1992), for instance, present an interesting account of teacher language choice and language switch in primary classrooms in Kenya. They claim that teachers are teaching prevailing patterns of multilanguage use as an unmarked choice – students learn when to use English, Swahili or the vernacular. At the same time they teach them how to manipulate language to make marked code-switches in the interest of successfully negotiating their way through society. In multilingual communities it seems that language switch patterning is learned at school and it is then used in the broader community. In examining language switch in in-group and inter-group situations two questions have preoccupied researchers: firstly, the actual distribution and function of language switch in the community,

L. van Lier and D. Corson (eds), Encyclopedia of Language and Education,
Volume 6: Knowledge about Language, 131–138.
© *1997 Kluwer Academic Publishers. Printed in the Netherlands.*

and, secondly, the speakers' awareness and acceptance of language switch as a normal way of speaking (Bathia & Ritchie, 1989; Garcia & Otheguy, 1989).

MAJOR CONTRIBUTORS

Besides bilingual and multilingual contexts, awareness and language switch have also been researched in S/FL learning contexts. In these contexts, language switch has usually been referred to as use of the 'mother tongue'. In the FL classroom, in particular, the L1 has been primarily used to provide grammar explanations, vocabulary explanations and to manage the class (Harbord, 1992). Use of the L1 in the S/F language classroom, however, has been viewed as evidence of some sort of deficit. It is an indication that learners who switch cannot as yet function well in the S/F language they are learning. In language teaching methodology, emphasis has usually been placed on the use of the S/F language-only principle. See for instance, Weinberg (1990) who reports how language students were penalized for speaking their L1 in an SL context.

Saville-Troike et al. (1984), however, refer to the L1 as a facilitating factor in SL interaction. They report ethnographic research in the SL classroom and describe how the SL young learners managed communication successfully among themselves although their SL production was minimal. They state that the learners achieved successful communication by making use of their awareness of the structure of the SL classroom situation as well as by switching to non-verbal language and their L1 to compensate for their poor L2. Furthermore, Aston (1983), arguing from an FL point of view, maintains that use of the L1 in the classroom helps to build a supportive and friendly environment for learners. He favours a more positive use of the L1, which can be negotiated between learners and teachers. Also Atkinson (1987), in reviewing the uses of the L2 in the FL classroom, concludes that the L1 should be sparingly used. He suggests that a ratio of 5% would be enough to cater for such cases as grammar explanations, etc., where its use can be considered necessary.

Moreover, studies of L2 speakers' use of communication strategies have shown that learners often resort to their L1 to solve problems in the L2 (Bialystok, 1983). Faerch & Kasper (1983) in particular discuss strategies in interlanguage communication, including use of the L1, and relate them to problems learners face. They consider them 'potentially conscious plans set up by the learner in order to solve problems in communication'. Furthermore, they argue that strategies as overt behaviours allow us to take a glimpse at the covert cognitive behaviour of learners, the way they think and cope in learning and communicating in the L2. Their views on strategies seem to embrace the Canale & Swain (1980) concept of strategic competence. Canale and Swain consider the learners' knowledge and abilities from L1 as a potentially valuable factor in L2 learning and communication. On the L2 acquisition issue in particular, Ringbom (1987) has shown that the L1 can have an important role to play in the context of cross-linguistic influence. In comparing the English learning processes of the Swedish speaking Finns with the Finnish speaking Finns he concludes that Swedish being closer to English seems to have facilitated learning English for Swedish speaking Finns considerably.

WORK IN PROGRESS

Monolingual views on S/FL learning/teaching have begun to be modified. S/FL learning is seen as a cross-cultural and a cross-linguistic experience. In this framework, language choice and awareness seem to play an important role. A variety of factors seem to contribute to language switch: linguistic, cognitive, affective, personal, personality, social, cultural, interactional and pedagogical. The function of language switch is to facilitate language learning and interaction and to build up learners' awareness about the L2 language and culture, the learning and communicating processes as well as the learning tasks, that the learners will have to carry out, in relation to their needs and purposes. Research about these factors and functions has been carried out in various learning environments, namely, in FL self-learning contexts, FL classroom situations as well as SL classroom settings.

Evidence from research in FL self-learning contexts indicates that language switch and awareness can help learners to combat cognitive, linguistic and cultural interference from L1. That is because students lack appropriate metalanguage as well as metacognitive and metacommunicative language in the L2. Besides, language switch and awareness seem to set learners at ease. After all, the learners are not under pressure to adopt a new identity or prove themselves competent L2 users as is the case of bilinguals, multilinguals or SL speakers (Myers-Scotton, 1993). Moreover, in these contexts, learners have been assigned many roles. They are participants and observers in the learning process, learners and teachers, recipients of knowledge but also assessors of the use of this knowledge. Not all learners can make the transition easily enough from one role to the other. Language switch and awareness make things easier for them. Furthermore, learners need to have general information as background knowledge concerning the country, the culture and the people. This can be achieved through language switch which thus becomes a means to develop L2 cultural awareness. Consequently, awareness and language switch are not only a matter of method, rather they indicate that specific factors are at work that can have a positive role to play in FL self-learning contexts. See Papaefthymiou-Lytra (*forthcoming*).

Similar factors and functions seem to determine language choice in teacher talk and learner talk in the FL classroom (Papaefthymiou-Lytra, 1990). Research indicates that learners and teachers switch languages for metalinguistic, metacognitive and metacommunicative purposes or for classroom management purposes. Being aware of their poor linguistic or communicative competence they override conformity to use-the-FL-only principle. Learners seem to prefer to switch languages to express motivation and interest in learning the L2, to express verbal humour and relaxation and to express attitudes and feelings. Teachers may also switch languages when they feel that tension and dissatisfaction are building up. Language switch is a means for teachers to impose their power and authority since their message cannot fail to reach their learners. Furthermore, when teachers are asked to talk about topics unrelated to the content of the lesson(s) or the procedures followed in class, they usually take refuge in the L1 as a strategy to save face. Similarly, learners switch languages to avoid displaying their poor L2 competence.

Language switch in the FL classroom also serves pedagogical purposes. It can be employed as an alternative teaching/learning strategy if teachers feel that other strategies, i.e. visual, linguistic, kinesic, etc., may not work. Little & Singleton (1992), for instance, consider language awareness an important aspect of pedagogical grammars that incorporate linguistic, sociolinguistic and pragmatic aspects. Language awareness, they maintain, is tied up with language switch in the early stages of FL learning in particular. In this context, awareness is often restricted to the intrapersonal, cognitive perspective emphasizing the reflective mode and how well the learner understands the relationships among form, function and meaning (Rutherford, 1987). Teacher talk and learner talk, however, are characterized by asymmetry in the use of language switch in classroom discourse. In teacher talk, there is a fluent authoritative L2 user (the teacher) present as a participant, who often regulates language switch in favour of the L2. When monolingual learners are involved in pair and group work, they seem to opt for language switch in order to fulfill a wider variety of roles and functions than their knowledge of the L2 and the situational constraints would permit. Poulisse & Bongaerts (1994) report research of a similar nature about Dutch learners' language switch at the lexical level. Their findings indicate that the occurrence of language switches in oral production is related to the learners' proficiency in English. Some of these switches, they argue, are intentional, others are unintentional. The researchers argue that intentional switches appear to be of two kinds: self-directed and other-directed. Self-directed switches are used by the learners in order to comment on problems, gain time or organize their thoughts. Other-directed switches are used by them in order to compensate for lexical problems or to mark asides.

There is evidence, however, that factors and functions encouraging language switch in SL contexts are not exactly the same as those that prompt language switch in FL contexts, mainly because the social and situational parameters are different. Under the influence of critical discourse studies (Fairclough, 1989), a new approach for adult SL learners has been developed. This approach aims at enabling the learners to critically examine the host society and its values and to become active in shaping their own roles in it (Auerbach, 1995: see her review in Volume 2). This participatory approach starts with the assumption that meaningful language learning must be centred on issues of importance to the learners in order to facilitate the shaping of the reality they are living in. Such an approach invites reflection, cultural comparison, and exploration of possible new practices, thus handing the power back to learners. In this way SL learners can maintain a stance of independence and choice in the learning process. In this context, language choice, Auerbach (1995) claims, seems to be an important issue. Whereas children, especially those coming from dominant L1 backgrounds, seem to benefit more from immersion programmes, adult SL learners, particularly those coming from low-prestige languages, find the bilingual approach more beneficial. A monolingual approach often leads them to frustration, lack of self-esteem and self-confidence. In this context, the use of the L1 seems to alleviate language shock and it allows for a safer transition from L1 to L2.

PROBLEMS AND DIFFICULTIES

Some of the difficulties in implementing awareness and language switch insights in S/FL contexts derive from the fact that social, ideological and economic factors have overridden affective, cognitive, cultural, personal, personality, interactive, pedagogical and other factors; indeed, the very factors that can lead to awareness and language switch. An orientation to L2 learning, where these factors gain prominence, involves a mainly educational process, where the linguistic, emotional and intellectual world of the learner becomes central to this process.

Language teachers, however, are not prepared to handle practices deriving from awareness and language switch insights in the language classroom, nor are the learners who study languages in self-learning contexts. Very often appropriate learning materials are not easy to obtain, nor are teachers trained to prepare them themselves. Moreover, some also claim that an over-indulgence in awareness and language switch practices may result in an unnecessary use of the L1 in the language classroom or in self-learning contexts. Although the L1 is employed by teachers and learners to perform a wider variety of functions than they can perform in the L2, it is likely that it may end up being used where it should not. Unrestricted use of the L1 may easily result in patterning language switch in S/FL discourse in a fashion similar to bilingual/multilingual societies. However, this is not the goal of S/FL learning and should be avoided.

Research and practice have not always taken into account that SL and FL contexts are two different learning environments. So language switch and awareness (among others) may not always serve the same purposes in those two contexts. In FL contexts, in particular, teachers are usually fluent users of the L2, though not as competent as native speaker teachers. However, they share the same L1, the same culture and similar learning experiences with their learners. Thus it makes it easier for them and their learners to adopt bilingual/bicultural practices in the classroom; it may not be as easy to incorporate similar practices in SL settings, if teachers are monolingual speakers. Moreover, FL learners may not share the same needs, interests and purposes as SL learners who live and work in the L2 social milieu.

FUTURE DIRECTIONS

Recent developments in the cultural and cross-cultural dimension to language learning and teaching have added extra value to the interplay of the L1 and the L2. Research will further investigate the factors and the functions of language switch and awareness in a wider variety of learning environments, i.e. different age groups, other socio-cultural groups, different L1 groups, etc. The aim is to determine more precisely the cognitive, linguistic and cultural influence of L1 on S/FL learning and language use in a variety of learning contexts and communicative situations. In this framework, language switch and awareness might have a central role to play in facilitating the learning and communication process.

Secondly, research should be carried out to investigate how awareness and language switch can promote tolerance and understanding between the various languages and cultures aiming at the learners' personal development and the enrichment of the learners' own culture. In this context, cross-cultural S/FL learning can be integrated with the learners' general educational and self-development goals or their more instrumental and professional objectives.

Thirdly, self-learning practices are closely related to learner training, autonomy and independence. They all seem to demand the use of awareness and language switch as special learning aids at the early stages of learning, in particular. Some educators, however, may argue that language switch can be as much an evil as a blessing for autonomous language learning. A lot of learners' time and effort is spent in working in the L1. Research is therefore needed to develop motivational practices and techniques as well as multi-media learning materials that promote use of the L2 rather than the L1 in these contexts.

It is hoped that research findings will eventually find their way into classroom, self-learning and distance learning materials and practices as well as into teacher training and learner training materials and techniques.

The University of Athens
Greece

REFERENCES

Aston, G.: 1983, 'The use of English and Italian in classroom management', in S. Holden (ed.), *Focus on the Learner*, ELT Publications, London, 101–105.
Atkinson, D.: 1987, 'The mother tongue in the classroom', *ELT Journal* 41, 241–147.
Auerbach, E.R.: 1995, 'The politics of the ESL classroom: Issues of power in pedagogical choices', in J.W. Tollefson (ed.), *Power and Inequality in Language Education*, Cambridge University Press, New York, 9–33.
Bhatia T.K. & Ritchie, W.C.: 1989, 'Introduction: Current issues in "mixing" and "switching" ', *World Englishes* 8, 261–264.
Bialystok, E.: 1983, 'Some factors in the selection and implementation of communication strategies', in C. Faerch & G. Kasper (eds.), *Strategies in Interlanguage Communication*, Longman, New York, 100–118.
Canale, M. & Swain, M.: 1980, 'Theoretical bases of communicative approaches to second language teaching and testing', *Applied Linguistics* 1, 1–47.
Faerch, C. & Kasper, G.: 1983, 'On identifying communication strategies in interlanguage production', in C. Faerch & G. Kasper (eds.), *Strategies in Interlanguage Communication*, Longman, New York, 210–238.
Fairclough, N.: 1989, *Language and Power*, Longman, London.
Garcia, O. & Otheguy R.J. (eds.): 1989, *English Across Cultures: Cultures Across English: A Reader in Cross-cultural Communication*, Mouton de Gruyter, Berlin.
Gumperz, J.: 1971, *Language in Social Groups*, Stanford University Press, Stanford, CA.
Harbord, J.: 1992, 'The use of the mother tongue in the classroom', *ELT Journal* 46, 350–355.
Heller, M. (ed.): 1988, *Code-Switching:Anthropological and Sociological Perspectives*, Mouton de Gruyter, Berlin.
Little, D. & Singleton, D.: 1992, 'Authentic texts, pedagogical grammar and language awareness in foreign language learning', in C. James & P. Garrett (eds.), *Language Awareness in the Classroom*, Longman, London, 123–132.
Merritt, M., Cleghorn, A., Abagi, O.J. & Bunyi, G.: 1992, 'Socializing multiligualism: Determinants of codeswitching in Kenyan primary classrooms', *Journal of Multilingual and Multicultural Development* 13, 103–121.
Myers-Scotton, C.: 1993, *Social Motivation for Codeswitching: Evidence from Africa*, Clarendon Press, Oxford.
Odlin, T.: 1990, *Language Transfer:Cross-linguistic Influence in Language Learning*, Cambridge University Press, New York.
O'Malley, J.M. & Chamot, A.U.: 1990, *Learning Strategies in Second Language Acquisition*, Cambridge University Press, New York.
Papaefthymiou-Lytra, S.: 1990, *Explorations in Foreign Language Classroom Discourse*, PAROUSIA Monograph Series No 11, The University of Athens, Athens.
Papaefthymiou-Lytra, S.: (*forthcoming*), 'Awareness and language switch in self-learning FL contexts', (mimeo).
Poulisse, N. & Bongaerts, T.: 1994, 'First language use in second language production', *Applied Linguistics* 15, 36–57.

Richards, J.C. &. Lockhart, C.: 1994, *Reflective Teaching in Second Language Classrooms*, Cambridge University Press, New York.
Ringbom, H.: 1987, *The Role of the First Language in Foreign Language Learning*, Multilingual Matters, Clevedon.
Rutherford, W.E.: 1987, *Second Language Grammar: Learning and Teaching*, Longman, London.
Saville-Troike, M., McClure, E. & Fritz, M.: 1984, 'Communicative tactics in children's second language acquisition', in F. R. Eckman, L.H. Bell & D. Nelson (eds.), *Universals of Second Language Acquisition*, Newbury House, Rowley, MA, 60–71.
Weinberg, J.: 1990, 'Pennies from He Vinh', *TESOL Newsletter* 24(5).

AVIVA FREEDMAN AND PAUL RICHARDSON

LITERACY AND GENRE

The word "genre" was rarely used with respect to literacy, at least in the sense of composition theory and pedagogy, until the late 1980's. "Genre," as a term, was reserved largely for literary texts, and was understood to refer to "text-types" – categories of texts marked by linguistic and formal similarities.

During the 1980's, however, the notion of genre was resurrected and redefined. Theorists on three separate continents, working quite independently in distinct traditions, seized on the notion of genre as central to an understanding of language use by imbuing the traditional definition with social, functional, and pragmatic dimensions. In 1984 in the U.S., Carolyn Miller's "Genre as Social Action" summarized, crystallized and foregrounded key aspects of a redefinition of "genre" that was emerging within the new rhetoric; in 1986, "Speech Genres and Other Late Essays" by Mikhail Bakhtin, although written considerably earlier, was translated from the Russian into English and became widely known and influential; and roughly within the same time frame, Sydney School linguists and language educators in Australia developed a notion of genre derived from the socially-oriented linguistics of M.A.K. Halliday (e.g., 1978). (Swales, 1990, working out of the tradition of applied linguistics and second-language teaching, also developed a congruent model, partly based on the work of both Halliday and Miller. Since his educational focus is primarily on second-language learning, his work will not be dealt with here.)

Common to all this work was the recognition that the textual regularities of genres (identified in traditional discussions of genres) are themselves correlates of pragmatic, social, political, and cultural regularities within the enveloping contexts of the discourse. At its base, then, this new theorizing involves the dual recognition that language is a way of getting things done, in response to the exigencies of the rhetorical situations or enveloping contexts; and that human beings tend to develop, within specific cultures and socio-economic groups, fairly conventionalized or regularized ways of getting similar things done through language.

'All our utterances' wrote Bakhtin (1986) 'have definite and relatively stable *typical* forms of construction'; and if 'we speak only in definite genres' (p. 87), this is at least in part because these primary speech genres 'correspond to typical situations of speech communication' (p. 87).

L. van Lier and D. Corson (eds), Encyclopedia of Language and Education,
Volume 6: Knowledge about Language, 139–149.
© *1997 Kluwer Academic Publishers. Printed in the Netherlands.*

Despite the similarities, there were important differences – especially between the notion of genre as developed in Australia, on the one hand, and the reconceptions by Bakhtin and the North American scholars, on the other. Certainly, only the ideas of the Sydney School have been translated directly into an educational project, and since that enterprise has had its own trajectory, and has remained fairly well contained within Australia, it will be treated separately and first in this chapter.

GENRE AND LITERACY IN AUSTRALIA

The development of a theory of genre in relation to language and education began in Australia in the late 1970's as a result of the influence of Michael Halliday's work in systemic functional linguistics on academic linguists, teacher educators and teachers. Over the last one and a half decades Jim Martin, Joan Rothery and Frances Christie have been central figures in the development of a genre-based theory of writing and writing pedagogy. Work by Kress (1982) and Kress & Hodge (1979) was initially appropriated as part of a theoretical scaffold in the formation of a "new" writing pedagogy designed to displace the process-writing pedagogy based on personal experience then influential in primary and junior secondary schools.

The systemic-functional model of genre theory privileges language and text as a system, locating meaning in the language as system and in text structure. Thus, while Martin, Rothery and Christie argue that texts are produced in a context of culture and situation, they insist that meaning is carried in the text structure and in the grammar of individual texts, and that it is through these that language users construct reality. Although Martin (1986) has posited ideology as a level beyond genre in a paradigmatic model which frames language, register, genre and ideology, his notion of genre as textual object which exists independently of social meaning-making practices has eclipsed questions of ideology. Little explicit attention has been paid to ideology beyond the belief that through the teaching of the powerful genres the powerless and the marginalised in society will gain access to distributed power.

Genre then, is defined as 'a staged, goal oriented social process', where genres are seen as social processes 'because members of a culture interact with each other to achieve them; as goal oriented because they have evolved to get things done; and as staged because it usually takes more than one step for participants to achieve their goals' (Martin et al., 1987, p. 59). This staged, purposeful cultural activity includes oral and written language genres and is characterised by having 'a schematic structure – a distinctive beginning, middle, and end' (Christie, 1984, p. 270).

In 1980, Martin and Rothery began an analysis of a collection of student writing which revealed that most texts were quite short, lacked development, and deployed only a few genres – labelling, observation/comments, reports, recounts, and narratives. Although these findings were not particularly new at the time, Martin and his colleagues were sufficiently alarmed to independently set about the task of devising a 'theoretically distinctive pedagogy to address this situation' (Cope et al., 1993, p. 233).

Their analysis began with a typology, based on Hallidayan linguistics, of the genres children wrote in school. Initially, the typology was represented by two strands branching off from observation/comment; one strand identified narrative genres, the other factual genres – both of which were further divided into subcategories. Eventually additional work (see Martin, 1985; Christie et al., 1990; Derewianka, 1990) produced a typology which accounted for the following genres, asserted to be those involved in learning all school subjects:

> **factual genres**: procedure (how something is done), description (what some particular thing is like), report (what an entire class of things are like), explanation (a reason why a judgement is made), argument (arguments why a thesis has been produced);
> **narrative genres**: recounts, narrative based on personal experience, narrative based on fantasy, the moral tale, myths, spoofs, serials and thematic narratives.

The textbook and teacher professional development materials devised by Christie et al. (1990–1992), Derewianka (1990), Callaghan & Rothery (1988), and Macken et al. (1989) ensured that teachers had access to materials and a model for teaching the identified types of texts. Text samples provided examples of the process by which the structural elements of text organisation and grammatical features could be analysed. An interventionist role was advocated for the teacher as an element in a curriculum cycle which required the teacher to model the social purpose of the text, jointly construct with students a model of the text, and to provide opportunities for consultation with students during their independent construction of a text. Systemic functional linguistics provided the analytical tools and frame through which to analyse the grammatical features of the identified text-types.

Not unexpectedly, the genre school initiated and developed by Martin, Rothery and Christie has spawned zealous disciples, critical friends and ardent opponents. A useful introduction is provided by Reid (1987) in which critical friends and spirited critics register their concerns about the apparent rigidity of genres, the process by which genres are learnt, the question as to whether particular forms of knowledge only embed in particular linguistic forms, and whether content can be separated from linguistic form.

Thibault (1989), Threadgold (1988), Threadgold & Kress (1988) and

Hasan (1995) have all cogently argued theoretical cases against the model of genre and language articulated by Martin, Rothery and Christie. Their critiques focus on the disjuncture between the claim that meaning is encapsulated in textual objects, genres as autonomous systems, and the avowal of a social constructionist functional model of language. Thibault observes that this instrumental view of genre 'both assumes and implicitly conveys the message that the world is organised in terms of an instrumental logic based on linear, one-way models of cause-and-effect or means-and-end' (p. 346), which may have the effect of socialising teachers and students into a reductionist one-way model of causality. Similarly Hasan (1995), in a long and highly technical study which assumes familiarity with her own work and Halliday's, along with that of Martin, systematically questions the model of language and genre proposed by Martin and seeks to reposition her own work and that of Michael Halliday in relation to the claims Martin and the genre educationists have made.

It was the pedagogical program initiated and developed by Martin and his colleagues which eventually led Kress (1989) to observe that 'genre theory in education is not, at this stage, a highly unified body of theory' (p. 10), and to distance his own work from that of the Sydney School genre educational enterprise. Knapp (1995) has recently reiterated this theme by outlining the differences between what he sees as two broadly different interpretations of genre in Australia: the systemic-functional model, and the "genre as social process" model – models drawn from significantly different views of language, epistemology and pedagogy. The latter model is more in tune with orientation and interests of North American genre studies.

NORTH AMERICAN GENRE STUDIES

Genre studies in Canada and the United States have taken a different course. Such work has been primarily theoretically and research-oriented, and both theory and research have revealed somewhat different shadings and understandings of the notion of genre from that displayed by the Sydney School work – different enough to have rendered the educational applications of the Sydney School project inappropriate.

Theory. As the seminal piece in North American work, Miller's "Genre as Social Action" (1984), suggests, the "social" has been foregrounded in genre studies, and more significantly, the notion of "social" has been broader in scope and more sweeping than that suggested in Sydney School work – not least because much of that work has remained inexorably tied to the text, and especially to the formal grammatical analysis of text developed by Martin and his colleagues from Halliday's systemic-functional grammar.

Indeed, perhaps the most seminal and generative insights in Miller's articles are those which tie the conventionalized textual regularities in genres to equally conventionalized typifications in the rhetorical situations. Miller argues cogently that the regularities in the rhetorical situation are not so much material, or objectively "out there" (as Bitzer, 1960, suggested) but rather socially constructed. She draws on Schutz in particular, and on the tradition of social theorists he represents, to point to the degree to which human beings tend to collaborate socially in defining certain situations as significant and recurrent. We simplify the vast inchoate mass of experience that must be confronted daily by tacitly agreeing communally that only certain sets of events or situation-types are to be noted as significant and hence responded to. (Inevitably, such situation-types vary by culture and often community.) Genre studies consequently have focussed as much on the social construction of rhetorical contexts as on the textual regularities elicited in response.

Furthermore, there has been throughout North American genre studies the same recognition of historicity and dynamism that one finds in Bakhtin's work (and it is significant that Bakhtin's influence has been felt far more strongly in North American genre studies than in Australia). Notions of situatedness within processes of socio-historical change are dominant, such that much work has in fact focussed precisely on the development and evolution of specific genres in response to changing epistemological, ideological, technological and political needs. Classic examples are Bazerman's *Shaping Written Knowledge* (1988), which describes the shaping and evolution of the research article in response to changing conceptions of scientific knowledge and proof; and Yates's *Control through Communication* (1989) which describes the evolution of the memo and the business report in response to changes in management philosophy and technology in American industry over the past century.

This awareness of dynamism also carries with it a recognition of the necessary blurring of genres (Geertz, 1983), the recognition and even the celebration of the fragility of genres – what Schryer (1993) refers to as the 'stabilized-for-now' aspect of genres – which allows for the power of agency, interactivity, and play.

As to the impact on education, the primary focus of genre studies in North America has been research-based. Several important studies have involved naturalistic research aimed at uncovering the range of genres elicited across the curriculum (See for example, Herrington, 1985; McCarthy, 1987.) Supporting this work has been the historical (Russell, 1991) and theoretical work on "writing in the disciplines" or "writing across the curriculum" in the United States. Much of this work has been animated by a recognition of the degree to which different disciplines evoke and necessitate different modes of thinking, different lines of reasoning, and ways of approaching data.

Further research has focussed on the nature of the gradual initiation of newcomers into classroom discourse communities as indicated by students' mastery of the relevant classroom genres, (e.g., Berkenkotter, Huckin & Ackerman, 1991; McCarthy & Fishman, 1991; Freedman, 1993). And yet other studies have been concerned to unpack the subtle complexities of the whole enterprise of genre acquisition and mastery within the university context. Thus, in differentiating among genres, scholars have pointed beyond the staples of traditional textual analyses to issues such as what counts as novelty (Kaufer & Geisler, 1989); what can be assumed as shared or background knowledge (Giltrow & Valiquette, 1994); what different communities are prepared to recognise as persuasive, using the classification of argument developed by Toulmin, Rieke and Janik in 1979 (Herrington, 1985; Currie, 1994; Freedman, 1995); and what is the essential social action undertaken in the texts (Freedman, Adam & Smart, 1995).

Throughout all this research, the complex interactive dynamics among the writer, the text, and the context have been unpacked, and this has had indirect but important applications to pedagogy. In a theoretical piece discussing classroom genres, entitled "Where is the Classroom" (1994), Bazerman has pointed to the many political, social, ideological, institutional, curricular factors that are at play in the negotiated creation of all classroom genres. Both Dias (1994) and Hunt (1994) have shown how new classroom genres can be created, not as a result of directives, but rather in response to fundamental reorientations in curricular and pedagogic goals undertaken by the instructor as negotiated with the students, as well as by the use of new technologies (in Hunt's case, the use of computers in their electronic-mail networking capacity).

Implicitly, all this research has underlined what Freedman (1993) argued: any pedagogic enterprise, insofar as it depends on the explicit teaching of genre features and rules, is doomed to failure because of the limited and naive notion of genre implied. To paraphrase and quote from this article, if we understand the full complexity of the notion of 'genres ... as actions, events, and/or responses to recurring situations or contexts' and if contexts are 'generally understood to involve a complex of social, cultural, and sometimes disciplinary dimensions,' then the question arises: 'can the complex web of social, cultural, rhetorical features to which genres respond be explicated at all, or in such a way that can be useful to learners?' (p. 225).

To make this argument Freeedman marshalls evidence from her own research and that of others describing the acquisition of genres by primary, secondary, and tertiary students, as well as the research literature into first and second-language acquisition in general, in order to argue against the usefulness of the explicit and decontextualized teaching of the rules of genres.

Instead of the explicit teaching of genre, Freedman draws on the model of acquisition developed in first and second-language theory, as well as the congruent model described in the recent literature on "situated learning." (For an overview of the latter, especially in the context of genre theory, see Berkenkotter & Huckin, 1993.) The underlying thrust of these models is that exposure to written discourse and immersion in the relevant contexts are both necessary (although not sufficient) conditions for acquiring new genres. Affective factors, such as degree of anxiety or motivation, and learning styles play a role as well. More significantly, learners must also be "pushed" to produce meaningful discourse in authentic contexts, through appropriate assignments and with appropriate feedback. Teacher intervention in the form of collaborative performance, as in early language learning, allows for growth within Vygotsky's "zone of proximal development."

At the same time, the modified model of second-language learning put forward by Ellis (1990; see also Ellis, this volume) allows for some explication and direct teaching, primarily as a form of consciousness-raising, – as long as the explication is accurate, appropriate to the learner's style, and offered in the context of an ongoing authentic task.

WORK IN PROGRESS

Work-in-progress is characterized by two thrusts. First, there is considerable research underway analysing and probing classroom and workplace genres. In North America, there is a large scale 6 year project in progress, supported by the Social Sciences and Humanities Research Council of Canada, and conducted by researchers at Carleton and McGill Universities. University and workplace discourse are compared in five different fields: social work (Anthony Pare); architecture (Peter Medway); business (Jane Ledwell Brown); public service (Aviva Freedman, Graham Smart, Christine Adam); and engineering (Ann Beer, Aviva Freedman, Christine Adam, Natasha Artemeva). In Australia, Paul Richardson has been studying the acquisition of the genres of writing in the economics class at Monash University, while Barbara Kamler and Rod McLean have been studying the writing of law students at Deakin University.

From a theoretic point of view, there is increasingly an attempt to relate genre studies to the work on Activity Theory that has developed in the Soviet Union and Russia out of the earlier work of Vygotsky. The two perspectives mesh because of their shared focus on the dynamic activities within complex networks created by agents acting socially (or as part of collectives) in response to their socially constructed worlds as mediated by, and created through semiotic tools. Berkenkotter, Russell, Bazerman, and the Carleton-McGill research teams are all involved in teasing out the theoretic implications of viewing genre from an activity perspective.

PROBLEMS AND DIFFICULTIES: FUTURE DIRECTIONS

A major weakness of the Australian approach is that, while espousing a commitment to effect social change, it in fact ignores the complex ecological realities of genres in context. Text is continually privileged, in analysis, over the intricate social world in which it plays a role. Despite its social manifesto, this project shares the same weakness that Corson (1997) pinpoints with respect to much work in applied linguistics in general: its epistemological and ontological underpinnings imply the hegemony of language and text – with insufficient attention to, and acknowledgement of those social realities foregrounded in allied fields that investigate the complex world of human interactions (based as they are on different epistemologies and ontologies).

A weakness of North American genre studies derives from the fact that, until recently, undue respect for this same ecological complexity has led to too great conservatism and a reluctance to suggest potential alternatives or limitations in the genres elicited in disciplinary classrooms. Far more needs to be done in North America, drawing on critical approaches, as Herndl (1993) in another context has argued.

As to research, given that the approach to such study has been quite naturally and appropriately naturalistic, there is a necessity to extend such studies into far more varied settings – with different mixes of populations and with genres at different stages of evolution. (Some pilot work at Carleton University has shown that genres in the classroom can be placed on a continuum: at one end are genres that are in the process of negotiated invention, as a result of new curricular goals or technologies; at the other end are genres so established that at least some of the "rules" have become enshrined in manuals.)

The pedagogic questions, as Freedman argued in 1993, still remain to be tested and answered. Insofar, for example, as any explicit teaching is profitable we need to know what kinds of formal features or underlying rules can be usefully explicated for use in monitoring. Furthermore, given that genres are responses to contexts, and given that most workplace and academic contexts are not only complex, but fluid, how much stability is necessary for any kind of explication to be useful? To what extent does the explication itself reshape the context? And is this to the benefit of the learner? Furthermore, are there social and cultural dimensions to learner amenability to explicit teaching? Such explication is typically recommended for students from disadvantaged backgrounds; however, an argument can be made (e.g., Bourdieu & Passeron, 1977) that it is only upper and middle class students (from highly literate backgrounds) who can profit from direct instruction. Presumably, this is testable.

A different question is the following. Is there some value to teaching about genres generally? If novices, especially adult novices, learn something about the nature of genre as social action and of the role of genres is discourse communities, will they be able to acquire new genres more quickly or less painfully when they enter new discourse communities? Can strategies for exploring new contexts and new genres be taught? (See Coe (1994) for a discussion of such strategies.) Alternatively, can such preparation at least lessen the anxiety of new entrants, so that they are more open to acquisition?

Clearly, the notion of "genre" is immensely powerful and illuminates much about what happens through discourse in general and in the classroom in particular (especially since so much that takes place in the classroom is embodied in language). It is equally clear that the theorizing that has so far taken place may be richly extended in a number of directions, and is consistent with intellectual work in a number of allied fields. And as to research and pedagogy, while the former is underway, many of the important questions with respect to the latter remain to be answered; the answers, however, may be more convincing and more soundly based if they are couched within a theoretic model of genre studies and based on relevant research.

Carleton University
Canada

&

Monash University
Australia

REFERENCES

Bakhtin, M.M.: 1986, 'The problem of speech genres', in C. Emerson & M. Holquist (eds.) and V.W. McGee (trans.), *Speech Genres and Other Late Essays*, University of Texas Press, Austin TX, 60–102.

Bazerman, C.: 1988, *Shaping Written Knowledge*, University of Wisconsin Press, Madison WI.

Bazerman, C.: 1994, 'Where is the classroom?', in A. Freedman & P. Medway (eds.), *Learning and Teaching Genre*, Heinemann Boynton/Cook Portsmouth, NH, 25–30.

Berkenkotter, C. & Huckin, T.: 1993, 'Rethinking genre from a sociocognitive perspective', *Written Communication* 10, 475–509.

Berkenkotter, C., Huckin, T. & Ackerman, J.: 1991, 'Social context and socially constructed text', in C. Bazerman & J. Paradis (eds.), *Textual Dynamics of the Professions*, University of Wisconsin Press, Madison, WI, 191–215.

Bitzer, L.: 1960, 'The rhetorical situation', *Philosophy and Rhetoric* 1, 1–14.

Bourdieu, P. & Passeron J.C.: 1977, *Reproduction in Education, Society, and Culture*, Sage, London.

Callaghan, M. & Rothery, J.: 1988, *Teaching Factual Writing* (Report of the DSP literacy project, Metropolitan East Region), NSW Department of Education, Sydney.

Christie, F. (ed.): 1984, *Children Writing: Study Guide and Reader*, Deakin University Press, Geelong, Australia.

Christie, F., Gray, B., Gray P., Macken, M., Martin, J.R. & Rothery, R.: 1990–1992, *Language: A Resource for Meaning* (Teachers' and Student Books), Harcourt Brace Jovanovich, Sydney.

Coe, R.: 1994, 'Teaching genre as process', in A. Freedman & P. Medway (eds.), *Learning and Teaching Genre*, Heinemann Boynton/Cook, Portsmouth, NH, 157–172.

Cope, B., Kalantzis, M., Kress, G., Martin, J. & Murphy, L.: 1993, 'Bibliographic essay: Developing the theory and practice of genre-based literacy', in B. Cope & M. Kalantzis (eds.), *The Powers of Literacy: A Genre Approach to Teaching Writing*, The Falmer Press, London.

Corson, D. 1997, 'Critical Realism: An Emancipatory Philosophy for Applied Linguistics', *Applied Linguistics* 18(2), 166–188.

Currie, P.: 1994, 'What counts as good writing?', in A. Freedman & P. Medway (eds.), *Learning and Teaching Genre*, Heinemann Boynton/Cook, Portsmouth, NH, 63–80.

Derewianka, B.: 1990, *Exploring How Texts Work*, Primary English Teaching Association, Sydney.

Dias, P.: 1994, 'Initiating students into the genres of discipline-based reading and writing', in A. Freedman & P. Medway (eds.), *Learning and Teaching Genre*, Heinemann Boynton/Cook, Portsmouth, NH, 193–206.

Ellis, R.: 1990, *Instructed Second Language Acquisition: Learning in the Classroom*, Blackwell, Oxford.

Freedman, A.: 1993, 'Show and tell? The role of explicit teaching in learning new genres', *Research in the Teaching of English* 27, 222–251.

Freedman, A.: 1996, 'Argument as genre and genres of argument', in D. Berrill (ed.), *Perspectives on Written Argumentation*, Hampton Press, Cresskill, NJ.

Freedman, A., Adam, C. & Smart, G.: 1994, 'Wearing suits to class: Simulating genres and simulations as genre', *Written Communication* 11, 193–226.

Geertz, C.: 1983, *Local Knowledge*, Basic Books, New York.

Giltrow, J. & Valiquette, M.: 1994, 'Genres and knowledge', in A. Freedman & P. Medway (eds.), *Learning and Teaching Genre*, Heinemann Boynton/Cook, Portsmouth NH, 47–62.

Halliday, M.A.K.: 1978, *Language as a Social Semiotic*, Edward Arnold, London.

Hasan, R.: 1995, 'The conception of context in text', in Peter H. Fries & Michael Gregory (eds.), *Discourse in Society: Systemic Functional Perspectives*, Ablex Publishing, NJ.

Herndl, C.: 1993, 'Teaching discourse and reproducing culture,' *College Composition and Communication* 44 (October), 349–363.

Herrington, A.: 1985, 'Writing in academic settings', *Research in the Teaching of English* 19, 331–361.

Hunt, R.: 1994, 'Traffic in genres, in class and out', in A. Freedman & P. Medway (eds.), *Genre and the New Rhetoric*, Taylor & Francis, London, 211–230.

Kaufer, D. & Geisler, C.: 1989, 'Novelty in academic writing', *Written Communication* 6, 286–311.

Knapp, P.: 1995, 'The trouble with genre', *Idiom* 29, 34–41.

Kress, G.R. & Hodge, R.: 1979, *Language as Ideology*, Routledge and Kegan Paul, London.

Kress, G.R.: 1982, *Learning to Write*, Routledge and Kegan Paul, London.

Kress, G.R.: 1989, 'Texture and meaning', in R. Andrews (ed.), *Narrative and Argument*, Open University Press, Milton Keynes.

Macken, M. et al.: 1989, *An Approach to Writing K-12: Introduction*, Literacy and Education Research Network, Directorate of Studies, NSW Department of Education, Sydney.

Martin, J.R.: 1985, *Factual Writing*, Deakin University Press, Geelong, Australia.

Martin, J.R.: 1986, 'Grammaticalizing the ecology', in T. Threadgold et al. (eds.), *Semiotic-Ideology-Language*, Pathfinder Press, Sydney.

Martin, J.R., Christie, F. & Rothery, J.: 1987, 'Social processes in education', in I. Reid (ed.), *The Place of Genre in Learning: Current Debates*, Deakin University Press, Geelong, Australia.

McCarthy, L.P.: 1987, 'A Stranger in strange lands: A college student writing across the curriculum', *Research in the Teaching of English* 21, 233–265.

McCarthy, L.P. & Fishman, S.: 1991, 'Boundary conversations', *Research in the Teaching of English* 25, 419–468.

Miller, C.: 1984, 'Genre as social action', *Quarterly Journal of Speech* 70, 151–167.

Reid, I. (ed.): 1987, *The Place of Genre in Learning: Current Debates*, Deakin University Press, Geelong, Australia.

Russell, D.: 1991, *Writing in the Academic Disciplines, 1870–1990*, Southern Illinois University Press, Carbondale, IL.

Schryer, C.F.: 1993, 'Records as genre', *Witten Communication* 10, 200–234.

Swales, J.: 1990, *Genre Analysis*, Cambridge University Press, Cambridge.

Thibault, P.: 1989, 'Genre as social action and pedagogy', *Southern Review* (Australia) 21, 338–362.

Threadgold, T.: 1988, 'The genre debate', *Southern Review* (Australia) 21, 315–330.

Threadgold, T. & Kress, G.: 1988, 'Towards a social theory of genre', *Southern Review* (Australia) 21, 215–243.

Toulmin, S., Rieke, R. & Janik, A.: 1979, *An Introduction to Reasoning*, Macmillan, New York.

Yates, J.: 1989, *Control through Communication*, Johns Hopkins University Press, Baltimore MD.

MARK FETTES

ESPERANTO AND LANGUAGE AWARENESS

Esperanto, designed as a neutral lingua franca (i.e. second language) for worldwide use, has been taught and learned for over a century, to such an extent that a flourishing oral and written culture is associated with the language. Although global linguistic hierarchies, in particular the hegemony of national languages within state borders and of a small subset of these languages in international communication, have ensured Esperanto's virtual exclusion from educational systems, a considerable number of Esperanto teachers and learners attest to exciting educational experiences in the language. Among the latter are a range of language awareness effects, including awareness of linguistic inequality, linguistic structure, and the sociocultural functions of language. Such experiences can transform students' perception of the world through the awakening of awareness and interest in other cultures, and lead to a reassessment of their own linguistic heritage together with the social practices and power relations in which it is enmeshed.

EARLY DEVELOPMENTS

The basis for Esperanto was published in 1887 by Dr. Lejzer (Ludovic) Zamenhof, a brilliant and idealistic Jewish ophthalmologist in Warsaw. The idea of a planned international language was not a new one, but Zamenhof contributed the crucial insight that it must develop through collective use; accordingly, he restricted his initial proposal to a minimalist grammatical sketch, a vocabulary of some 900 words, some samples of poetry and prose, and a persuasive introductory essay. He believed that people from any background could learn the language 'as if in play', thanks to a transparent morphology and syntax freed from most of the complexities and inconsistencies of European languages (for an accessible overview, see Janton, 1993, p. 41–89). Linked to Zamenhof's linguistic work was a progressively developed and refined critique of the links between language and nationalism (Zamenhof, 1929; Lieberman, 1979).

Over the fifteen years following its launch, Esperanto's written norms slowly developed through its use in correspondence, periodicals and printed works by a small but growing community of users scattered throughout Europe and the European colonies. Its use in spoken communication was rare in this period, but grew rapidly following the first international congress in 1905. By the outbreak of the First World War, the

L. van Lier and D. Corson (eds), Encyclopedia of Language and Education,
Volume 6: Knowledge about Language, 151–159.
© 1997 Kluwer Academic Publishers. Printed in the Netherlands.

language and its speech community were firmly established, and there were many instances in the war years of Esperanto speakers and organizations helping one another across national divides. After the war, there was a surge of interest in Esperanto among working-class and socialist movements both in Europe and elsewhere (e.g. China, Japan), and an inspirational teacher, Andreo Cseh, founded an adult education movement based on the direct instruction of Esperanto without the use of the learner's first language (Lapenna, Lins & Carlevaro, 1974).

In 1922 the Rousseau Institute of Educational Science in Geneva organized the first International Conference on the Teaching of Esperanto in Schools, with the support of the League of Nations. The conference report drew attention to Esperanto's effectiveness in arousing interest in other peoples and cultures, as well as its use as an introduction to foreign language study (Lapenna, Lins & Carlevaro, 1974). Shortly afterwards, the noted educational psychologist E.L. Thorndike undertook the first of several studies at Columbia University on the acquisition of Esperanto (Thorndike et al., 1933). This research confirmed the relative ease with which Esperanto could be learned (an estimated one-fifth of the time required by 'an average college senior or graduate' to learn French, German, Italian or Spanish to the same level), and suggested that the prior study of Esperanto facilitated the learning of French, a so-called 'propaedeutic' effect. However, the experimental conditions were not adequate to allow strong conclusions to be drawn (Fantini & Reagan, 1992).

MAJOR CONTRIBUTIONS

The Second World War had dramatic consequences for the teaching and learning of Esperanto. Two of the most vigorous national movements, in Germany and the Soviet Union, had been persecuted to the brink of extinction; the onset of the Cold War divided the European movements; and the rise of the United States to superpower status enhanced the status of English throughout the democratic and colonized worlds. The tale of Esperanto's survival is a gripping one, although it cannot be recounted here. It is important to note, however, that global politics have marginalized the scholarly study of the language, including research into its use in education. There are no comprehensive studies available in Esperanto of its instruction in Central and Eastern Europe, or in China, although these countries have probably accounted for the majority of Esperanto learners and teachers over the last half century. The present review draws on reports of a small number of educational experiments, primarily in Western Europe, and a larger number of narrative accounts and essays.

The 'experiments' in question resemble the Columbia study mentioned above, in that they have usually set out to measure the effects of Esperanto instruction on the subsequent learning of other languages. The logic behind this approach is easy to understand. Esperanto's marginal position in the global language order has meant that teachers have often seen their strongest argument as presenting it as a 'modern Latin' for the beginning language learner. In justification it is argued that Esperanto's regularity and morphological transparency provide an ideal model for students to take the first tentative steps away from their mother tongue. In other words, learning Esperanto leads to an *awareness of linguistic structure* which can be built on in learning other languages.

The experimental data offer some support for this view. The headmaster of a secondary school near Manchester, England, found consistently over an 18-year period that pupils who learned Esperanto for a year acquired a level of fluency in the language equivalent to four years of French study, and subsequently achieved a higher level in French after three years of study than those pupils who learned only French for four years. These conclusions were based on tests of pupils' ability to translate phrases of equivalent meaning from Esperanto or French into English, since comparing the quality of their translations into French or Esperanto proved to be difficult. The same teacher also found a strong positive effect of Esperanto study on results in General English (Williams, 1965). The effects were strongest for pupils who scored low on a range of intelligence tests, and extended to eight of 11 categories of language skills tested (Halloran, 1952).

Similar results have since been reported for Finnish pupils learning Esperanto followed by German; German pupils learning Esperanto followed by English; Japanese pupils learning Esperanto followed by English; and Italian pupils learning Esperanto followed by French (Maxwell, 1988; Corsetti & La Torre, 1995; and references therein). The finding that the learning of Esperanto positively influences students' awareness of their mother tongue has been reported independently in a number of contexts, most notably the Hawaii English Program, where several units in Esperanto were introduced in approximately one-third of all sixth grade classes in the early 1970s (Wood, 1975; Piron, 1986; Fantini & Reagan, 1992).

On the negative side, all of these studies suffer from the usual limitations of educational research, and collectively they clearly represent only a fraction of the situations in which Esperanto has been or might be taught. Controls have frequently been inadequate, and in propaedeutic studies the 'target language' (L3) in all cases has been a Western European language lexically related to Esperanto. A strong argument can therefore be made that detailed conclusions about the propaedeutic value of Esperanto must await more sophisticated studies which would measure a range of linguistic skills for various combinations of L1 and L3 (Corsetti & La Torre, 1995).

The translator and psychologist Claude Piron, in the course of a broader sociolinguistic study, has nonetheless developed a persuasive theoretical foundation for the propaedeutic hypothesis (Piron, 1986, 1994). For second language learners in a non-immersion setting, according to Piron's analysis, language learning occurs through a lengthy process of cognitive and motor deconditioning and reconditioning, in which the student's urge to generalize from limited data is constantly frustrated. Esperanto, because of the extreme productiveness of a small number of rules and morphemes, allows students to freely employ both convergent and divergent forms of reasoning, and thereby stimulates *linguistic confidence* and *linguistic creativity*, with all that these may entail for language learning and language use in general. By contrast, other second languages involve 'propelling the student from one complex, rigid and arbitrary system to another equally complex, rigid and arbitrary system, with no attempt to facilitate the articulation between the systems in any concrete way' (Piron, 1994, p. 322).

Interesting though propaedeutic effects are, they are not of central relevance to the broader goals of language awareness, particularly the critical variety advocated by Fairclough and his colleagues (Clark et al., 1990; Fairclough, 1992). These aspects of Esperanto pedagogy have received little attention from researchers. Indeed, Esperanto's marginal status tends to make its defenders (and teachers, perhaps, more than others) play down any suggestions that it might lead students to question existing linguistic hierarchies. Yet this is precisely what Esperanto can do, in a variety of ways that provide a valuable complement to other language awareness strategies.

To begin at the least controversial level, the fact that learners rapidly acquire basic communicative skills distinguishes Esperanto from virtually any other approach to *awareness of linguistic difference*. Rather than simply learning *about* difference, students can be enabled to *experience* it for themselves. Important concepts that lack meaning and relevance to monolingual students, such as the constraints on translatability and the links between language and culture, are a natural part of Esperanto pedagogy (Lee, 1993; Piron, 1994). Although it is frequently asserted, or assumed, that Esperanto 'lacks a culture' (e.g. Mead & Modley, 1967; Steiner, 1974), from the start Esperanto has been viewed by its speakers as a cultural project as well as a linguistic one (Auld, 1982a), dedicated both to cultivating an indigenous, non-national tradition (Dasgupta, 1987; Richmond, 1993) and to providing a forum for multicultural exchange (Auld, 1982b; Cool, 1993). A broader approach to language study at the post-secondary level, ending the traditional divide between the study of languages and the study of linguistics, would find Esperanto an ideal instrument for bridging the gap (Tonkin, 1987).

This brings us to the claim that Esperanto can provide

an important complement to the depth of study of a single foreign language and culture such as German or Russian. It avoids the danger of replacing a monocultural view merely with a bicultural one, and it can instead make a major contribution to helping students perceive the pluralistic nature of our new world (Sherwood, 1982, p. 410).

Implicit here is a goal of *multilingual awareness*, a concept generally overlooked in the language awareness literature but which, along with *awareness of linguistic inequality*, forms an inseparable part of most textbooks and courses in Esperanto (e.g. Richardson, 1988). This is easy to understand, since Esperanto's existence is premised on the multilingual nature of the world and the importance of the language of communication in establishing or reinforcing power relations between individuals and groups (Tonkin, 1979). In this respect Esperanto provides a counterweight to received views of English as 'the' international language, an aspect of 'critical language awareness' familiar in the developing world but typically ignored in English-speaking countries (Lopes, 1993).

In appropriate conditions, the access to reciprocal, egalitarian communication in a worldwide community can effect the type of *transformative awareness* that Freire (1972) referred to as 'conscientization'. For example, a young Chinese Malaysian woman learns Esperanto in her home country and in Poland. After a few weeks, she notes that 'one result is . . . that I now want to learn my mother tongue, Chinese. In Malaysia I never studied it, because there are few Chinese schools. . . . Esperanto has made me regret my illiteracy in the language of my ancestors' (Piron, 1994, p. 271). A young American is motivated by his experience of Esperanto to study linguistic discrimination among the indigenous peoples of the Americas and Asia; an African teacher discovers an international audience for his moving and humorous portrayals of village life; a Japanese journalist becomes involved with the restoration of daily life in Sarajevo (personal observations). Such odysseys of discovery are part of the accepted background to everyday communication in Esperanto, and point to the language's potential for enabling learners to reevaluate and transform their relationship with the world.

PROBLEMS AND DIFFICULTIES

Suggestive though the anecdotal evidence is, major obstacles remain to the effective deployment of Esperanto in the language awareness classroom. These obstacles are rooted both in external language hierarchies and in the discourse of the Esperanto community itself.

Since its inception, and particularly since the 1920s, Esperanto has been the object of many of the same kinds of prejudice as other non-national languages, for instance (in the U.S. context) Black English and American Sign Language (Reagan, 1996). Esperanto can also be perceived as deeply threatening to monolinguals' sense of identity (Piron, 1982). Educators, administrators and researchers are not immune to such influences, nor are they generally anxious to explore phenomena which the reigning discourse subjugates as 'marginal' or 'atypical'. As a result, most worthwhile knowledge about Esperanto has been generated in the language itself, rendering it inaccessible to outside observers (Edwards, 1993). Since knowledge which is not available in English or other national languages is frequently assumed not to exist, many scholars have felt entitled to make pronouncements about Esperanto which have little basis in reality, yet reinforce its marginal status (Auld, 1982a; Piron, 1994).

The lack of a broad social base has in turn directed much of the energy of the Esperanto community to fostering its internal cohesion rather than engaging in broader public debates about education, linguistic rights and related issues. Although awareness of linguistic diversity and discrimination is accepted as important by virtually all Esperanto speakers, it is not perceived as a truth that can or should be promoted on its own merits, since this might detract from the goal of recruiting new speakers to contribute to the community's survival and development. Indeed, a significant proportion of Esperanto speakers holds that a preoccupation with changing the world is actually a burden that the community would be better off without (Jordan, 1987; Fettes, 1996). Such discourses have made it difficult for the community to clearly articulate a rationale for the classroom use of Esperanto that is premised not on the learning of the language *per se*, but on the attainment of other educational goals (Fantini & Reagan, 1992).

FUTURE DIRECTIONS

Clearly, the future development of Esperanto pedagogy depends crucially on how the obstacles identified in the previous section are resolved.

On the one hand, the dominant modernist discourse on language is being eroded in a variety of ways, ranging from post-structuralist critiques to the resurgence of small languages and a growing interest in multilingualism and linguistic rights (see my article on language planning in Volume 1). In the field of Esperanto studies, this has been accompanied by the involvement of a small but growing number of professional researchers, and the beginnings of a substantive dialogue with educational institutions at both the national and international levels. In the European Union, for instance, the effectiveness of Esperanto in mediating a balance of awareness between local linguistic identities and participation in an international community of nations fits well with contemporary rhetoric (Chiti-Batelli, 1987). A proposal for an international experiment in teaching Esperanto as the first foreign language has been developed by a group of Italian researchers (Corsetti & La Torre, 1995), building on the recent establishment of a national training program for Esperanto teachers under the auspices of the Ministry of Education (La Torre, personal communication). Similarly, in the United States the feasibility of articulating a compelling rationale for Esperanto instruction in a language awareness framework, e.g. within

English programs, courses in multicultural and global education, or as an introduction to foreign language study, is supported by preliminary research (Fantini & Reagan, 1992).

Such initiatives can be viewed through the prism of postmodern sociology (Bauman, 1992). One of the legacies of modernity is that countries throughout the world are now grappling with similar educational challenges. In the case of language awareness, these may be formulated as the need to educate about indigenous diversity, often in opposition to the hegemony of a single national language, and about global diversity, often in opposition to the hegemony of English. For Esperanto educators, these two sets of issues are intimately linked. An awareness of indigenous diversity that leaves English hegemony unchallenged is as partial a response as an awareness of global diversity that takes only national languages into account. Recent developments within the Esperanto community suggest a growing readiness to engage in constructive debate on these issues (Fettes, 1997).

Two general priorities can be identified. First, to integrate Esperanto studies, and interlinguistics more generally, within established research programs in the social sciences including education. Second, to develop high-quality teaching materials and courses for teachers which make full use of Esperanto's potential as it is currently understood. This article has reviewed evidence that both developments are amply justified and may lead to long-term benefits for language teaching and language awareness in general.

OISE, University of Toronto
Canada

REFERENCES

Auld, W.: 1982a, 'Myth and fact About Esperanto', in R. & V.S. Eichholz (eds.), *Esperanto in the Modern World*, Esperanto Press, Bailieboro, 159–170.
Auld, W.: 1982b, 'The international language as a medium for literary translations', in R. & V.S. Eichholz (eds.) *Esperanto in the Modern World*, Esperanto Press, Bailieboro, 111–158.
Bauman, Z.: 1992, *Intimations of Postmodernity*, Routledge, London.
Chiti-Batelli, A.: 1987, *Communication internationale et l'avenir des langues et des parlers en Europe*, Presses d'Europe, Nice.
Clark, R., Fairclough, N., Ivanic, R. & Martin-Jones, M.: 1991, 'Critical language awareness. Part II: Towards critical alternatives', *Language and Education* 5(1), 41–54.
Cool, J.: 1993, 'Esperanto and literary translation: Its potential as a vehicle for the study of comparative literature', in I. Richmond (ed.) *Aspects of Internationalism: Language and Culture*, University Press of America, Lanham, 67–84.
Corsetti, R. & La Torre, M.: 1995, 'Quale Lingua Prima? Per un Esperimento CEE Che Utilizzi l'Esperanto', *Language Problems and Language Planning* 19(1), 26–46.
Dasgupta, P.: 1987, 'Towards a dialogue between the sociolinguistic sciences and Esperanto culture', *Language Problems and Language Planning* 11, 305–334.

Edwards, J.: 1993, 'Esperanto as an international research context', in I. Richmond (ed.), *Aspects of Internationalism: Language and Culture*, University Press of America, Lanham, 21–34.

Fairclough, N. (ed.): 1992, *Critical Language Awareness*, Longman, London.

Fantini, A. & Reagan, T.: 1992, *Esperanto and Education: Toward a Research Agenda*, Esperantic Studies Foundation, Washington.

Fettes, M.: 1996, 'The Esperanto community: A quasi-ethnic linguistic minority?', *Language Problems and Language Planning* 20(1), 53–59.

Fettes, M.: 1997, 'Esperanto and language policy: Exploring the issues', *Language Problems and Language Planning* 21(1), in press.

Freire, P.: 1972, *Pedagogy of the Oppressed*, Penguin, Harmondsworth.

Halloran, J.H.: 1952, 'A four year experiment in Esperanto as an introduction to French', *British Journal of Educational Psychology* 22, 200–204.

Janton, P.: 1993, *Esperanto: Language, Literature, and Community*, ed. H. Tonkin, trans. H. Tonkin, J. Edwards & K. Johnson-Weiner, SUNY Press, Albany.

Jordan, D.: 1987, 'Esperanto and Esperantism: Symbols and motivations in a movement for linguistic equality', *Language Problems and Language Planning* 11, 104–125.

Lapenna, I., Lins, U. & Carlevaro, T.: 1974, *Esperanto en perspektivo: Faktoj kaj analizoj pri la Internacia Lingvo*, Universala Esperanto-Asocio & Centro de Esploro kaj Dokumentado pri la Monda Lingvo-Problemo, London-Rotterdam.

Lee, M.: 1993, 'The separation of language and culture', in I. Richmond (ed.), *Aspects of Internationalism: Language and Culture*, University Press of America, Lanham, 41–56.

Lieberman, E.J.: 1979, 'Esperanto and trans-national identity: The case of Dr. Zamenhof', *International Journal of the Sociology of Language* 20, 89–107.

Lopes, L.P.: 1993, 'Critical language awareness' (review of Fairclough 1992), *Language and Education* 7(4), 290–292.

Maxwell, D.: 1988, 'On the acquisition of Esperanto', *Studies in Second Language Acquisition* 10, 51–61.

Mead, M. & Modley, R.: 1967, 'Communication among all people, everywhere', *Natural History* 76(12), 56–63.

Piron, C.: 1982, 'The psychological resistance to Esperanto', in R. & V.S. Eichholz (eds.), *Esperanto in the Modern World*, Esperanto Press, Bailieboro.

Piron, C.: 1986, 'L'espéranto vu sous l'angle psychopédagogique', *Education et Recherche* 8(1), 11–41.

Piron, C.: 1994, *Le défi des langues: Du gâchis au bon sens*, L'Harmattan, Paris.

Reagan, T.: 1996, 'Language diversity in the twenty-first century: The educational dimension', in H. Tonkin (ed.) *Languages in International Organizations: A Half-Century of International Order?*, Center for Research and Documentation on World Language Problems, University of Hartford, 39–45.

Richardson, D.: 1988, *Esperanto: Learning and Using the International Language*, Orcas, Eastsound.

Richmond, I: 1993, 'Esperanto literature and the international reader', in I. Richmond (ed.), *Aspects of Internationalism: Language and Culture*, University Press of America, Lanham, 103–118.

Sherwood, B.: 1982, 'The educational value of Esperanto study', in R. & V.S. Eichholz (eds.) *Esperanto in the Modern World*, Esperanto Press, Bailieboro, 408–413 (also no. 31A in the series Esperanto Documents, Universala Esperanto-Asocio, Rotterdam).

Steiner, G.: 1974, *After Babel*, Oxford University Press, Oxford.

Thorndike, E., Kennon, L. & Eaton, H.: 1933, *Language Learning: Summary of a Report to the International Auxiliary Language Association in the United States*, Division of Psychology, Institute of Educational Research, Teachers College, Columbia University, New York.

Tonkin, H.: 1979, 'Equalizing language', *Journal of Communication* (Spring), 124–133.

Tonkin, H.: 1987, 'Grassroots and treetops: Collaboration in post-secondary language programs', in J.M. Darcey & C.L. Brown (eds.), *The Language Teacher: Commitment and Collaboration*, Northeast Conference on the Teaching of Foreign Languages, Middlebury.

Williams, N.: 1965, 'A language teaching experiment', *Canadian Modern Language Review* 22(1), 26–28.

Wood, R.: 1975, 'Teaching the interlanguage: Some experiments', *Lektos: Interdisciplinary Working Papers in Language Sciences*, University of Louisville, Louisville, 61–81.

Zamenhof, L.L.: 1929, *Originala verkaro* (ed. J. Dietterle), Ferdinand Hirt, Leipzig.

Section 4

Teacher Development

CHRISTOPHER BRUMFIT

THE TEACHER AS EDUCATIONAL LINGUIST

Language is the teacher's central resource. Whether the school is seen as the main agency for the promotion of literacy, as the location for expert to novice dialogue in the Socratic tradition, or as the source of exploratory talk among students to facilitate learning, the management of linguistic interaction is crucial to effective pedagogy. Explicit consideration of the role of language in institutionalised education is, however, a relatively recent phenomenon. Only in the last third of the twentieth century, centred on newly professional teacher educators for mother tongue or foreign language teachers, has there been systematic interest in the role of language in classrooms in schools or colleges. This period has coincided with major developments in linguistic and educational research, but, as this article will show, work on the central role of teachers as educational linguists (i.e. as conscious analysts of linguistic processes, both their own and others'), has scarcely begun.

This review is not a history of language in education, nor of language teaching methods which implicitly exploit language knowledge, for linguists are defined by their explicit awareness of language. This review concentrates on research into teachers' explicit beliefs about, and understanding of, language. Because the field is so new, there are no authoritative statements, though much incidental and small scale research. Where possible, citations of overviews are provided, but many references in this article are indicative of approaches or findings, and could be replaced equally by others without altering the main argument (see the review by Widdowson in Volume 4).

EARLY DEVELOPMENTS

The formal tradition of language in education derives from the teaching of classical languages, emphasising literacy, translation, a canon of approved literary texts, and grammatical instruction. Outside formal education, more naturalistic methods for effective development of foreign language skills co-existed, while the democratisation of schooling led to an increasing role for mother tongue education. As primary education expanded, basic courses developed to train teachers, and language study began to respond to the impact of psychological and sociological research as these disciplines established themselves through the twentieth century. Thus Piaget's and Vygotsky's work underlay notions of child development and socialisation.

L. van Lier and D. Corson (eds), Encyclopedia of Language and Education,
Volume 6: Knowledge about Language, 163–172.
© *1997 Kluwer Academic Publishers. Printed in the Netherlands.*

The development of pedagogy for teaching languages illustrates clearly the recurrent tension between a pedagogy based on accuracy, requiring from teachers an explicit understanding of formal linguistics, and one based on fluency with its emphasis on process and classroom interaction.

As education systems on western models spread throughout the world, debates about the appropriate content for teacher education proliferated. In Britain these concentrated on the establishment of certain 'foundation' disciplines, and out of the 1960s a consensus arose that in addition to subject knowledge and pedagogy for the teaching of that subject, teachers should have an understanding of the history, philosophy, psychology and sociology of education. The intellectual boundaries had thus been drawn without linguistics, and even in the United States, linguistics took second place to other disciplines. Nonetheless, the potential relevance of linguistics to the direct teaching of languages was recognised, in the US through Charles Fries's 1950s marriage of structural linguistics with audiolingual procedures in foreign language learning, and in Britain by the establishment of the Linguistics and English Teaching Project (1964–70), under Michael Halliday's direction, in English mother tongue work; both produced theoretical statements and teaching materials.

Yet the impact of new 1960s initiatives remained slight, partly because their greatest influence coincided with a retrenchment of government spending on teacher education, and applied linguistics departments proved vulnerable to cuts.

Nonetheless, a number of forces combined to provide a substantial, though disorganised impetus to teacher awareness of language from the 1970s onwards. These factors were:

1. The increased impact of linguistics as a discipline deriving from the influence of transformational generative grammar, together with the attempts of its critics to promote alternative, socially sensitive models of language – providing an intellectual basis;

2. The thriving international market for English as a Foreign Language following the 1973 oil crisis, creating a need in many countries for linguistically sensitive teachers, and for the research and scholarship to support their training, teaching materials, and curricula – providing cross-cultural experience and financial investment in pedagogically-orientated research and development;

3. The increasingly powerful representation of linguistic minorities in the industrialised countries leading to a greater awareness of multilingualism in state education systems, coinciding with moves towards greater international co-operation such as the European Union – providing an incentive for educational policy to address linguistic issues more seriously than before;

4. The questioning of progressive educational ideas which accompanied political shifts towards the right-wing parties, leading to reassertion of

claims for the teaching of formal grammar and 'standard' languages – providing a counter to the forces in 3 above and ensuring that language remained significant in educational debates.

But these factors also reflected tensions in the wider community which created difficulties for work on language in general education. On the one hand, work with teachers within the education systems of particular countries was distorted by the greater financial base and strong neo-colonial pressures of EFL; on the other internal political pressures caused direct interference by politicians into linguistic work with teachers. Thus the major linguistically-based courses for teachers were frequently aimed at overseas markets and the teachers' associations with closest links to linguistics and applied linguistics were those for EFL/ESL (e.g. TESOL in the United States, IATEFL in UK). Examples of political pressure include the 'English Only' movement in the US, and the banning of the Language in the National Curriculum (LINC) programme in the UK in 1991.

Nonetheless, one effect of the dominance of English was to bring into dialogue a range of national traditions that had had only slight contact in the early years of the cold war. In the Soviet Union and Eastern Europe, for example, indigenous traditions of language curriculum development continued, informed by local schools of linguistics. In other areas the demand for communication across linguistic boundaries led to cross-linguistic and cross-national schemes for the development of language teaching, supported by substantial teacher education programmes (e.g. Council of Europe). Meanwhile, international agencies promoted programmes for the teaching of ex-colonial languages which included substantial teacher development components, and most industrial countries designed in-service programmes to educate teachers in language-teaching methodology. Simultaneously, government initiatives to renew the curricula of state educational systems (UK in 1988; Spain in 1990), or attempts to develop national language policies (in Australia, New Zealand, South Africa, for example) raised major linguistic issues for teachers and teacher education, though governments did not always accept, or even recognise, the significance of their own initiatives.

Thus by the beginning of the 1990s teachers had to respond to educational linguistics in different ways, depending on their personal roles. Teachers of foreign languages, teachers of the major national languages taught as 'mother tongues', and teachers of bilingual learners had training programmes which incorporated and exploited linguistic knowledge to varying degrees, but other teachers did not normally receive such training.

Work on teachers' explicit understanding in this period was rarely empirical; teachers' knowledge, attitudes or understanding about language appears marginal in both educational and linguistic research, with the exception of work on attitudes to language varieties, reviewed below. Thus major surveys of language in education research (e.g. Young, Arnold & Watson, 1987) make no references to teachers' knowledge or attitudes, and surveys of teacher beliefs (e.g. Fang, 1996), while referring to the recent interest in think-aloud protocols, teacher biographies and focused interviews as means of understanding teachers' knowledge, cannot locate empirical work on language beyond views about the nature of reading.

Empirical work usually served teacher education (e.g. attitude surveys to help teachers uncover their own assumptions: English, Mittins, 1970; foreign languages, De Garcia et al., 1976), or was incidental to larger studies (e.g. Naiman et al., 1978, exploring teachers' views for consistency with their empirical study of good language learners; Mitchell, 1988, pp. 12–47, analysing definitions of communicative language teaching). Other references to language teachers' knowledge and beliefs are more typically programmatic, proposing programmes of development or (more rarely) investigation.

WORK IN PROGRESS

It will be clear from earlier discussion that there is no recognised research field central to the role of 'Teachers as Educational Linguists'. Indeed, insofar as linguists are expected to theorise and make explicit the underlying principles of their beliefs about language, there is a potential conflict with the teaching role. The implicit linguistic beliefs of teachers could be derived from the investigation of classroom discourse and language teaching methodology, but teachers have rarely needed to make their own beliefs and attitudes explicit and two decades of 'reflective practice' as an in-service slogan have produced many small scale and local studies of individual professional development, few of which have taken language as a focus (for an exception, see Bain et al., 1992). As for teachers' knowledge, this has been a politically sensitive area for investigation since as in any profession it was assumed to be a direct consequence of effective training and admission procedures, while the 'craft knowledge' tradition has not addressed language issues. Only rarely, as in commentaries on the mismatch between the literary training and linguistic needs of English mother tongue teachers in the UK (DES, 1988) has the issue been raised explicitly. There are also very few studies of the practice of teachers that relate these to their views of language. For these reasons, the possibility of generalisation from empirical evidence is reduced.

Yet the next decade is likely to see a change. The impact of interests such as those outlined above, interacting with wider concerns about the role of minority languages, demands for 'linguistic rights', and geo-political protective measures in defence of linguistic communities that feel themselves beleaguered, push teachers towards linguistic self-consciousness with irresistible force.

Thus a survey of 1990s work can illustrate the nature of work in progress, but is unable to call upon authoritative findings which synthesise the current position; rather, there is a range of studies, exploring small areas of a wide terrain, often with different prime interests, and with serious theorising as yet undeveloped.

The key components of a comprehensive study of teachers as linguists would need to encompass the following:

1. Teachers' knowledge and beliefs about language, language acquisition, the role of language in society, in learning, and in power structures

    a) across age levels

    b) across subject areas

    c) across cultures;

        related to

2. Teachers' practices in classrooms, and within their institutions, described both individually and corporately;

        related to

3. Children's developmental beliefs and practices in all these areas, as they mature, across cultures;

        related to

4. Learners' practices and beliefs in their roles as pupils/students across levels of learning and cultures.

Each of these constitutes a substantial research agenda in its own right, but even the issues addressed under 3 above, where children's metalinguistic understanding has been (at least at the early stages) subject to much research (Gombert, 1992), do not provide us with any easily described account of how children perceive language, from birth to school-leaving.

There is, however, current empirical work relevant to heading 1, though it is frequently embedded in more general studies with larger goals.

The characteristics of language teachers have been examined (similar work with teachers in other subject areas has ignored language altogether). Teachers of English as a mother tongue have been characterised by Protherough (1989) in a study whose main focus is the attitudes of learners to the subject 'English'. However, although 'just under a hundred' teachers and university lecturers filled in questionnaires and an unspecified number were interviewed on their views on English as a subject, assessment, literature, etc. no significant views of language are reported and the term does not appear in the index. Only a few stray comments indicate that they have any views on linguistic matters at all: advanced language work at the top end of secondary school would be desirable (p. 63), and university lecturers feel that schools provide inadequate training in basic language skills (p. 64). A further questionnaire study of 110 teachers (Protherough & Atkinson, 1991) is similarly lacking in language-based discussion, while Davies' (1996) analysis of English teachers' statements of aims, drawing on educational sociologists' work on subject sub-cultures, reveals similar lack of linguistic concern. Goodwyn (1993) notes the lack of interest in linguistic models by English teachers responding to proposals for a national curriculum, a view confirmed by Poulson et al. (1996) reporting that English teachers discuss language in terms of pedagogy, not of technical features. Higher in the education system, Evans (1993) also indicates a marginalisation of language and linguistics, within university English departments.

More generally, across mother tongue classes in a range of European countries, the role of grammar is seen as both central and problematic (Herrlitz et al., 1984, pp. 13–14), but what is meant by 'grammar' varies from parsing on the model of classical languages to more sophisticated analysis based on twentieth century linguistics.

For foreign language teachers the role of descriptive linguistics is less obviously problematic. Evans (1988, pp. 65–7) sees foreign language teachers at university level as more convergent and less creative than English teachers, but – as in his later study of English – he notes recurrent tensions between those with literary and those with linguistic interests.

Attempts to explore the attitudes and practices of teachers have frequently made use of the opportunity provided by teacher education, though it is difficult to generalise from such studies to the knowledge and thought-processes of experienced teachers. These vary from high inference studies based on current social theory and data such as trainee diaries to detailed work on specific aspects of language-teaching practice (e.g. Palfreyman's (1993) detailed analysis of lesson planning discussions, and Chandler et al. (1989) on student teachers' approaches to children's writing). Van Lier (1996) synthesises theory and practice in this area, but again with little reference to explicit knowledge.

Bloor (1986) has attempted to define the grammatical and sociolinguistic knowledge of language students; similar work with trainee teachers is very limited (though Chandler et al. (1988) and Andrews (1994) for pre-service, and Williams (1994) for in-service provide some evidence).

Following discussions of 'Language Awareness' by British English and foreign language teachers, Brumfit et al. (1994) document the practices of English mother tongue and foreign language teachers in three schools, and relate these to interview studies of their beliefs about language, using five categories:

1. Language as system
2. Language learning and development
3. Styles and genres of language

4. Social and regional variation

5. Language change through time.

They find that foreign language teachers are most committed to 1, while English teachers orient themselves to 3 and 4. Both groups value explicit knowledge only insofar as it directly contributes to learner performance. Similar work in a cross-linguistic context (Spanish, Catalan and English) is in progress at the University of Lleida in Spain. More limited studies by Mitchell & Hooper (1992) explore the views of heads of English and foreign language departments, and Merchant (1992) examines the views on linguistic diversity of British primary school teachers, confirming in a cross-linguistic context the positive views on category 4 above of English teachers.

Internationally, work on language attitudes of teachers is most fully developed, with studies of American varieties, particularly black vernaculars, Spanish, and Hawaiian; creoles, Australian varieties, bilingual learners' English and dialects of Welsh English (Garrett et al., 1995). Cheshire et al. (1989, p. 6) provide summaries of European work in this area, and McGroarty (1996, pp. 16–18) of American. In general, teachers tend to reflect the class or ethnic attitudes of non-teachers, but still report themselves as having positive attitudes; however they may act discriminatively against non-standard forms in classroom practice.

Work in the EFL/ESOL community is still geared to teacher awareness, but, with increased numbers of diary studies becoming available from development work, meta-statements are beginning to emerge (Pennington, 1995), and interpretation of teachers' subjective rationales will be a continuing theme.

Finally, Woods (1996) has produced the first full-length study of 'teacher cognition in language teaching'. Concentrating on university level ESL teachers in Canada, he examines the relationship between beliefs, knowledge and practical decision-making. He concludes that the important issues for learners coincide with those that are crucial for teachers in his study: 'the balance between support and independence, discipline and freedom, pre-active (decontextualized) and in-situational (contextualized) learning, form and function/meaning' (pp. 298–9). How these relate to teachers' and learners' beliefs constitutes a substantial future research agenda.

FUTURE DIRECTIONS

As we have noted, the major weakness of this field is the lack of a strong research basis. As language education research moved since 1960 from method studies to learner-centred work, to classroom discourse, the teacher's role was taken for granted, either as a passive purveyor of 'method', or as a distraction from concerns with learning (why do learners not learn what teachers teach?), or a participant in the construction of learning discourse. Simultaneously, teacher educators concerned themselves with learner teachers, but limited discussion to the reporting and analysing of experience, rather than empirical studies of teacher cognition. The situation is changing, but it is too soon for an authoritative overview. Not only is too little known about all the areas listed above as key components, but the language teaching profession remains relatively isolated from educational research, and the ESOL profession from practice in mother tongues and with languages other than English. Yet understanding teachers is important, for they are the most crucial agents in successful education, and language is their fundamental (and cheapest) resource. As Evans (1988, 1993) indicates, 'language people' and 'English people' are tribes with distinct territories and cultures. ESOL/EFL people intersect these groups, and their culture awaits its ethnographer. What global categories will predominate in such teachers' sub-cultural self-definitions ('adult v. school level teacher, native speaker v. non-native speaker, proficient linguist v. linguistically ignorant, humanist v. functionalist'?) remain to be seen, but the power of English and the global claims of ESOL may have diverted our understanding from the groundedness of local language work in other traditions: 'global and decontextualised v. local and specific' may be the crucial defining distinction.

Against this sociology of the language teaching professions must be set the wider question of the role of language in the general educational process. How teachers operate as educational linguists must reflect their views of language in learning that have received virtually no empirical investigation. Yet the intersection of that research programme for all teachers with the one outlined here on teachers of languages will eventually be a necessary precondition for understanding both teaching and educational linguistics.

University of Southampton
England

REFERENCES

Andrews, S.J.: 1994, 'The grammatical knowledge/awareness of native-speaker EFL teachers – What the trainers say', in M. Bygate, A. Tonkyn & E. Williams (eds.), *Grammar and the Language Teacher*, Prentice Hall, Hemel Hempstead, 69–89.
Bain, R., Fitzgerald, B. & Taylor, M. (eds.): 1992, *Looking into Language: Classroom Approaches to Knowledge about Language*, Hodder & Stoughton, London.
Bloor, T.: 1986, 'What do language students know about grammar?', *The British Journal of Language Teaching* 24(3), 157–162.
Brumfit, C., Mitchell, R. & Hooper, J.: 1994, ' "Grammar", "language" and classroom practice', in M. Hughes (ed.), *Teaching and Learning in Changing Times*, Blackwell, Oxford, 70–87.

Chandler, P., Robinson, W.P. & Noyes, P.: 1988, 'The level of linguistic knowledge and awareness amongst students training to be primary teachers', *Language in Education* 2(3), 161–173.

Chandler, P., Robinson, W.P. & Noyes, P.: 1989, 'The treatment of children's writing by student teachers', *Language in Education* 3(1), 1–12.

Cheshire, J., Edwards, V., Münstermann, H. & Weltens, B. (eds.): 1989, *Dialect and Education*, Multilingual Matters, Clevedon.

Davies, C.: 1996, *What is English Teaching?* Open University Press, Buckingham.

De Garcia, R., Reynolds, S. & Savignon, S.: 1976, 'Foreign-Language Attitude Survey', *Canadian Modern Language Review* 32, 302–304.

DES (Department of Education and Science): 1988, *Report of the Committee of Inquiry into the Teaching of English Language* (The Kingman Report), HMSO, London.

Evans, C.: 1988, *Language People*, Open University Press, Milton Keynes.

Evans, C.: 1993, *English People*, Open University Press, Buckingham.

Fang, Z.: 1996, 'A Review of research on teachers' beliefs and practices', *Educational Research* 38(1), 47–66.

Garrett, P., Coupland, N. & Williams, A.: 1995, ' "City harsh" and "the Welsh version of RP"': Some ways in which teachers view dialects of Welsh English', *Language Awareness* 4(2), 99–108.

Gombert, J.: 1992, *Metalinguistic Development*, Harvester Wheatsheaf, New York.

Goodwyn, A.: 1993, 'The impersonal growth of national curriculum English', *NATE News* (National Association for the Teaching of English), 9–11.

Herrlitz, W., Kamer, A., Kroon, S. Peterse, H. & Sturm, J (eds.): 1984, *Mother Tongue Education in Europe*, International Mother Tongue Education Network, Enschede, Netherlands.

McGroarty, M.: 1996, 'Language attitudes, motivation, and standards', in S.McKay & N. Hornberger (eds.), *Sociolinguistics and Language Teaching*, Cambridge University Press, Cambridge, 3–46.

Merchant, G. 1992: 'Linguistic diversity and language awareness: The views of primary school teachers', in C. James & P. Garrett (eds.), *Language Awareness in the Classroom*, Longman, London, 51–61.

Mitchell, R.: 1988, *Communicative Language Teaching in Practice*, Centre for Information on Language Teaching, London.

Mitchell, R. & Hooper, J.: 1992, 'Teachers' views of language knowledge', in C. James & P. Garrett (eds.), *Language Awareness in the Classroom*, Longman, London, 40–50.

Mittins, W: 1970, *Attitudes to English Usage*, Oxford University Press, Oxford.

Münsterman, H.: 1989, 'Language attitudes in education', in J. Cheshire, V. Edwards, H. Münstermann & B. Weltens (eds.), *Dialect and Education*, Multilingual Matters, Clevedon, 166–181.

Naiman, N., Fröhlich, M., Stern, H. & Todesco, A.: 1978, *The Good Language Learner*, Multilingual Matters, Clevedon.

Palfreyman, D.: 1993, ' "How I got it in my head": Conceptual models of language and learning in native and non-native trainee EFL teachers', *Language Awareness* 2(4), 209–223.

Pennington, M.: 1995, 'The teacher change cycle', *TESOL Quarterly* 29(4), 705–731.

Poulson, L., Radnor, H. & Turner-Bisset, R.: 1996, 'From policy to practice: Language education, English teaching and curriculum reform in secondary schools in England', *Language and Education* 10(1), 33–46.

Protherough, R.: 1989, *Students of English*, Routledge, London.

Protherough, R. & Atkinson, J.: 1991, *The Making of English Teachers*, Open University Press, Buckingham.

van Lier, L.: 1996, *Interaction in the Language Curriculum*, Longman, London.

Williams, E.: 1994, 'English grammar and the views of English teachers', in M. Bygate, A. Tonkyn & E. Williams (eds.), *Grammar and the Language Teacher*, Prentice Hall, Hemel Hempstead, 105–18.

Woods, D.: 1996, *Teacher Cognition in Language Teaching*, Cambridge University Press, Cambridge.

Young, R., Arnold, R. & Watson, K.: 1987, 'Linguistic Models', in M.J. Dunkin (ed.), *The International Encyclopedia of Teaching and Teacher Education*, Pergamon, Oxford, 49–58.

TONY WRIGHT AND ROD BOLITHO

LANGUAGE AWARENESS IN IN-SERVICE PROGRAMMES

Language awareness (LA) (see James & Garrett (1991) for definitions of the scope and fields of LA) is an integral part of any in-service (INSET) programme for language teachers concerned with continuing professional development. Just as professional development may be seen as a career-long process (Lange, 1990; Hargreaves & Fullan, 1992) it can be argued that no teacher of any language should ever stop learning about their subject. In addition, the processes involved in LA work are entirely consistent with the best traditions of experiential learning (Kohonen, 1992), or learning from practice (Schön, 1983, 1987). Here, we describe and trace the connections between LA and experiential learning, and examine some of the potential benefits to teachers of LA work in INSET. Finally we suggest some ways in which LA work can be usefully incorporated into INSET programmes.

EARLY DEVELOPMENTS

Language Teachers, Initial Training and INSET Needs

Many language teachers of all nationalities enter the language teaching profession on the basis of a 'philological' first degree, in some cases topped up with a concurrent or subsequent initial teacher training (ITT) programme. An integral part of this kind of preparation is the formal study of language. In the case of non-native speakers of the target language, this will frequently include language proficiency work in addition to linguistics and a thorough study of language systems. By the time they start teaching, graduates of such programmes are, in Edge's (1988) terms both proficient **users** and skilled **analysts** of the target language. However, **pedagogically-oriented** LA work is not always included in ITT programmes, or even later in Masters' programmes, and this frequently results in the transfer of the fairly formal approaches to language, acquired during university studies, to the classroom. In an era of rapid change in the linguistic basis for syllabus design and materials writing (Howatt, 1984; White, 1988), this has often meant that teachers are less than adequately equipped to teach English for communicative purposes. Thus, while some non-native teachers may lack both spontaneity in their own language use and an awareness of the linguistic principles underlying communicative

L. van Lier and D. Corson (eds), Encyclopedia of Language and Education,
Volume 6: Knowledge about Language, 173–181.
© *1997 Kluwer Academic Publishers. Printed in the Netherlands.*

materials, they do bring to their work a very thorough knowledge of the target language and its systems (Medgyes, 1995). This, in itself, is an excellent starting point for LA work. While native speaker teachers may be natural and spontaneous *users* of their own language, only a minority have any real *analytical* perspective on it. Once again, however, this basic user competence provides a promising basis for LA work.

It is this prior use and knowledge of a language, coupled with subsequent classroom work with learners' language and with textbooks, which form the experiential basis for LA work in INSET courses, and teachers' classroom experiences with language can provide a useful starting point in INSET courses. By the time they enrol in an INSET course, many teachers will have begun to uncover some of the shortcomings in the presentation and practice of language in coursebooks they use regularly, and will have developed a better understanding of their own learners' particular difficulties with the target language (interference problems, in many cases). They may even have begun to realise that grammar reference books and dictionaries are finite and cannot offer answers to all the questions about language which concern both them and their learners. Such questions may be raised directly, in class, by learners, or indirectly, as teachers correct learners' work or prepare lessons. When they arise, teachers quickly realise that they need a means of thinking about the questions for themselves, and that there may not always be a 'cut-and-dried' answer to all of them. Opportunities in INSET programmes to share experiences of problems of this sort provide an appropriate, experientially-based point of departure for LA work in INSET.

Language Awareness Activities: Awareness Raising and Learning

In INSET programmes, teachers' classroom experiences with language and the problems these encounters raise are the basis for a great deal of language awareness work. The central processes in this work are awareness-raising and discovery. A carefully-organised series of tasks forms the essential scaffolding (Bruner, 1966) for the teachers in their work on language issues.

A typical 'problem-based' sequence may then be carried out as follows:

Step 1 A language problem is raised by participants derived from their teaching experience, with the assistance of the trainer. The problem may be a grammatical difficulty either they or their students face, or a query about aspects of vocabulary usage or about how texts are structured.

Step 2 The trainer aids teachers' clarification of the problem through focus questions, specially written activities using real texts and examples (Wright (1994), Bolitho & Tomlinson (1995) and Thornbury (1996) have a range of tasks for use at this stage of the work). The aim at this stage is to explore the linguistic and pedagogic dimensions of the problem.

Step 3 There is full exploration of the problem through discussion, analogizing, and reference to grammars and dictionaries where necessary. At this stage, there may be explicit statements of rules of grammar or principles for use of vocabulary items, for example.

Step 4 Participants work out a remedial strategy or a fresh teaching approach to try out when they return to their own classrooms.

It will readily be seen that these four steps closely parallel the stages in most versions of an experiential learning cycle (Kolb, 1984), viz: Experience (doing), reviewing, learning (making meaning or conceptualising) and planning. Aspects of participants' **experience** of teaching the language are brought out and articulated in *Step 1*. This experience is analysed and **reviewed** in *Step 2*. It is very likely that new awareness of the point under consideration will emerge as participants review their experiences. These are then refined through a process of discovery. Participants **learn** (or engage in more abstract thought processes) through further exploration at *Step 3*, gaining deeper insights into the aspect of language they are considering. Finally, they **plan** collaboratively or individually for future classroom action at *Stage 4*.

Language awareness activities in INSET thus proceed from teachers' direct experience of language and language teaching and learning through a series of activities which enable them to think about the experiences and their linguistic dimensions in different ways, to form or reformulate concepts about language and finally to return to the classroom, refreshed by the new insights they have gained.

In a sequence like this, the trainer's role is likely to be essentially facilitative: providing a secure environment for learning, helping participants to keep focused, listening carefully and responding appropriately, probing with questions at the right moment, ensuring that the necessary learning resources are available, setting relevant tasks, negotiating deadlines and outcomes etc. A key aspect of this approach to awareness-raising about language is that participants are encouraged to articulate their ideas about the language point being worked on. It is through this public discussion of teachers' 'practical theories', or theories of action (Argyris & Schön, 1974) about language and language teaching and learning that enables teachers to review their own and each others' understanding of various language points – grammar, lexis, discourse and usage among others. Only at Step 3 is there likely to be a reason for a trainer to provide 'technical' input of any kind to underpin the learning which is taking place. As with all discovery-oriented learning, participants will gain confidence through the value which is accorded to their own ideas, and in this way the personal and internal understanding of language which is any teacher's most vital resource will be strengthened and developed. These procedures draw from the same broad views of teacher education as those proposed within the tradition of 'reflective practice' (Schön, 1983; Freeman, 1996)

CURRENT VIEWS: THE BENEFITS OF LA IN INSET

Increased Confidence

As well as the development of cognitive and intellectual knowledge about language that LA activities can produce, and the sense of immediacy in transfer of ideas to classroom activities, there is also a strong affective dimension in LA. Feeling confident and positive about the subject one teaches is a prerequisite for development. A valuable function of LA work in INSET is to enable teachers to develop this confidence, and a positive attitude towards the language, something which can only be achieved if their existing knowledge is respected and valued. This means that "top-down" lectures from experts may not be appropriate in INSET programmes, as they usually serve only to persuade participants of how little they really know, thus undermining their confidence. Far more appropriate and helpful is an approach which encourages enquiry and discovery, thus encouraging participants to become researchers of language themselves, and to set the parameters of their work on language around their own working situations rather than depending upon external definitions of what is important to them. This, in turn, will lead to the evolution of their own individual 'theories' of language for teaching purposes, and to an acknowledgement of the rich ambiguity and diversity of language, rather than its reduction to a rigid and simplified system. The presence of LA work in INSET courses is thus an acknowledgement of teachers' professional need to **talk about** language and, as such, is an indispensable element in their professional development.

Strengthening the Teacher's Position in Relation to Published Materials

Novice teachers often have little option but to follow the language syllabus of a prescribed textbook, and to accept all its explanations of language unquestioningly. LA work can help teachers to develop a more robust attitude to textbooks and other published materials, by helping them to establish criteria for the evaluation of textbooks prior to selection, and of the material (texts, exercises etc.) in a textbook prior to teaching any lesson. This process of evaluation can then inform teachers' decisions about omission, adaptation and supplementation to meet the needs of a particular group of learners. In short, continuing attention to LA in INSET programmes can help teachers to become 'masters of' rather than 'slaves to' their textbooks.

As a Basis for Materials Writing

A logical consequence for most teachers of a more critical attitude to textbooks is that, sooner or later, they will wish to write learning materials for their own learners. The more linguistically aware a teacher is, the more likely such materials are to be successful. It almost goes without saying that this linguistic awareness, in materials writing, needs to be complemented by pedagogical awareness: a sense of what will work in the classroom. LA work in INSET programmes seeks to develop both linguistic and associated pedagogic awareness. Linguistically aware teachers will develop criteria for selecting and exploiting texts for teaching purposes, for creating appropriate socio-cultural contexts for learning particular aspects of the target language (a key area in communicative materials design), and will become better at writing tests which focus on what has been taught.

Attitudes to the Target Tanguage

A teacher who sees the target language as a closed system is likely to present the language to her/his learners as a series of right/wrong choices. Sooner rather than later, however, every teacher finds out that language is more complex than this. There are ambiguities, overlaps, exceptions, instances where lingering doubts about correctness or appropriacy cannot be dispelled. A teacher may choose to ignore all this in the interest of maintaining the semblance of an orderly system (and a quiet life!) or may take the honest course and acknowledge it as a challenge inherent in the subject. If a teacher is prepared to remain a 'lifelong student' of the language, and to accept that there is always more to learn about it, there is a chance that this enquiring attitude will transfer itself to learners, who will benefit equally from becoming independent 'explorers' of language rather than mere recipients of a school subject. Recent developments in corpus studies have opened up many possibilities for challenging long-held views about language in general (particularly spoken/written differences) and also specific points of grammar and lexical patterning. Awareness of these trends and the study and analysis of real text will assist greatly in helping teachers to review and question their own and others' attitudes to language.

Language Proficiency in Non-Native Teachers

While there is no research evidence that LA work brings about measurable improvement in the competence or performance of *any* second language learners, we have certainly found that the fresh challenge of LA work on INSET courses has often had a positive effect on the *attitude* of teachers towards the target language, and on their *understanding* of it as a socioculturally rooted means of communication rather than as a set of abstract systems. This, coupled with the joy of discovery which LA work can bring about, has often brought fresh impetus to non-native speaker teachers' own attempts to grapple with the intricacies of the language as advanced learners, and has resulted, over time, especially on longer courses, in improved written and spoken performance. Non-native teachers are often their own fiercest critics when it comes to language proficiency (both in terms of grammatical accuracy and usage). The vast majority of language teachers have, in our experience, wanted to become better users of the target language, as well as more knowledgeable about how it works, and LA work can satisfy their need to 'do something about their own language' on an INSET course without exposing them directly to didactic language learning situations in which they might 'lose face' by making an error or appearing 'out of date' in their language use.

To sum up this section, while there are benefits in LA work to the teacher as a **user** and as an **analyst** of the target language, we see the main benefit to the teacher as a **teacher**, boosting confidence, reinforcing subject knowledge with a sharp pedagogical perspective at the level of the classroom and also in associated work with materials. The post-experience nature of INSET programmes makes them an ideal setting in which to work on this pedagogical perspective, providing both the means and the setting for new professional development.

FUTURE DIRECTIONS

Above we outlined a procedure, based on experiential learning, for LA work in INSET. There are, of course, other possible procedures, though a commitment to the notion of **exploring** language autonomously is a common thread in published LA materials (Bolitho & Tomlinson, 1995; Wright, 1994) and in much of the writing about LA in a second or foreign language classroom (for example, Borg, 1994; Maestri, 1995; Pohl, 1995). We are also not the first (James & Garrett, 1991) to point out that L.A. remains, in general, an under-researched area. In this section we suggest some potentially fruitful fields of enquiry for LA work in INSET.

The Language System

Since we see LA as a training/teaching methodology or as a mode of enquiry rather than as a subject or an academic discipline, we have found that an awareness-raising approach has enabled INSET participants to take a fresh look at their beliefs about how language works, and to indulge in some healthy re-examination of some of the traditional descriptions of language systems and the influences of these beliefs and descriptions on teaching and learning. (See Hall & Shepheard (1991) for an example from

English Language teaching) This is also an area in which trainers and linguists could usefully find a common research focus.

Contrastive Studies

We have often found that LA work has helped INSET participants to become more conscious of the relationship between L1 and L2 – both the contrasts (which often cause interference problems) and the overlaps (such as cognates) which help the learning process. (See James, 1997) This is a further area in which research will bring new perspectives, and to which an L.A. approach can usefully contribute.

Authentic Language Use vs Textbook Language

It is useful, in the security of an INSET course, both to question the authenticity and value of 'predigested' samples of language which appear in textbooks and to become more aware of the benefits (and perils!) of using authentic samples of language as teaching material. (Torres (1993) provides an example of discussion of some of these issues in the context of coursebook construction.)

Learner Language

We have found it useful to work, on INSET courses, with samples of spoken and written language produced by learners, both from the point of view of error analysis and from the more positive perspective of understanding the stage of learning they have reached and what they may be capable of expressing. This type of work could usefully draw upon the types of consciousness-raising ideas suggested by Rutherford (1987). Learner language in its own right could usefully be researched from an L.A. angle.

Lesson Data

Looking at video recordings or examining the transcripts of language lessons from an LA point of view (with the help, perhaps, of a few focusing questions provided by the trainer) can throw helpful light on the teaching and learning process. The teacher's classroom language and her/his ability to present or explain language points can also be scrutinized, as can, for example, learners' responses and questions. Here we see an opportunity to create links between classroom research (for example Allwright & Bailey (1991); Brumfit & Mitchell (1991)) and teacher development issues (see Edge & Richards (1993) for explicitly made connections). This area could provide an interesting focus for in-course action research projects.

The Relationship between Language and Culture

The boundaries between language awareness and cultural awareness are far from distinct. Our cultural identity is often expressed through language, and many see a 'natural' link between the two. In INSET courses, the study of literary texts, off-air videos, the press and other sources can serve to emphasise the complementarity of these two areas of enquiry, and to help teachers be more confident about introducing an appropriate cultural component into their own classroom work. Cultural awareness raising is still neglected on many training programmes.

Non-Verbal Communication

Video recordings can provide a powerful source of data on which to base an exploration of the various aspects of body language and paralinguistic communication which are often so difficult for non-natives to understand and respond to (van Lier, 1995).

There are certainly many more fields of enquiry appropriate to INSET-based LA work, for example Critical Language Awareness (Fairclough, 1989, 1991). Elsewhere (Wright & Bolitho, 1993) we have listed some of the processes which may usefully be adopted in LA work in teacher education. Most of them belong firmly within an enquiry-oriented or 'reflective' tradition. We believe that the feeling of being at ease with the subject one is teaching is vital to any teacher. The knowledge about language in teachers' heads is ultimately a far more important and useful resource to her/him than anything produced in a publishing house. It is this 'inner resource' which LA work in INSET seeks to strengthen.

College of St Mark and St John
England

REFERENCES

Allwright, D. & Bailey, K.: 1991, *Focus on the Language Classroom*, Cambridge University Press, Cambridge.
Argyris, C. & Schön, D.: 1974, *Theory in Practice: Understanding Professional Effectiveness*, Jossey-Bass, San Francisco.
Bolitho, R. & Tomlinson, B.: 1995, *Discover English* (second ed.), Heinemann, Oxford.
Borg, S.: 1994, 'Language awareness as methodology: Implications for teachers and teacher training', *Language Awareness* 3(2), 61–71.
Brumfit, C.J. & Mitchell, R. (eds.).: 1991, *Research in the Language Classroom*, MEP, London.
Edge, J.:1988, 'Applying linguistics in English language teacher-training for speakers of other languages', *ELT Journal* 42(1).
Edge, J. & Richards, K. (eds.).: 1993, *Teachers Develop Teachers Research*, Heinemann, Oxford.
Fairclough, N.: 1989, *Language and Power*, Longman, Harlow.

Fairclough, N. (ed.): 1991, *Critical Language Awareness*, Longman, Harlow.

Hall, P. & Shepheard, D.: 1991, *The Anti-Grammar Grammar Book*, Longman, Harlow.

Hargreaves, A & Fullan, M. (eds.): 1992, *Understanding Teacher Development*, Cassell, London.

Howatt, A.:1984, *A History of English Language Teaching*, Oxford University Press, Oxford.

James, C.A (ed.).: 1997, *Contrastive Approaches to Language Awareness*, Special Edition, *Language Awareness*.

James, C.A. & Garrett, P. (eds.).: 1991, *Language Awareness in the Classroom*, Longman, Harlow.

Kohonen, V., 1992, 'Experiential language learning: Second language learning as cooperative learner education', in D. Nunan (ed.), *Collaborative Language Learning and Teaching*, Cambridge University Press, Cambridge.

Kolb, D.A.: 1984, *Experiential Learning: Experience as a Source of Learning and Development*, Prentice-Hall, Englewood Cliffs, NJ.

Lange, D.L.: 1990, 'A blueprint for a teacher development programme', in J.C. Richards & D. Nunan (eds.), *Second Language Teacher Education*, Cambridge, Cambridge University Press.

Maestri, F.: 1995, 'Exploring structure and discovering meaning', *Language Awareness* 4(2).

Medgyes, P.: 1995, *The Non-Native Teacher*, Macmillan, Basingstoke.

Pohl, J-U.: 1995, 'The process side of language awareness: a Hungarian case study', *Language Awareness* 3&4(3), 151–160.

Rutherford, W.: (1987) *Second Language Grammar*, Longman, Harlow.

Schon, D.: 1983, *The Reflective Practitioner*, Temple-Smith, London.

Schon, D.: 1987, *Educating the Reflective Practitioner*, Jossey-Bass, London.

Thornbury, S.: 1996, *About Language*, Cambridge University Press, Cambridge.

Torres, E.: 1993, 'A fish's story: Insights from investigating use of a fisheries-based ESP textbook in classrooms', in J. Edge & K. Richards (eds.), *Teachers Develop, Teachers Research*, Heinemann, Oxford.

van Lier, L.V.: 1995, *Introducing Language Awareness*, Penguin, Harmondsworth.

White, R.V.: 1988, *The ELT Curriculum*, Blackwell, Oxford.

Wright, T.: 1994, *Investigating English*, Edward Arnold, London.

Wright, T. & Bolitho, R.: 1993, 'Language awareness: A missing link in teacher education?', *ELT Journal* 47(4).

AMY B.M. TSUI

AWARENESS RAISING ABOUT CLASSROOM INTERACTION

The term classroom interaction as used in this review covers all forms of interaction that take place in the classroom, both verbal and non-verbal. The dimensions of classroom interaction that will be discussed include the language used by the teacher and the learners, the interaction generated between the teacher and the learners, and among the learners themselves, and the effects of the interaction on opportunities for teaching and learning. They constitute the observables of classroom interaction. The discussion will also include the underlying factors which have a critical role to play in shaping classroom interaction. They include the socio-cultural background of the teacher and the learners, their psychological state, their beliefs about teaching and learning, and the context of interaction. They constitute the unobservables of classroom interaction.

EARLY DEVELOPMENTS

Studies of interactions and events that go on inside the classroom originated in the 1950s for teacher education purposes. Firstly, supervisors of student teachers were looking for a relatively objective way of assessing teachers' performance in the classroom. Secondly, teacher educators wanted to find out what constituted effective teaching so that the findings could be used as input for teacher education. The first major attempt to examine classroom interaction systematically was Flanders' Interaction Analysis Categories (FIAC) which analysed teachers' use of language in the classroom, the affective dimension of the language used, and the mode of participation by students (see Flanders, 1960).

The analysis of interaction in ESL (English as a second language)/EFL (English as a Foreign Language) classrooms began in the sixties with the aim of distinguishing and monitoring the effectiveness of different methods in foreign language teaching in the hope that the findings would show the 'best' method for teaching a foreign language. The inconclusive findings led researchers to question the basic tenets of these studies. There was a general recognition that what goes on in the classroom is extremely complex, and that research on language teaching should focus on describing events in the classroom. It was also pointed out that the descriptions should not just focus on teachers' behaviour, but also students' contributions.

L. van Lier and D. Corson (eds), Encyclopedia of Language and Education,
Volume 6: Knowledge about Language, 183–193.
© *1997 Kluwer Academic Publishers. Printed in the Netherlands.*

The focus of classroom interaction analysis, therefore, changed from evaluating teacher trainees' classroom teaching to raising their awareness of their own and their students' classroom behaviour. Teachers were trained to use interaction analysis systems to analyse their own teaching and to use the findings as a guide to change their classroom behaviour. There were a number of attempts to adopt Flanders' interaction analysis for language teacher training, the most well-known being Moskowitz's (1968) Foreign Language Interaction (Flint) (see Allwright (1988) for a detailed account of the development of classroom observation in ESL/EFL teaching).

Parallel to the development of classroom interaction analysis was the 'language across the curriculum' movement which began in Britain, also in the sixties, with a strong emphasis on the importance of language in education. Britton (1970) pointed out that language is a means of organising and representing the world, and therefore is crucial to learning. Barnes (1969) examined the language used by teachers in various first language (L1) content classrooms, and pointed out that the types of question asked by the teacher affect the opportunities for learning. Barnes (1976) investigated the kinds of talk that were generated in the classroom and pointed out that exploratory talk in which pupils organise their thinking as they talk should be encouraged in the classroom.

MAJOR CONTRIBUTIONS

Major contributions in classroom interaction consist of analyses at the macro-level and the micro-level. The former examine classroom interaction structures and patterns. Prominent work in this area includes Bellack et al.'s study (1966) which borrowed Wittgenstein's (1953) the concept of "move" in games to describe interaction in the classroom. They proposed that there are four types of moves, "structure", "solicit", "respond", and "react". Their conception of classroom interaction as a sequence of "moves" was adopted by Sinclair & Coulthard (1975) in their linguistic description of classroom discourse which perceives classroom discourse as organized in terms of a hierarchical rank scale of "act", "move", "exchange", "transaction" and "lesson". The strongest impact that Sinclair and Coulthard's work had on classroom interaction analysis was their proposal that a typical classroom exchange consists of an "initiating" move, usually from the teacher, a "responding" move, usually from the student, and a "follow-up" move from the teacher which evaluates the response. This IRF exchange structure has been widely adopted for analysing classroom data.

Major contributions of classroom interaction at the micro-level examine what actually goes on at the move level, or the turn level, and the exchange level. Studies in this area pertain roughly to three main aspects: input, interaction and output. Input refers to the language used by teachers, output refers to the language produced by learners, and interaction refers to the way input affects the output, and vice versa. These three aspects are intertwined; the study of one necessarily involves the other two. The terms "input" and "output" are used as a convenient means of classifying aspects of classroom interaction for discussion purposes. There is no assumption of a linear "cause-effect" relationship between them. (See van Lier 1996 for a discussion of the input-output metaphor.)

Studies of input included features of teacher speech, teacher questions and teacher feedback. Research on features of teachers' speech to learners investigated phonological, lexical and syntactic features and how they differ from those in teachers' speech to native-speakers (NS). The differences between NS to NS speech and NS to non-native speaker (NNS) speech, referred to as 'foreigner talk' in conversations, were also examined. The findings showed that, in order to make the input comprehensible to learners or NNSs, teachers or NSs modified their speech by exaggerating the articulation, lengthening the pauses, slowing down the speech rate, simplifying the syntax, using fewer contractions and reductions, less colloquial expressions and more basic vocabulary (see Chaudron (1988) for a detailed summary of the studies).

Studies of teacher questions investigated the types of question asked by the teacher and whether they restricted or enhanced learner response. An influential study on teacher questions in content L1 classrooms was Barnes (1969). He proposed a classification of questions differentiating 'closed' questions and 'open' questions, as well as 'genuine questions' to which the teacher does not have an answer, and 'pseudo-questions' to which the teacher does. Subsequent studies on teacher questions in ESL classrooms made a similar distinction between 'display questions' (which correspond to pseudo-questions) and 'referential' questions (which correspond to display questions). These studies found that ESL teachers used more display than referential questions, more display questions with ESL learners than with L1 learners, and more display questions than NSs with NNSs (see for example Long & Sato 1983; Pica & Long 1986). They argued that 'referential questions' were more likely to elicit lengthier and more complex verbal responses from learners and should therefore be used more in the classroom.

Another aspect of teacher questions that was investigated was how teachers modified their questions and whether the modifications were effective in eliciting responses. Tsui (1995) made a distinction between modifications which are comprehension-oriented, that is, they help learners to understand the question, and those which are response-oriented, that is, they help learners to respond. The former include syntactic modifications such as making the topic salient (Long & Sato, 1983) and semantic modifications such as paraphrase or disambiguation. The latter include modifying wh-questions into yes-no questions, providing clues and Socratic questioning.

In studies of teacher feedback, the function of teacher feedback was initially construed as positive or negative reinforcement. With the advances in theories of cognitive learning and second language acquisition, teacher feedback is now understood as providing information for learners to confirm or disconfirm the hypotheses that learners are formulating about the language that they are trying to master. Allwright and Bailey pointed out the need for teachers and researchers alike to re-consider the notion of 'error' from a developmental perspective and to attend to the cognitive as well as the affective dimensions of teacher feedback (see Allwright & Bailey (1991, p. 6) for a summary of findings in this area). Van Lier (1988) subsumed "error correction" under the broader notion of "repair" which he defined as the treatment of trouble in interactive language use and perceived as useful input for language learning (p. 183). He distinguished between didactic repair and conversational repair. The former refers to repairs for teaching purposes, and the latter refers to repairs for social interactional purposes. He observed that both types of repair operate in L2 classrooms. He further observed that while some repairs serve to help speakers respond when they have problems or to establish common ground, others serve to evaluate the response. He referred to the former as conjunctive repair and the latter as disjunctive repair. He pointed out that this classification of repair types could be a useful framework for investigating the role of repair in language learning.

Early studies of input and modified input were very much focused on the teacher, with the assumption that modifications made by teachers would help learners' comprehension. There was little or no evidence from the students to support this assumption. More recent studies of classroom interaction pointed out the need to investigate interaction rather than just the input. Subsequently, apart from teacher questions and their modifications, studies were also conducted on how interaction was modified as a result of trying to make the input comprehensible. Long (1983) proposed a list of modification devices commonly used by NSs in NS-NNS conversations, which include confirmation checks, comprehension checks, clarification requests, repetition requests, decompositions, and self-repetition. These modification devices have been used in a number of studies to analyse classroom data to determine the amount of input that was made comprehensible to the learner (see for example Varonis & Gass, 1985).

The study of interaction necessarily involves the study of output, which includes learners' turn-taking behaviour and oral participation in different classroom settings. Seliger (1983) examined learners' turn-taking behaviours and how they relate to learners' English achievement. He proposed that there are two types of learners, 'high input generators' (HIGs) and 'low-input generators' (LIGs). The former frequently initiate turns and by doing so obtain high levels of input from other people. The latter are very passive and speak only when they are allocated turns. He found that HIGs had much higher English achievement than LIGs, and concluded that HIGs were more effective language learners. Seliger's position, however, was questioned because firstly his findings were not confirmed in subsequent studies, and secondly he did not take into consideration important factors such as the cultural background of the learners which often affect learners' interaction behaviour (see Sato 1982).

Studies of learners' oral participation examined the effect of pair work, group work and teacher-fronted teaching on the amount and kinds of contribution made by learners. Long et al. (1976) found that in pair work students not only produced more speech, but also performed a larger variety of speech acts than in teacher-fronted settings. Doughty & Pica (1986) found that while there was no significant difference between pair and group interactions, there was significantly more negotiation of meaning in both when compared to teacher-fronted interaction. Furthermore, they found that task type was a crucial variable in learner interaction. A task where information exchange was obligatory generated more conversational adjustments in pair and group interactions than one where information exchange was optional (see also Plough & Gass, 1993).

WORK IN PROGRESS: PROBLEMS AND DIFFICULTIES

In most of the major contributions in classroom interaction reviewed so far, there seem to be three major weaknesses. Firstly, as Allwright & Bailey (1991) observe, most of them focused on what is observable in the classroom. Relatively little attention has been paid to the unobservable. Secondly, most of them were conducted from an observer's perspective rather than from the participants' perspective. Finally, most of these studies tend to focus on particular aspects of classroom interaction without taking into consideration the entire context of situation in which the interaction occurred.

Let us take for example studies of student participation. Most of them examined the ways in which students participated orally in the classroom without investigating the underlying factors. There are many factors which may affect students' behaviour in the classroom. One of them is learning style (see the review by Jones in this volume). Some learners prefer to listen and internalize rather than to verbalize. Teachers who force these learners to participate verbally may adversely affect their learning success.

Another factor is the psychological state associated with learning a second or foreign language. One kind of psychological state is language learning anxiety. Horwitz, Horwitz & Cope (1991) pointed out that performing in a second language is likely to threaten one's self-concept as a competent communicator and will lead to reticence. Closely related to language learning anxiety is students' self-esteem. Whether students see themselves as competent learners affects their learning success. A study is currently being conducted on the relationship between Hong Kong school students' oral participation in the classroom, their language learning anxiety level, and their self-esteem in speaking Chinese, in speaking English and in academic performance.

Yet another factor is cultural background. As mentioned in the previous section, learners' cultural background and their beliefs about what constitutes proper behaviour in the classroom often affect the kind of interaction that takes place. Sato (1982) studied the turn-taking behaviour of Asian and non-Asian students and found that the former took significantly fewer turns. A study of the sociocultural factors affecting student participation in Hong Kong classrooms observed that students who knew the answer were not expected to volunteer answers until they were called upon by the teacher (Tsui, 1995; see also Johnson (1995) on Vietnamese and Taiwanese students).

Similar to studies in student participation, studies in teacher talk and teacher behaviour also tend to focus on the observable and neglect the unobservable. For example, studies of teacher questions tend to focus on the types of questions that teachers asked, but not why they asked those questions, and why they directed a particular question to a particular student. Although observations have been made by various researchers that teacher questions may be used to perform a variety of functions in the classroom, such as focusing attention, moving the lesson forward, exercising disciplinary control, and so on (see Tsui, 1995), relatively little has been done in teacher thinking and teacher decision-making in their questioning behaviour.

A plausible reason for the lack of attention to the unobservable is that studies of classroom interaction were mostly conducted from an observer's perspective where insights from the participants were not available. Yet, unobservable information provided by participants is often crucial to understanding the complexities of classroom interaction. For example, in a study conducted on Hong Kong ESL students' communication strategies in group discussion tasks, it was found that agreement had a very high frequency of occurrence in the data. It was only from interviews with students that the researcher discovered that agreement was in fact used by students as an avoidance strategy when they did not understand what the group members were saying or when they did not know how to express themselves.

Since most studies were conducted from an observer's point of view, and since it is impossible for the observer to gain an understanding of the entire context by simply observing a lesson or a small number of lessons, it is inevitable that these studies failed to take the entire context into consideration when interpreting classroom data. Consequently, the researcher will miss or fail to make sense of highly meaningful classroom events (see Walker & Adelman, 1976; Nunan, 1996).

Recent classroom research strongly advocates an ethnographic approach which investigates an event from the participants' perception ('emic'), rather than from an outsider's perception ('etic'), in a naturalistic rather than an experimental setting, and in its entire context, that is, 'holistic' (see Hammersley, 1990; see also van Lier (1988) for an ethnographic approach to classroom observation).

The first substantial ethnographic study of classroom interaction is Mehan (1979) which made a holistic examination of the organization of teacher-pupil interaction in an elementary classroom by taking into consideration both the formal and informal activities that went on in the classroom when interpreting the data. The study, however, was very much conducted from the observer's perspective.

A classroom study which fully exemplifies the ethnographic approach is one by Hammersley who studied the issue of classroom deviant behaviour and the extent to which culture conflict theory applied to all schools. His approach to the issue of classroom order was not just confined to identifying incidents of disruptive behaviours in the classroom, but conducted holistically in the context of the school and classroom culture. He obtained data not only from classroom observations, but also from staffroom conversations, and observations of teacher-pupil interactions outside the classroom. Apart from his own perception of classroom order, he also obtained the teachers' perspectives. By triangulating these sources of data, Hammersley concluded that the culture conflict theory did not apply to the particular school being studied and that there seemed to be other factors such as the teacher's strategies in maintaining classroom order which led to the relatively low level of pupil resistance (see Hammersley, 1990).

Two recent publications on classroom communication research which depart from the 'etic' and quantitative tradition are Johnson (1996) and Bailey & Nunan (1996), the latter being a collection of studies. Johnson's work includes students' perception of classroom events as an important part of understanding classroom communication. Bailey and Nunan's collection of studies used a variety of sources of data, including lesson transcripts, observer's fieldnotes, teachers' and learners' journals, stimulated recall protocols, interview data, and lesson plans. The participants' voices, both the teachers' and the students', were either central to the studies or were brought in as part of the analytic procedures. The issues covered pertain mostly to the unobservable in the classroom. The studies in this volume demonstrate a significant step towards an ethnographic approach in classroom communication research.

FUTURE DIRECTIONS

As many classroom researchers have pointed out, classroom processes are extremely complex. It would be simplistic to think that an observer can understand the why and wherefore of classroom events by just observing and analyzing a number of recorded lessons. As can be seen from the issues dealt with and findings reported in Bailey & Nunan (1996), studies using an ethnographic and qualitative approach yielded more interesting insights than studies which are quantitative and experimental. Having said that, it must be borne in mind that qualitative and quantitative approaches should not be seen as mutually exclusive research paradigms. As Hammersley observed when comparing quantitative studies of classroom events by using systematic classroom observation instruments and ethnographic studies, "if ethnographers are to justify their claims about what happens in classrooms and why, they cannot avoid the measurement issues which have preoccupied systematic observers – notably the question of the typicality of the cases studied, and the relative frequency of different types of action" (1986, p. 47; see also Hammersley, 1990). He pointed out that we are more likely to find solutions to problems of classroom research if we maintain an "open-ended attitude towards research, in which eclectic combinations of research methods can be used" (ibid.).

The involvement of teachers in conducting action research on their own classroom has been practised for some time in teacher education. For language classrooms research, the involvement of teachers is a fairly recent endeavour. Getting teachers to reflect on their own lessons and to comment on their own classroom data not only provides valuable insights to classroom events and interactions, but also raises teachers' awareness of their own classroom practices and helps them to develop professionally. As Nunan points out, "In this way, theory, research and practice are bound together and become mutually reinforcing" (1996, p. 54).

Studies of classroom interaction seldom take into consideration the wider educational and socio-political contexts which include dimensions like educational policies, the school curriculum, the school culture, the socio-economic background of students, the expectations of parents. These dimensions often affect the classroom directly or indirectly. A number of studies collected in Bailey & Nunan (1996) examine the language classroom from this wider perspective and are a welcome addition to the classroom research literature.

ESL/EFL classroom interaction research started off by drawing on insights from teacher education research. Because of the linguistic focus of the research, it soon turned to first and second language acquisition research for insights and generated numerous interesting studies which enhanced our understanding of the linguistic aspects of classroom interaction. However, it is becoming more and more apparent that merely focusing on the linguistic aspects is not enough to understand and explicate the complexities of classroom processes. ESL/EFL classroom researchers are beginning to recognize the importance of taking into consideration dimensions like teacher beliefs, teacher thinking and teacher decision-making in understanding teacher behaviour in the classroom. There is a very rich body of knowledge in the recent teacher education literature which can be drawn upon to illuminate classroom interaction phenomena. Recent research on second language classrooms has already begun to tap this resource (see for example Richards & Lockhart, 1994; see also Bailey & Nunan, 1996). There is also a very rich body of research in L1 classrooms on the relationship between language and learning which is highly relevant to ESL/EFL classroom interaction studies (see for example Wells, 1985; Norman, 1992). The work by Johnson (1996) is a recent endeavour to draw upon this body of knowledge.

Recent work on classroom interaction has also begun to draw on theories in neighboring disciplines to illuminate phenomena in classroom interaction. One such piece of work is van Lier (1996). To explicate and understand classroom interaction and its relation to language learning, van Lier drew on social interaction theory (Rommetveit's notion of "prolepsis", adopted by Rogoff & Gardner (1984) in their explication of "proleptic instruction" which emphasizes learner's participation in the learning activity), learning theory (Vygotsky's (1978) theory of "zone of proximal development" and Bruner's (1983) closely related notion of "pedagogic scaffolding" which sees learning as development with assistance and guidance from adults and more competent peers; Tharp & Gallimore's (1988) notions of "responsive teaching" and "recitation teaching", the former being characterized by two-way interaction in which the direction of talk is determined by all participants, and the latter being characterized by teacher-led interaction), discourse analysis (Sinclair & Coulthard's (1975) IRF exchange structure), and conversational analysis by ethnomethodologists who perceive conversation as symmetrical talk which is locally managed by participants (see for example Sacks, Schegloff & Jefferson, 1974). Van Lier proposed a multi-layered view of classroom discourse in which classroom interaction was seen as varying on a cline along the following dimensions: from monologic to conversational; from elliptic to proleptic; from authoritarian to exploratory; from externally controlled to self-determined; from product-oriented to process-oriented; from asymmetrical to symmetrical; and from non-contingent to contingent, the last dimension being one which plays a crucial role in learning. Van Lier maintains that unfolding the many aspects of classroom interaction will enable educators to make informed choices about the kinds of classroom talk that would be beneficial for learning at different times and for different purposes.

The recent developments outlined above show that classroom interaction research is heading towards a joint-venture between researchers and practitioners to try to understand the complexities of the classroom by conducting both quantitative and qualitative research, tapping resources from a number of disciplines.

University of Hong Kong
China

REFERENCES

Allwright, D.: 1988, *Observation in the Language Classroom*, Longman, London.
Allwright, D. & Bailey, K: 1991, *Focus on the Language Classroom*, Cambridge University Press, New York.
Bailey, K. & Nunan, D. (eds.): 1996, *Voices from the Language Classroom*, Cambridge University Press, New York.
Barnes, D.: 1969, 'Language in the secondary classroom', in D. Barnes, J. Britton & H. Rosen (eds.), *Language, the learner and the school*, Penguin, Harmondsworth, 11–77.
Barnes, D.: 1976, *From Communication to Curriculum*, Penguin, Harmondsworth.
Bellack, A.A., Kliebard, H.M., Hyman, R.J. & Smith, F.L.: 1966, *The Language of the Classroom*, Teachers' College Press, New York.
Britton, J.: 1970, *Language and Learning*, Penguin, Harmondsworth.
Bruner, J.: 1983, *Child's Talk: Learning to Use Language*, Norton, New York.
Chaudron, C.: 1988, *Second Language Classrooms*, Cambridge University Press, New York.
Doughty, C. & Pica, T.: 1986, ' "Information gap" tasks: Do they facilitate second language acquisition?', *TESOL Quarterly* 20, 305–325.
Flanders, N. A.: 1960, *Interaction Analysis in the Classroom: A Manual for Observers*, University of Michigan Press, Ann Arbor.
Hammersley, M.: 1986, 'Revisiting Hamilton and Delamont: A cautionary note on the relationship between 'systematic observation' and ethnography', in M. Hammersley (ed.), *Controversies in Classroom Research*, Open University Press, Milton Keynes, 44–48.
Hammersley, M.: 1990, *Classroom Ethnography*, Open University Press, Milton Keynes.
Horwitz, E., Horwitz, M. & Cope, J.: 1991, 'Foreign language classroom anxiety', in E. Horwitz & D. Young (eds.), *Language Anxiety: From Theory and Research to Classroom Implications*, Prentice Hall, Englewood Cliffs, NJ.
Johnson, K.: 1995, *Understanding Communication in Second Language Classrooms*, Cambridge University Press, New York.
Long, M.: 1983, 'Native-speaker/non-native speaker conversation and the negotiation of comprehensible input', *Applied Linguistics* 4, 126–141.
Long, M.H., Adams, L., McLean, M. & Castanos, F.: 1976, 'Doing things with words: verbal interaction in lockstep and small group classroom situations', in J. Fanselow & Y. Crymes (eds.), *On TESOL '76*, TESOL, Washington, DC, 137–153.
Long, M.H. & Sato, C.: 1983, 'Classroom foreigner talk discourse: Forms and functions of teachers' questions', in H.W. Seliger & M.H. Long (eds.), *Classroom-Oriented Research in Second Language Acquisition*, Newbury House, Rowley, Mass., 268–285.
Mehan, H.: 1979, *Learning Lessons: Social Organization in the Classroom*, Harvard University Press, Cambridge, Mass.
Moskowitz, G.: 1967, 'The FLint system: An observational tool for the foreign language class', in A. Simon & E.G. Boyer (eds.), *Mirrors for Behaviour: An Anthology of Class-*

room *Observation Instruments*, Center for the Study of Teaching, Temple University, Philadelphia, 1–15.

Norman, K. (ed.): 1992, *Thinking Voices*, Hodder & Stoughton, London.

Nunan, D.: 1996, 'Hidden voices: Insiders' perspectives on classroom interaction', in K. Bailey & D. Nunan (eds.), *Voices from the Language Classroom*, Cambridge University Press, New York, 41–56.

Pica, T. & Doughty, C.: 1985, 'Input and interaction in the communicative language classroom: A comparison of teacher-fronted and group activities', in S.M. Gass & C.G. Madden (eds.), *Input and Second Language Acquisition*, Newbury House, Rowley Mass., 115–132.

Plough, I. & Gass, S.: 1993, 'Interlocutor and task familiarity: Effects on interactional structure', in G. Crookes & S. Gass (eds.), *Tasks and Language Learning: Integrating Theory and Practice*, Multilingual Matters, Clevedon, 35–56.

Richards, J. & Lockhart, C.: 1994, *Reflective Teaching in Second Language Classrooms*, Cambridge University Press, New York.

Rogoff, B. & Gardner, W.: 1984, 'Adult guidance in cognitive development', in B. Rogoff & J. Lave (eds.), *Everyday Cognition: Its Development in Social Contexts*, Harvard University Press, Cambridge, MA.

Rommetveit, R.: 1974, *On Message Structure*, Wiley, New York.

Sacks, H., Schegloff, E. & Jefferson, G.: 1974, 'Towards a simplest systematics for the organization of turn-taking for conversation', *Language* 50(4), 698–735.

Sato, C.: 1982, 'Ethnic styles in classroom discourse', in M. Hines & W. Rutherford (eds.), *On TESOL '81*, TESOL, Washington, DC.

Seliger, H.W.: 1983, 'Learner interaction in the classroom and its effect on language acquisition', in W. Seliger & M. H. Long (eds.), *Classroom Oriented Research in Second Language Acquisition*, Newbury House, H. Rowley, Mass., 246–267.

Sinclair, J. & Coulthard, M.: 1975, *Towards an Analysis of Discourse*, Oxford University Press, London.

Tharp, R. & Gallimore, R.: 1988, *Rousing Minds to Life*, Cambridge University Press, Cambridge.

Tsui, A.B.M.: 1995, *Introducing Classroom Interaction*, Penguin, London.

van Lier, L.: 1988, *The Classroom and the Language Learner*, Longman, London.

van Lier, L.: 1996, *Interaction in the Language Curriculum: Awareness, Autonomy and Authenticity*, Longman, London.

Varonis, E.M. & Gass, S.: 1986, 'Nonnative/nonnative conversations: A model for negotiation of meaning', *Applied Linguistics* 6, 71–90.

Vygotsky, L.: 1978, *Mind in Society*, Harvard University Press, Cambridge, MA.

Walker, R. & Adelman, C.: 1976, 'Strawberries', in M. Stubbs & S. Delamont (eds.), *Explorations in Classroom Observation*, John Wiley, Chicester.

Wittgenstein, L.: 1953, *Philosophical Investigations*, Blackwell, Oxford.

Wells, G.: 1985, *The Meaning Makers*, Hodder & Stoughton, London.

BRUCE MAYLATH

ASSESSORS' LANGUAGE AWARENESS IN THE EVALUATION OF ACADEMIC WRITING

To date, Language Awareness and the evaluation of academic writing have focused primarily on learners and how their awareness of language can help them achieve better results in their writing for the academy. Only secondarily have researchers asked how assessors' awareness of language might affect evaluations of academic writing. Since 'language awareness' has been thought to raise 'sensitivity to and conscious awareness' of language in action (van Lier, 1991, p. 532; citing Donmall, 1985), and since it has been seen as 'a means to bridge the consciousness gap within the individual' (James & Garrett, 1991, p. 5), one can consider research on writing assessors' evaluation practices as an attempt to gauge assessors' sensitivity and consciousness to language and its variation. To that end, the research in this area can be seen as attempts to answer the following questions: What factors influence writing assessors? How and why do these factors influence them? Are they aware of language and language variation? Are they aware of language's effects on their judgements?

EARLY DEVELOPMENTS

Two studies, one in Italy by Remondino (1959) and one in the USA by Diederich, French & Carlton (1961), mark the beginnings of research investigating the factors influencing assessors' evaluations of academic writing. Interestingly, the results of both studies pointed to nearly identical factors influencing assessors. As dubbed by Diederich (1964), they include, in descending order of popularity, 1) ideas ('clarity, quality, and fertility'), 2) mechanics, 3) organization, 4) wording, and 5) 'flavor' ('style, interest, and sincerity'). Assessors were found to base their judgements primarily and sometimes solely on one factor above all others. Which factor depended on the assessor. The highest correlations with the test-factor were mechanics and wording.

Of the two studies, the Diederich et al. (1961) study has gained far more recognition and influence on later studies, perhaps in part because of Diederich's high-visibility position at Educational Testing Service, in part because the language studied was English, in part because of wider dissemination (Diederich, 1964, 1974), and in part because of methodology that was conducted and repeated with a wider range of assessors. Diederich

L. van Lier and D. Corson (eds), Encyclopedia of Language and Education,
Volume 6: Knowledge about Language, 195–203.
© 1997 Kluwer Academic Publishers. Printed in the Netherlands.

et al. (1961) included not only college- and high school-level English teachers but also teachers in the social sciences and natural sciences, writers and editors, lawyers, and business executives.

For many years these two studies remained the lone landmarks in research in this area. Despite their lack of direct comment on language awareness – a term that had not yet come into use – they did provide a view of how textual features affect assessors' evaluations of academic writing. However, they did not reveal whether the assessors were unaware, semi-aware, or fully aware of the textual features' influence on the assessors' judgements.

MAJOR CONTRIBUTIONS

The 1970s saw the rise of both the Language Awareness movement, centered in Britain, and the field of composition, centered in North America. With the increased interest in written communication grew curiosity about teachers' evaluations of writing. The first published major study to move well beyond Remondino (1959) and Diederich et al. (1961) was Harris (1977), which produced some eye-opening results. Examining the assessment patterns of high school writing teachers in the USA, Harris discovered that 1) the criteria that teachers believed were most important for evaluating writing were not the criteria that influenced them most when they actually marked essays, 2) there was an inverse relationship between the criteria thought to be used and those actually used, 3) despite individual differences, teachers taken as a whole used similar criteria, 4) teachers concerned themselves primarily with 'technical correctness', and 5) changes in form affected the teachers' perception of quality of content. The study appeared to deliver a devastating repudiation of writing teachers' assessment and evaluation methods. Writing teachers seemed not only unaware of the full picture of language in the writing they read but also seemed unaware of their own intentions and behavior.

A more heartening study was conducted by Freedman (1979), who tested writing assessors' evaluations of rewritten essays in four categories: content, organization, sentence structure, and mechanics. Freedman found that content and organization affected ratings most, while mechanics and sentence structure had smaller effects. Freedman's study was important in that it turned attention again to some of the specific textual factors identified by Remondino (1959) and Diederich et al. (1961). Surprisingly, however, it omitted a factor that was gaining increased attention: wording and phrasing.

How a text is worded and phrased, at least in English, has been shown to be a potent factor in assessors' evaluations of academic writing, whether the assessors are consciously aware of variations in language or not. The first inklings within structured research that such was the case came to the fore in Sloan's (1978) informal experiment with 'plain' vs. 'erudite' vocabulary and in the groundbreaking Hake & Williams (1981) investigations of verbal and nominal styles. In an early report from the latter, Williams (1975) announced that the versions of papers written with vocabulary of mainly Romance origins were preferred by writing assessors over the versions using vocabulary with mainly Anglo-Saxon origins, despite the common classroom advice to avoid Romance words where Anglo-Saxon words will do. Similarly, the report of the full investigations (Hake & Williams, 1981) revealed that writing teachers at nearly every level of instruction tended to favor essays with nominalized sentences over similar versions with verbalized sentences, despite frequent classroom advice to prefer verbal over nominal styles. Hake & Williams concluded that, to many teachers, 'profound style = profound content' (1981, p. 440). The teachers gave no evidence that they were aware of how the variation in language had affected their evaluations.

At about the same time, other studies appeared to support what Hake & Williams were finding. Stewart & Grobe (1979) found that writing assessors' evaluations were influenced much more by an essay's length and absence of spelling errors than by syntactic maturity and mechanics. This study was then replicated by Grobe (1981), revealing similar results but also showing that teachers' perceptions of good writing were closely tied to what he termed 'vocabulary diversity'. Focusing on 'lexical maturity' and nominal complexity, Nielsen & Piché (1981) found that writing assessors favored essays with 'mature synonyms' over 'simple synonyms'. They concluded that 'the lexical factor exerts a significant effect on judged quality of writing' (p. 71). Later, reviewing research done to date on reading difficulty, Graves (1986) concurred: 'Writing that employs more mature vocabulary has repeatedly been judged as superior to that with less mature vocabulary' (p. 59). Although these studies did not define 'mature', 'simple', or 'diverse', Maylath (1996) took the terms as cues for Williams' (1975) distinction between Romance and Anglo-Saxon vocabulary, a distinction whose ramifications were laid bare in a series of studies Corson had conducted in the meantime. Best summed up in Corson (1995), these investigations suggested that students' writing containing high levels of Greco-Latinate vocabulary impressed assesors far more than writing with low levels. Refining earlier measuring instruments, and building especially on Corson's work, Maylath (1996) discovered that essays high in Greco-Latinate vocabulary tended to receive higher evaluations from novice writing teachers, while versions high in Anglo-Saxon vocabulary tended to receive higher evaluations from veteran writing teachers. Through interviews, Maylath identified increased level of security as the factor that turned preference for the Greco-Latinate vocabulary to preference for the Anglo-Saxon. Notably, while the teachers revealed some awareness that the language in the essays varied, few were aware of the degree to which the variations had influenced their evaluations.

Another line of research has investigated the effect of dialectal features on writing assessors' evaluations. The vast majority of studies in this area have been finding that dialect features spotted by writing assessors within a text have little influence on evaluation, although assessors' awareness of the student-writer's ethnicity can have an overwhelming effect on the evaluation an essay receives. Perhaps the most cited among these studies are a pair led by Piché (Piché, Michlin, Rubin & Sullivan, 1977; Piché, Rubin, Turner & Michlin, 1978), which, focusing on African-American dialect features, overturned assumptions held by previous language-attitude researchers. The Piché investigations concluded 'that a general ethnocentric bias exists which affects teachers' judgments of the quality of students' composition, but that it bears no close relation to specific linguistic features of such writing' (Piché et al., 1978, p. 116f.). In a more comprehensive investigation of African-American rhetoric in writing, Balester (1993) appears to have found similar results in an informal test of writing teachers, as have Krater, Zeni & Cason (1994) when they explored the reasons why male African-American children were failing at writing. Language awareness alone appears inconsequential when faced with deep ethnic bias, a conclusion with which Chandler, Robinson & Noyes (1988) appear to concur based on their studies of language teachers in Britain. Meanwhile, in France, Dannequin (1987) found teachers denying any recognition of dialectal features and demanding that conventions of standard written French be applied even to children's speech, while in Italy, native English-speaking teachers of Italian university students expected essays in English to conform to British and North American rhetorical conventions, unaware that conventions in Italian differ markedly or that most testing in Italian universities is conducted orally. Taken as a whole, the research findings seem to indicate that language awareness must be broadened to rhetorical and cultural awareness, if it is to affect the evaluation of writing.

WORK IN PROGRESS

Work in this area has occurred only sporadically in the past. The present appears no different. At the time of this writing, a telephone and e-mail survey of editors of scholarly journals to which researchers might submit their research on this topic revealed that nothing has been submitted for publication in recent months.

Nevertheless, the survey did uncover a study underway on university-level writing assessors' awareness of 'academic register' in their students' writing and how the register's inclusion, absence, or 'hyperfluency' influences evaluation. This study by Neal in the USA builds on an earlier investigation conducted by Balester (1991).

In addition, Maylath is completing a study of tertiary-level technical writing instructors that replicates the one he conducted earlier (1996) with tertiary-level general writing instructors. Although technical writing has not traditionally been viewed as academic writing, it is increasingly gaining a place in the academic curriculum in several locations, most notably in the Canadian province of Manitoba, where Ronald Blicq has led efforts to include it at all levels of education.

PROBLEMS AND DIFFICULTIES

Research on writing assessors' awareness of language and its effect on evaluation is scant when compared to the research on learners' awareness of language and assessment/evaluation generally. The reasons why are several but can be narrowed to these: Teachers are more difficult than students to recruit as research subjects. Not only do they number far fewer than students, but they are more scattered; they rarely are part of a captive audience (as are students in a classroom); they often expect some sort of remuneration for their participation, thereby driving up research costs; and they sometimes display resistance to acting as subjects. Indeed, because of these difficulties, several of the studies cited above relied for their subjects on students training to be teachers, and then assumed that the results would hold valid for teachers of any longevity. However, studies using teachers already trained might find that the results differ radically from those obtained with student-teachers, as Maylath's (1996) research suggests.

Gathering research in this area from foreign language teaching is especially difficult, given the field's emphasis on speech rather than writing. Commenting on the teaching of French in England, Crawshaw (1984) says that '... the increasing priority given to the oral over the written language has had as one of its most glaring consequences the denigration of formal linguistic knowledge as a necessary component of foreign language acquisition' (p. 67). The same could be said of foreign language teacher training. That the foreign language might be English appears not to matter: '... it is true that many teachers of EFL concern themselves little with writing at all' (Brumfit, 1980, p. 9). When a language field neglects the teaching of writing, it is a rare researcher who will attempt to investigate assessment practices of writing in that field.

Perhaps an even greater barrier to research in this area is the general lack of awareness of Language Awareness. Even though many of the studies cited above were conducted in the USA, the phrase 'Language Awareness' is rarely heard or used in America. Indeed, not one of the studies cited uses the term in its published reports. The program schedules for the 1995 and 1996 conventions of the Conference on College Composition and Communication, the chief organization in the USA for teachers and researchers of academic writing at the tertiary level, do not list a single session using the phrase 'Language Awareness' in its title, nor do any of the sessions listed deal with research on writing assessors' language awareness in the evaluation of academic essays. One has to go back to the 1994 program to find even one (a conference presentation of Maylath's [1996] findings). Of course, a phrase does not have to be in common currency for the topic which the phrase names to be researched, as the presence of the studies cited above indicates.

Nevertheless, research in this area has been at least partially stymied by a lack of attention to the Language Awareness movement and its goals, programs, and successes, even in Britain, where the movement originated. On the one hand, Balboni (1993) reports that the teaching of two foreign languages in middle schools in the north of Italy 'has proved a major factor in including teachers of Italian as well ... in [giving attention to] language awareness' (p. 188). On the other hand, Candelier (1992) says that while secondary-level teachers of foreign languages in France have gained awareness of language, 'it is very likely that primary school teachers or teachers of French (as mother tongue) have not acquired a similar aware- ness' (p. 27). Van Lier (1991) notes both the lack of attention to language awareness in the USA and the 'serious inadequacies in language education in the British teacher training establishment as well' for their dampening effect (p. 529f.), a view that Brumfit (1991) echoes for the United King- dom. In addition, Mittins (1991) calls attention to a semi-official trend in the UK to shy away from focusing Language Awareness assessment and research on teachers and to keep the focus solely on learners.

Despite Hawkins' (1987) assertion that 'since 1981 interest in 'aware- ness of language' has grown rapidly', at least in Britain, one has to admit that interest in the movement has waned in many countries. Reports in Evans (1985) indicate that interest in Language Awareness in Canada trailed off by the 1980s, while Quinn & Trounce (1985) state that '... the Australian Language Awareness movement peaked in 1976 and declined steadily after that ... ' (p. 132), a result, perhaps, of a lack of appropriate teacher education. Of course, any movement can be revived, but until the Language Awareness movement resuscitates more fully, research on assessors' language awareness in the evaluation of academic writing is likely to remain thin and sporadic.

FUTURE DIRECTIONS

With the Language Awareness movement poised for a possible revival, research in the area of writing assessment and evaluation stands a chance to widen and deepen, and, of course, more research bears the promise that findings will affect assessment and evaluation practice. Of the factors identified by Remondino (1959) and Diederich et al. (1961), wording remains the area most closely identified with linguistics and language awareness, while such factors as ideas and organization are more closely linked with rhetorical awareness. Although linguistic awareness of wording deserves more investigation – with teachers at more levels and in more disciplines, with readers at large, and with more languages than English – writing assessment research is likely to veer more and more away from language variation and awareness and toward awareness of ethnicity, culture, and rhetoric, a move already well underway in North America. Even the research in such seemingly obvious language areas as the effect of dialect features on writing assessment has been proving more fruitful when directed toward cultural and rhetorical sources and causes, rather than linguistic ones. Other linguistic features, such as syntax, may perhaps draw renewed attention, although studies to date on such features as syntactic maturity have not shown that such features have as much influence on assessment practices as do other features, like wording or ideas. (The studies of syntactic maturity done in the 1960s and 1970s by Kellogg Hunt, Roy O'Donnell, and Frank O'Hare, among others, focused on learners while merely assuming that writing assessors valued syntactic complexity.)

The larger question may be whether research can change writing assessment practice substantially. As noted in the 'Problems and Difficulties' section above, teacher education programs have not yet proved adept at incorporating linguistics and language awareness research to date, yet it is in just such programs that changes in practice are most likely to be realized. Even with greater success in teacher education programs, however, writing assessors' behavior has been shown to stand dismayingly at odds with the assessors' conscious beliefs and intentions regarding their behavior. It remains to be seen whether language awareness, not to mention awareness of the discrepancies between assessors' intentions and actual behavior, can change practice or whether assessors' deeply held subconscious beliefs and biases will cause assessors to resist and prevent change.

The University of Memphis
USA

REFERENCES

Balboni, P.E.: 1993, 'Language awareness in the national curriculum for language education for Italy', *Language Awareness* 2, 187–192.
Balester, V.M.: 1991, 'Hyperfluency and the growth of linguistic resources', *Language and Education* 5, 81–94.
Balester, V.M.: 1993, *Cultural Divide: A Study of African-American College-Level Writers*, Boynton/Cook, Portsmouth NH.
Brumfit, C.J.: 1980, *Problems and Principles in English Teaching*, Pergamon Press, Oxford.

Brumfit, C.J.: 1991, 'Language awareness in teacher education', in C. James & P. Garrett (eds.), *Language Awareness in the Classroom*. Applied Linguistics and Language Study series, C. N. Candlin (general ed.), Longman, London and New York, 24–39.

Candelier, M.: 1992, 'Language awareness and language policy in the European context: A French point of view', *Language Awareness* 1, 27–32.

Chandler, P., Robinson, W. P. & Noyes, P.: 1988, 'The level of linguistic knowledge and awareness amongst students training to be primary teachers', *Language and Education* 2, 161–173.

Corson, D.: 1995, *Using English Words*, Kluwer Academic Publishers, Dordrecht, The Netherlands.

Crawshaw, R.: 1984, 'Information, awareness and context as factors in foreign language learning', *British Journal of Language Teaching* 22, 67–73.

Dannequin, C.: 1987, 'Les enfants baillonnés (gagged children): The teaching of French as mother tongue in elementary school', *Language and Education* 1, 15–31.

Diederich, P.B.: 1964, 'Problems and possibilities of research in the teaching of written composition', in D.H. Russell, E.J. Farrell, M.J. Early, D.V. Gunderson, R. Braddock & J. R. Squire (eds.), *Research Design and the Teaching of English: Proceedings of the San Francisco Conference 1963*, National Council of Teachers of English, Champaign IL, 52–73.

Diederich, P.B.: 1974, *Measuring Growth in English*, National Council of Teachers of English, Urbana IL.

Diederich, P.B., French, J.W. & Carlton, S.T.: 1961, *Factors in Judgments of Writing Ability*, Research Bulletin RB-61-15, Educational Testing Service, Princeton NJ.

Donmall, B.G. (ed.): 1985, *Language Awareness: National Council for Language in Education Reports and Papers, 6*, Centre for Information on Language Teaching and Research, London, 132–142.

Evans, P.J.A. (ed.): 1985, *Directions and Misdirections in English Evaluation*, Canadian Council of Teachers of English, Ottawa.

Freedman, S.W.: 1979, 'How characteristics of student essays influence teachers' evaluations', *Journal of Educational Psychology* 71, 328–338.

Graves, M.F.: 1986, 'Vocabulary learning and instruction', *Review of Research in Education* 13, 58–89.

Grobe, C.H.: 1981, 'Syntactic maturity, mechanics, and vocabulary as predictors of quality ratings', *Research in the Teaching of English* 15, 75–85.

Hake, R.L. & Williams, J.M.: 1981, 'Style and its consequences: Do as I do, not as I say', *College English* 43, 433–451.

Hargan, N.: 1995, 'Misguided expectations: EFL teachers' attitudes towards Italian university students' written work', *Language and Education* 9, 223–232.

Harris, W.H.: 1977, 'Teacher response to student writing: A study of the response patterns of high school English teachers to determine the basis for teacher judgment of student writing', *Research in the Teaching of English* 11, 175–185.

Hawkins, E.W.: 1987, *Modern Languages in the Curriculum* (revised edition), Cambridge University Press, Cambridge.

James, C. & Garrett, P.: 1991, 'The scope of language awareness', in C. James & P. Garrett (eds.), *Language Awareness in the Classroom*, Applied Linguistics and Language Study series, C.N. Candlin (general ed.), Longman, London and New York, 3–20.

Krater, J., Zeni, J. & Cason, N. D.: 1994, *Mirror Images: Teaching Writing in Black and White*, Heinemann, Portsmouth NH.

Maylath, B.A.R.: 1996, 'Words make a difference: The effects of greco-latinate and Anglo-Saxon variation on college writing instructors', *Research in the Teaching of English* 30, 220–247.

Mittins, W. H.: 1991, *Language Awareness for Teachers*, Open University Press, Milton Keynes, England, and Philadelphia PA.

Neal, H.M.: 1996, *Hyperfluency, Academic Register, and the Acquisition of Academic Discourse*, Unpublished manuscript.

Piché, G.L., Michlin, M.L., Rubin, D.L. & Sullivan, A.: 1977, 'Effects of dialect-ethnicity, social class and quality of written compositions on teachers' subjective evaluations of children', *Communication Monographs* 44, 60–72.

Piché, G.L., Rubin, D.L., Turner, L.J. & Michlin, M.L.: 1978, 'Teachers' subjective evaluations of standard and black nonstandard English compositions: A study of written language and attitudes', *Research in the Teaching of English* 12, 107–118.

Quinn, T.J. & Trounce, M.: 1985, 'Some aspects of Australian experience with language awareness courses', in B.G. Donmall (ed.), *Language Awareness: National Council for Language in Education Reports and Papers*, 6, Centre for Information on Language Teaching and Research, London, 132–142.

Remondino, C.: 1959, 'A factorial analysis of the evaluation of scholastic compositions in the mother tongue', *British Journal of Educational Psychology* 29, 242–251.

Sloan, G.: 1978, 'Predilections for plethoric prose', *College English* 39, 860–865.

Stewart, M.F. & Grobe, C.H.: 1979, 'Syntactic maturity, mechanics of writing and teachers' quality ratings', *Research in the Teaching of English* 13, 207–215.

van Lier, L.: 1991, 'Language awareness: The common ground between linguist and language teacher', in J.E. Alatis (ed.), *Georgetown University Round Table on Languages and Linguisitics 1991*, Georgetown University Press, Washington DC, 528–546.

Williams, J.L.: 1975, 'Nominal and verbal styles: Some affective consequences', *Journal of the Midwest Modern Language Association* 8.2, 63. (Presented as a conference paper at the 1975 Midwest Modern Language Association convention, 7 November, Chicago IL).

SALLY MITCHELL

TEACHING, LEARNING AND ASSESSING ARGUMENT

In broad terms, studies in argument can be ranged on a continuum between formal 'internal' notions of argument (e.g. 'evidence supporting a conclusion'), to argument as action aimed at belief and behaviour within communicative situations. A number of divisions can be discerned in these studies. The first stems from early Greek thought and results in, on the one hand, the philosophical tradition in which language is used transparently in the pursuit of truth and, on the other, a rhetorical tradition concerned with the style and arrangement of language for the production of effects. The second is roughly a division between 'nature and nurture': the nature view, in various forms generally held by psychologists, is that the ability to argue is acquired developmentally; whilst the nurturers (generally educationalists) are concerned with the way argument may be developed through teaching and learning strategies (see the review by Costello).

EARLY DEVELOPMENTS

The distinctions outlined above have tended to blur as researchers and teachers have drawn from the various traditions contributing to the study of argument. Two early trends are discernible.

One is a move away from normative definitions of argument influenced by the rules of formal logic in philosophy. In the 1960s, it began to be recognised that principles of formal logic did not account for everyday extended arguments. 'Informal logic' turned attention to 'real' arguments, though methodologically, it continues to reconstruct examples according to logical principles (e.g. Fisher, 1988). Social and psychological factors, such as the role of belief and the impact of communicative situations, began to be included in accounts of argument (Voss & Means, 1991).

Recognition of the non-equivalence of logic and argument is associated with what has been called the 'rhetorical turn', beginning with Burke in the 1950s and emphasising the suasive nature and communicative functions of language. Important landmarks here are Toulmin's (1958) theory of argument, which, by defining validity in terms of *effectiveness* within a given field of operation, shifted the emphasis from rationality to 'the reasonable'; and that of Perelman & Olbrechts-Tyteca (1958; trans. 1969) which emphasises the dialogic dimension of argument.

The other discernible trend is the influence of psychology on language education. For instance, Piaget's linking of reasoning abilities with formal

L. van Lier and D. Corson (eds), Encyclopedia of Language and Education,
Volume 6: Knowledge about Language, 205–213.
© *1997 Kluwer Academic Publishers. Printed in the Netherlands.*

logical principles and explicitness about interpropositional relations was used as a measure in assessing students' written arguments. Forms of language use came to be associated with certain stages in cognitive development. Moffett (1968), for example, posited a hierarchy of discourse types: from 'what is happening' and 'what happened' (dramatic and narrative modes) to 'what may happen' (argument and theorising modes). Narrative was associated with the localised 'centred' view of the young child whilst argument came only with 'decentring'. The argumentative essay in particular was associated with high level cognitive skills and, in turn, was a measure of 'being literate' (see Street, 1984). Though the Piagetian influence is still apparent in some studies of argument, more social and constructivist models have also emerged. These have often promoted talk and oral argument as important means by which learning takes place (e.g. Barnes, Britton & Rosen, 1969), and have also created interest in the dialogic aspects of writing.

MAJOR CONTRIBUTIONS

The developmental connection between narrative and argument has been challenged by pointing out the ability of even very young children to engage in argument, at least orally (e.g. Wilkinson, 1990). In addition, it has been suggested that the category of argument can be more widely defined as a function as well as a mode of discourse and that argument can, for example, be embedded within narrative (see a collection edited by Andrews, 1989).

Dolz, Pasquier & Bronckart (1993) dispense with a developmental relation, pointing out that narrative and argument have specific discursive characteristics that can be learned independently. The concern then is to trace the developmental stages *within* argument from its early manifestations as childish speech to the production of substantial written texts. Brassart (1989), for instance, observes the development of the ability to use counter-arguments in children between eight and thirteen years old; and Berrill (1992) looks at the different ways in which egocentricity features in the writing of eleven year old and university students. Coirier & Golder (1993) describe three stages, from no stance being taken in relation to a topic through to the taking of a stance supported by two related arguments. In an experimental study, they show that the third stage is only produced by a large percentage of students at age fifteen to sixteen.

Such findings echo those of large-scale studies of writing abilities in the 1970s and 80s which brought to light problems in the written argument of secondary age students. In Canada, Freedman & Pringle (1985) studied the writing abilities of school children in Grades 5, 8 and 12 using a definition of argument text as having 'a clear thesis ... substantiated logically and through illustration'. They found a clear development over the age range, but considered there to be a confusion between argumentative and persuasive discourse. It was recommended that students have 'more exposure to good argumentative models at all levels' (p. 125).

In Britain, studies by Britton et al. (1975) and Gorman et al. (1988) noted that students were more adept at additive ordering in their writing than logical selection and that 'breakdown' tended to occur when argument structure was attempted. However, Britton et al. also noted that the writing students produced did not necessarily reflect their innate abilities but was heavily influenced by the requirements of the school system. Dixon & Stratta (1986) have taken up this point and challenged the contrived and formulaic opportunities for written argument in the classroom. They suggest that argument should be a means of discovering as well as defending positions and they offer a checklist for assessing development.

Acknowledging that writing – and, indeed, argument – is shaped by social and cultural forces as much as by the stages in cognitive development leads to overlapping areas of interest. First, there is interest in the process of writing itself, including how different writers interpret the *same* task as, for example, an invitation to summarise material or to put forward an argument (Flower et al., 1990). Second, there is interest in the cultural or institutional salience of texts: what makes acceptable academic discourse. An example here would be the study by Mathison (in Costello & Mitchell, 1995) which showed that teachers rated texts which offered negative critiques of sources more highly than those which took a positive stance towards them. Other studies (e.g. Greene, 1995), show how student writers' sense of personal authority in relation to views expressed in authoritative texts can effect their ability to construct an argument. In such studies, the notion of 'authorship' is frequently used to describe the argumentative goal of participating in a scholarly conversation. An in-depth investigation of how argument constitutes participation, together with strategies for helping students, is recorded in Geisler (1994). Comparative approaches also shed light on the cultural specificity of argument practices. Watanabe (1993), for example, identifies different characteristics in the way American and Japanese students structure arguments in group discussions.

In terms of students' own awareness of language practices differing pedagogical emphases can be discerned. In Australia, there has been concern that 'progressivist pedagogy' (privileging narrative) fails to give students access to socially powerful genres such as argument. As a consequence moves have been made to identify and make explicit the grammatical features of curriculum genres (in the case of argument these are 'exposition' and 'discussion'), and to develop approaches which teachers can use in the classroom. Explanations of the genres, teaching approaches and illustrated accounts of what can be expected at progressive stages of schooling are given in a number of publications (e.g. Knapp & Watkins, 1994). A shift has occurred to describe genres and their grammars as enacting processes rather than textual products: so the most recent work describes 'the genre of arguing' rather than 'argument'.

In Britain moves to develop language awareness in schools have been criticised as naturalising language practices and as promoting social integration in the interests of existing social norms. Critical Language Awareness, on the other hand, aims to place students in a position to work for improved language practices by developing their 'consciousness of the socially structured and structuring nature of discourse' (Clark et al., 1991, p. 46: see the review by Clark & Ivanič). There are particular resonances here for the teaching and learning of argument. On the one hand CLA is rhetorical in its approach to language as purposeful; on the other, its emancipatory goal may suggest the possibility of escape from 'dirty' rhetoric into 'truer' ways of communicating.

It is reasoning rather than rhetoric that is the primary concern of the expanding and influential critical thinking and philosophy for children movements, which have produced studies and materials to show that children can, at very young ages, engage in philosophical modes of reasoning (e.g. Costello, in Costello & Mitchell, 1995). This approach was combined with the more rhetorical English teaching tradition in an action research project for primary and secondary teachers based at Hull University from 1991–1993 (summarised in Andrews, 1995). Both Costello and Andrews, the joint directors of the project, are interested in the implications of argument for democracy and citizenship (see Costello, 1997).

WORK IN PROGRESS

Argument as a form of 'social action' has an important role to play in the collaborative work of a community literacy centre and Carnegie Mellon University in Pittsburgh. Here urban teenagers join with mentors to construct texts, videos and 'community conversations' which address the issues they feel are important (Long et al. in Costello & Mitchell, 1995). They make use of argument strategies, such as 'rival hypothesis thinking', that are characteristic of academic discourse.

Academic discourse came under scrutiny in a study of argument (both spoken and written) which took place at the University of Hull from 1991–1994 (Mitchell, 1994; Mitchell in Costello & Mitchell, 1995; Andrews, 1995). The project took a broadly ethnographic approach to a number of disciplines in post-compulsory education, taking account of the social, contextual and epistemological factors which appeared to shape the nature and role of argument in learning. It concluded that argument played an important role in developing disciplinary identity, but that the forms it took were often conservative (for example, the 'default genre' of the essay; see Womack, 1993). A number of alternative forms for writing were explored.

A further finding of this project was that though the term 'argument' was highly valued in academic contexts, it was rarely the subject of explicit discussion in teaching, nor did teachers have many strategies to allow it to develop. Further funding has now become available for another project which aims to address these issues and to find ways of 'Improving the Quality of Argument in Higher Education'. This new project is based at Middlesex University, London and runs from 1995–1998. A collaborative approach has been adopted in which teaching staff work with the researcher to explore problems and develop materials and strategies that have practical pedagogical applications.

A more formally experimental approach to developing teaching strategies is being trialled in Switzerland. An article in a recent issue of the journal *Argumentation* records how an instructional approach combining a situational view of argument with aspects of formal text organisation was tested with 2 experimental groups of 11–12 year olds (Dolz, 1996). Analysis of the results showed, amongst other things, that the approach increased the length of the students' texts, the number of arguments employed and the degree of orientation towards the addressee. In addition, each task produced differing argumentative demands. Dolz concludes that systematic teaching of argument should begin early, but that if it is to be effective teachers will need to improve their specific knowledge of what argumentative discourse entails.

Much the same belief lay behind the 'Language in the National Curriculum' project which was developed in Britain between 1989 and 1992 as an inservice programme for teachers. An example of how argument was addressed in a primary classroom is given by Monk (1992). Although the LINC project faltered through lack of government support, efforts to meet the needs of teachers continue, an example being the current project to transform the Australian genre materials for use in the British educational context.

Other practical work to improve the quality of argument includes a project at the University of Utrecht from 1997–1999 where computer interfaces are being developed that will facilitate interaction between learners working on argumentative tasks. The work is forward-looking in so far as it is felt that the roles of collaboration and telematic environments will become increasingly significant in learning.

Research continues on the role of argument in current educational contexts. Projects underway in Britain include a study at King's College London, which assesses the extent to which secondary science students engage in argument in group discussions and the degree to which the teacher's framing of the activity supports this. (For earlier work on science see Boulter & Gilbert, in Costello & Mitchell, 1995.) At Lancaster University, researchers are looking at the full range of writing produced by students at the upper junior level. The study will provide useful comparative data with the earlier studies of writing in 1975 and 1988, shedding light on the changes made by the introduction of a national curriculum in Britain and the current place of argument in the work set for students at this level.

At a more theoretical level Coirier (1996) offers a useful summary of experimental work in psychology and linguistics within Europe and the recent issue of *Argumentation* referred to above also contains articles on this work. For example, Feilke's work on syntactical development is challenging the long held association of writing with explicit referencing and logical entailment by revealing that the argument texts of older students are characterised less by syntactical complexity and more by increased framing and contextualising of the subject matter.

PROBLEMS AND DIFFICULTIES

A major difficulty when addressing the teaching and learning of argument resides in finding consistent meanings and uses for the term. In its everyday uses 'argument' is frequently associated with passion and heated debate, whilst in more specialised contexts, it is the recourse to reason that distinguishes argument from 'mere' persuasion. Some people prefer to retain this distinction; others include persuasion within the category of argument. Argument can also be thought of either as a mode of discourse ('this text has the features that show it to be an argument') or as a function (in which case, one could ask of a *poem* for instance: 'What does this argue?').

Within educational settings argument can be constrained by the powerful agendas of the institution, convention and the teacher. For example, though argument may be thought of as adversarial or at least as a means of exposing difference, consensus is often the aim of the teacher who sets up a group discussion. Then there is the difficulty of moving from spoken situations – where an interlocutor is present – to written argument where a point of view must be sustained and alternative positions engaged. (See Coirier (1996) for the heavy 'cognitive load' imposed by the combination of argumentative and textualising operations). Beyond this, the written forms that argument takes in schools often bear no relation to those of 'real life'.

How to translate research results into knowledge and techniques that are usable by teachers is always a problem. A number of studies have concluded that teachers – of all subjects, not just of language – should have clearer linguistic and procedural knowledge of argument. Concerns are raised, however, that providing textual prototypes will leave writers little scope for creativity and experimentation and may exclude consideration of their cultural contexts and purposes of texts. It is possible, for example, to take a feminist standpoint towards conventional forms of argument (based on the notion of a unified thesis), and argue that they are patriarchal and exclude or subsume dissident voices. Yet developmental models often use the conventional 'essayist' form as an assessment yardstick.

Those who advocate explicit teaching argue that without some knowledge of how language works to achieve certain ends, students have no basis from which to exercise real creativity, nor to meet the very real demands that academic institutions make of them. The difficulty lies in deciding what constitutes appropriate knowledge for argument and then in giving teachers a level of competence and confidence to use it in their classrooms. In Australia there has been funding for the training of teachers, but this is by no means the case elsewhere. Nor would such a move be met without resistance, since switching attention to language forms and ways of processing information will inevitably be to the detriment of covering content.

FUTURE DIRECTIONS

Although there is no consensus about what knowledge teachers need in helping their students learn to argue, interest in explicit approaches to teaching are growing. In part this is a recognition of cultural diversity in classrooms, which makes tacit knowledge amongst students harder to assume. At the same time, in a rapidly changing world, the shift away from subject content is highlighting skills such as 'communication' and 'problem solving' which are associated with argument. In Britain, where there is now a mass system of higher education, tutors of English for Academic Purposes are increasingly called upon to support native as well as non-native speakers in developing academic skills amongst which argument is highly valued.

At the same time, and due to some of the same factors, standard traditional forms of argument are being challenged and greater diversity introduced. There is growing interest in the differences made by culture and gender to the way argument is conducted. Additionally, increased awareness of workplace requirements is highlighting a need for students to be able to develop arguments that address a wider range of audiences and to present a case in speech as well as writing. Critiques of the essay and its conflation with the highest forms of cognitive development are also opening up new possibilities for writing, though diversity will make the job of assessing more difficult. Andrews (1995) argues that exploiting the dialogic potentials of writing will bring with it a shift in the role of teachers from judge to interlocutor.

A major potential for future work will come with multimedia technologies which enable words, pictures and sound to be combined in an interactive environment. In challenging ideas of what constitutes text, these will perhaps force an expanded view of argument which incorporates the visual as well as the verbal. Diversification may of course present a challenge to the project of explicit teaching, since it will set in flux present notions of what counts as argument.

Middlesex University
England

REFERENCES

Andrews, R, (ed.): 1989, *Narrative and Argument*, Open University Press, Milton Keynes.
Andrews, R.: 1995, *Teaching and Learning Argument*, Cassell, London.
Barnes, D., Britton, J. & Rosen, H.: 1969, *Language, the Learner and the School*, Penguin, Harmondsworth.
Berrill, D.: 1992 'Issues of audience: Egocentrism revisited', in Andrews, R. (ed.), *Rebirth of Rhetoric*, Routledge, London, 81–101.
Brassart, D.G.: 1989, 'La gestion des contre-arguments dans le texte argumentatif ecrit chez les eleves de 8 a 12 ans et des adultes competents', *European Journal of the Psychology of Education* 1, 51–69.
Britton, J., Burgess, T., Martin., McLeod, A. & Rosen, H.: 1975, *The Development of Writing Abilities (11–18)*, Macmillan, London.
Clark, R., Fairclough, N., Ivanic, R. & Martin-Jones, M.: 1991 'Critical language awareness. Part 2: Towards critical alternatives', *Language and Education* 5, 41–54.
Coirier, P.: 1996 'Composing argumentative texts: cognitive and/or textual complexity', in G. Rijlaarsdam, A. van den Berg & M. Couzijn (eds.), *Theories, Models and Methodology in Writing Research*, Amsterdam University Press, Amsterdam, 317–338.
Coirier, P. & Golder, C.: 1993, 'Writing argumentative text: A developmental study of the acquisition of supporting structures', *European Journal of Psychology ofEducation* 2, 169–181.
Costello, P.J. & Mitchell, S. (eds.): 1995, *Competing and Consensual Voices: The Theory and Practice of Argument*, Multilingual Matters, Clevedon.
Costello, P.J.: 1997, *Liberating Children's Minds; Education, Citizenship and Critical Thinking*, Multilingual Matters, Clevedon.
Dixon, J. & Stratta, L.: 1986 'Argument and the teaching of English: A critical analysis', in A. Wilkinson (ed.), *The Writing of Writing*, Open University Press, Milton Keynes, 8–21.
Dolz, J., Pasquier, A. & Bronckart, J.P.: 1993, 'L'aquisition des discours: Emergence d'une compétence ou apprentissage de capacités langagieres?', *Etudes de Linguistique Appliquée*, 89.
Dolz, J.: 1996, 'Learning argumentative capacities: A study of the effects of a systematic and intensive teaching of argumentative discourse on 11–12 year-old children', *Argumentation* 10(2), 226–251.
Fisher, A.: 1988, *The Logic of Real Arguments*, Cambridge University Press, Cambridge.
Flower, L., Stein, V., Ackerman, J., Kantz, M.J., McCormick, K. & Peck, W.C.: 1990, *Reading to Write: Exploring a Cognitive and Social Process*, Oxford University Press, New York.
Freedman, A. & Pringle, I.: 1985, *A Comparative Study of Writing Abilities in Two Modes at the Grade 5, 8 and 12 Levels*, Ministry of Education, Ontario.
Geisler, C.: 1994, *Academic Literacy and the Nature of Expertise: Reading, Writing, and Knowing in Academic Philosophy*, Lawrence Erlbaum Associates, New Jersey.
Gorman, T.P., White, J., Brooks, G., MacLure, M. & Kispel, A.: 1988, *Language Performance in Schools: A Review of APU Language Monitoring 1979–83*, HMSO, London.

Greene, S.: 1995 'Making sense of my own ideas: The problems of authorship in a beginning writing classroom', *Written Communication* 12(2), 186–219.

Knapp, P. & Watkins, M.: 1994, *Context/Text/Grammar*, Text Productions, Broadway NSW.

Mitchell, S.: 1994, *Teaching and Learning Argument in Sixth Forms and Higher Education: Final Report*, University of Hull, Hull.

Moffett, J.: 1968, *Teaching the Universe of Discourse*, Houghton Press, Boston.

Monk, J.: 1992, 'The language of argument in the writing of young children', *Looking into Language: Classroom Approaches to Knowledge About Language*, R. Bain, B. Fitzgerald & M. Taylor, Hodder & Stoughton, London.

Perelman, C. & Olbrechts-Tyteca, L.: 1969, *The New Rhetoric: A Treatise on Argumentation*, J. Wilkinson & P. Weaver (trans. from French, 1958), University of Notre Dame Press, Notre Dame.

Street, B.: 1984, *Literacy in Theory and Practice*, Cambridge University Press, Cambridge.

Toulmin, S.E.: 1958, *The Uses of Argument*, Cambridge University Press, Cambridge.

Voss, J.F. & Means M.L.: 1991, 'Learning to reason via instruction in argumentation', *Learning and Instruction* 1, 337–350.

Watanabe, S.: 1993, 'Cultural differences and framing: American and Japanese group discussions', in D. Tannen (ed.), *Framing in Discourse*, Oxford University Press, New York, 176–209.

Wilkinson, A.: 1990, 'Argument as a primary act of mind', *English in Education* 24(1), 10–22.

Womack, P.: 1993, 'What are essays for?', *English in Education* 27(2), 42–59.

Section 5

Critical Language Awareness

ROMY CLARK & ROZ IVANIČ

CRITICAL DISCOURSE ANALYSIS AND EDUCATIONAL CHANGE

Critical Discourse Analysis (C.D.A.) can contribute to educational change for individuals, for institutions and for societies. At the personal level, C.D.A. aims to empower learners by providing them with a critical analytical framework to help them reflect on their own language experiences and practices and on the language practices of others in the institutions of which they are a part and in the wider society within which they live. Learners have to decide whether to accommodate to all or some of the dominant practices (including the discoursal and generic conventions) which they encounter, or to challenge these by adopting alternative practices. By turning awareness into action – by choosing to adopt alternative practices in the face of pressure to conform to norms – people can contribute to their own emancipation and that of others by opening up new possibilities for linguistic behaviour. These new possibilities can contribute to change not only in the classroom but also in the wider institution of education and within societies as a whole.

C.D.A. is also a powerful means of analyzing and explaining change in educational practices. For example, Fairclough's (1995) critical analysis of policy documents and educational promotional material can lay bare the increasing tendency towards the commodification of education in the UK (see the review by Wortham in this volume). This use of C.D.A. makes the issue of critical language awareness-raising in educational settings all the more urgent.

Before discussing early developments of C.D.A. and its applications in the classroom, it is important to explain the use of the word 'critical' in relation to discourse analysis. According to Fairclough (1992a), it means:

> ...not just describing discursive practices but also showing how discourse is shaped by relations of power and ideologies and the constructive effects discourse has upon social identities, social relations and systems of knowledge and belief. (p. 12)

Later in the same book he stresses the importance of the dialectical relationship between discourse and social structure (p. 65). With reference to educational change, this means that awareness of discourse practices must include awareness of the power relations within the classroom, within the institution, and in the wider social structure in which the institution of education is embedded. Benesch (1993) distinguishes different meanings of 'critical reading': she argues that 'critical' means more than 'analytical',

L. van Lier and D. Corson (eds), Encyclopedia of Language and Education,
Volume 6: Knowledge about Language, 217–227.
© *1997 Kluwer Academic Publishers. Printed in the Netherlands.*

and that 'critical' reading involves recognizing how texts maintain or challenge social structures.

EARLY DEVELOPMENTS

Critical Linguistics

The first major development was the approach of Fowler and colleagues at the University of East Anglia in the late 1970s (Fowler et al., 1979; Kress & Hodge, 1979). Kress & Hodge argue that linguistics:

... must be concerned with the relations between language and society, since language is so distinctly a social phenomenon. It is a key instrument in socialization and the means whereby society forms and permeates the individual's consciousness. (1979, p. 1)

They argue that the insights of linguistics should therefore be part of a democratic process of raising consciousness about how language works in society. They provide a practical instrument, originally intended for and developed with undergraduates who had no knowledge of linguistics, for the critical analysis of texts, with a view to uncovering their ideological underpinnings. This takes the form of a checklist of features, drawn from Halliday's functional approach to grammar: transitivity (the aspect of grammar which serves the ideational function of language); modality (the aspect of grammar which serves the interpersonal function of language); transformations; the ordering, coherence and unity of discourse (the aspect of grammar which serves the textual function of language). They stress that there is no one-to-one relationship between linguistic feature and meaning, and that grammar interacts with lexis to convey meaning. However, as Fairclough points out (1992a, pp. 28–30), this early approach placed too much emphasis on the text as product and too little on the processes of producing and interpreting texts. It also neglected discourse as an arena of struggle and social change. Critical linguists are themselves critical of their early work: in more recent publications they have paid more explicit attention to a social theory of discourse, of social struggle, and of social and discoursal change (see, for example, Hodge & Kress, 1988).

In the early 1980s, Kress took the insights of critical linguistics beyond the academic study of texts, concerning himself with the processes of reading and writing, and with the role of education in these processes. He criticized dominant practices in the teaching of reading:

The teacher's function – and that of the education system at large – is ... to construct her or his students as particular kinds of readers, to construct for them reading positions vis-à-vis a very large set of texts, those of the culture as a whole. (1985, p. 18)

He showed how this is done in school textbooks. He recognized that readers need not comply with the demands of a reading position constructed for them, suggesting that

... the best reader will be ... one who sees both the constructedness of text and of the reading position and who can at the same time reconstruct the text in a manner useful for herself or himself. (p. 40)

However, he claimed that reading in schools actually serves to counteract the engendering of such modes of reading because ultimately

Education is that social institution which is about the change and progression of its client members in the direction of mainstream culture, and into its classifications. (p. 94)

Earlier, Kress (1982) had made a similar point in relation to the teaching of writing in schools, claiming that in the process of acquiring the conventional forms of written language

the genre comes to control the child. Given the cognitive and social implications of these generic forms, the consequences for the child are immense. (p. 11)

Early C.D.A.: Fairclough 1989

In the early 1980s Fairclough was developing, through seminars at Lancaster University and in conference papers and articles, a more complex understanding of the role of discourse in society than the one proposed by the critical linguists of the previous decade. Replacing the word 'linguistics' with the term 'discourse analysis' was significant in making connections with sociological and philosophical theories of 'discourse' which are broader-ranging than the term 'linguistics' implies. The word 'discourse' explicitly encompasses both the social practices associated with the distribution, circulation and consumption of texts, and the ideologies and power relations which are inscribed in linguistic conventions, in addition to the linguistic conventions themselves.

Fairclough's book *Language and Power* (1989) brought together linguistic analysis and social theory, focusing on the connections between language, power and ideology, and providing a practical procedure for the critical analysis of discourse, aimed at a wide range of users. The book ends with a chapter called: 'Critical language study and social emancipation: language education in schools'. In this chapter Fairclough argues that:

The point of language education is not awareness for its own sake, but awareness as a necessary accompaniment to the development of the capabilities of children as producers and interpreters of discourse. (p. 239)

He goes on to stress that he is not just referring to the capabilities of each individual child:

... but also to developing the collective capabilities of children from oppressed social groupings. I would regard this as the primary emancipatory task of language education: critical language awareness is a facilitator for 'emancipatory discourse' which challenges, breaks through, and may ultimately transform the dominant orders of discourse, as part of the struggle of oppressed social groupings against the dominant bloc. (same page)

Fairclough offers a model of language learning (1989, p. 240) which is based on two guiding principles which are fundamental to the critical approaches to education:
  i) marrying awareness and practice
  ii) building on experience.

MAJOR CONTRIBUTIONS

Concurrently, Fairclough and a group of colleagues at the Centre for the Study of Language in Social Life at Lancaster University focused their attention on how to apply the insights of critical discourse analysis in the classroom. The first public formulation of 'Critical Language Awareness' was presented in a paper critiquing the dominant understandings of Language Awareness. This critique was first presented to the profession at a meeting of the British Association of Applied Linguists in 1987, and widely circulated in an unpublished article. It was not published until 1990/1991 (Clark, Fairclough, Ivanič & Martin-Jones), by which time its contents had already had considerable impact on the teaching profession. The authors present the view that language use is part of a wider social struggle, and that language education has the opportunity to raise learners' awareness of this. In this article they summarize Fairclough's critical approach to discourse analysis in a way which might be useful for educators, and compare a more neutral approach to language awareness-raising with one which is informed by a critical view of language. The article compares the objectives of the two types of language awareness-raising, their proponents' respective views of schooling, their views of language and their views of language learning.

One key point of this comparison is to suggest that language awareness-raising should concern the way in which language constructs ideologies and power relations, rather than just presenting a 'rich tapestry' view of language as if it were an ideologically neutral subject on the curriculum. C.L.A. has to address the intrinsically ideological nature of language and language use. Another key point is that the objectives of language awareness-raising should be to equip learners to contribute, through their language use, to challenging and ultimately changing social inequities, rather than reproducing the status-quo. With this article the term 'Critical Language Awareness' (C.L.A.) was born.

There were several immediate sequels to the writing of this article. Firstly, the article in its unpublished form contributed to the debate about the model of language which was presented by the Kingman Committee, and about the role of knowledge about language in the National Curriculum in the U.K. It was widely read within the Language in the National Curriculum (LINC) working party which was set up to coordinate efforts to increase teachers' knowledge about language, and it had a significant influence on the development of the LINC materials for teacher development (LINC Coordinators, 1992). Fairclough and Ivanič also entered the debate with an article specifically discussing the importance of CLA in any future curriculum for the teaching of English (Fairclough & Ivanič, 1989).

Secondly, Ivanič published an article entitled *Critical Language Awareness in Action* in a journal circulating among teachers of English and community languages to adults (Ivanič, 1988). In this article she gave examples of the differences between a neutral and critical approach to language awareness, and discussed how critical language awareness can give learners more control over their own situation. She focused particularly on the dilemma people face as to whether to conform to conventions which might be disempowering or to resist these conventions and thereby challenge the status quo and contribute to emancipation and social change. In some situations the immediate personal consequences of resistance may be too damaging, but some people in some situations might feel the risks involved in challenging the conventions for language use are worth taking in order to preserve their identity and integrity.

Thirdly, Ivanič and Clark began to investigate the possibilities of using critical language awareness-raising in the teaching of academic writing in higher education and in research in this field (Clark, Constantinou, Cottey & Yeoh, 1990; Ivanič & Roach, 1990). They worked in group situations and individual tutorials, raising students' awareness of the way in which language use positions them in terms of power relations, ideological affiliations and literacy practices. They brought into the classroom discussions of the way in which language constructs hierarchies and relationships among members of the academic community, and of the way in which knowledge and understanding can be presented relatively objectively or relatively subjectively. They discussed with students the ways in which different types of language use in academic settings can be relatively inclusive or exclusive, offering or denying access to understanding. They also developed a way of introducing students to academic writing which integrated critical awareness of language into a representation of all the complex aspects of the writing process (Clark & Ivanič, 1991). Academic literacy has continued to be a major site for the developing C.L.A., as we discuss in the next section.

Concurrently classroom applications of a critical views of language were being developed by Hilary Janks at the University of Witwatersrand, South Africa, who was taking up the ideas of critical linguists and social theorists, particularly Althusser, and seeing the same sorts of applications of these ideas to classroom practice as the Lancaster Group (see the review by Janks in Volume 1). She developed the argument for explicit study of texts from a critical perspective in a South African context.

WORK IN PROGRESS

These movements culminated in the publication of a collection of articles edited by Fairclough and entitled *Critical Language Awareness* (Fairclough ed., 1992b). The main point of this book was to go beyond theoretical discussions of possible CLA practice to explore practical possibilities and implications for real classroom experience, and to report on some attempts to put theory into practice. In the first paper Fairclough critically examines the concept of 'appropriateness' which, he argues, underpins current educational policy and practice, including non-critical language awareness-raising. He criticizes the Cox Report (Department of Education and Science, 1989), arguing that it draws on an 'appropriateness' model of language variety to achieve a compromise between its declared respect for other languages and dialects while stressing the need to teach standardized English. He claims that the 'appropriateness' model 'gives a misleading picture of sociolinguistic variation' and 'confuses sociolinguistic realities with ideologies' (p. 18). The book brings together contributions from educational practitioners and researchers in the U.K. and Southern Africa who have explored possibilities for critical language awareness-raising in a range of settings from primary school to HE and adult training courses. They all argue that more attention needs to be paid to social aspects of language, and that the relationship between language and power should be highlighted in language education. Particularly Clark & Ivanič and Janks argue that CLA can have both empowering and emancipatory outcomes. Students are provided with the means for emancipation through the development of alternative conventions, thus also contributing to change in what are acceptable discourse practices within the institution of education and, ultimately, in society as a whole.

Janks remains in the forefront of the field, as the pioneer of developing practical applications of critical discourse analysis in the classroom. She was responsible for the publication of the Critical Language Awareness Series: a set of six books of classroom materials designed for use in South African secondary schools (Janks ed., 1993a). This series is, as far as we know, the only published set of materials which attempts to draw learners' attention to the way in which language constructs identities and power relations, and positions its users. The activities are based around real texts, in which Janks and her collaborators raise critical questions about the ideological underpinning of particular discoursal features. Janks researched teachers' and learners' responses to these materials as part of the process of piloting them, concluding that the raising of critical language awareness varies according to learners and environments for learning (Janks, 1993b, 1995). She has no illusions about the difficulties involved in raising critical language awareness in educational settings, recognizing that it is a complex undertaking, and risky for all concerned in that it makes explicit the tensions and inequities which might otherwise have been left to smoulder beneath the surface. Janks concludes that CLA needs to be introduced carefully, in full knowledge of these possible consequences, and that teachers need preparation for dealing with a full range of reactions from learners, including anger, denial, and personal confrontations.

In Australia, similar work is being developed under the title 'critical literacy'. Barbara Comber provides an overview of this field, summarizing the 'three key principles of critical literacy' as:

- repositioning students as researchers of language
- respecting student resistance and exploring minority culture construc- tions of literacy;
- problematizing classroom and public texts (Comber, 1994, p. 661)

Other key contributors to this field in Australia focus on the way in which school texts construct subject positions for readers, particularly gender positions, and on pedagogical strategies for drawing this positioning to learners' attention (see Lee, 1993, and the review by Luke in Volume 2).

Raising awareness of the sorts of critical issues which emerge from C.D.A. is of continuing interest to researchers and practitioners concerned with academic literacy. Jenny Clarence in South Africa, Romy Clark and Roz Ivanič in the U.K. are among those who have developed courses to raise students' awareness of the way in which they are positioned by the discourses of higher education institutions (see Clark, 1992, 1995; Clarence, 1994; Clark & Ivanič, 1997, Chapter 10). Ivanič has investigated subject positioning using critical language awareness-raising both as a pedagogic strategy and as a research methodology (Ivanič, 1994, 1995, forthcoming). Theresa Lillis is currently undertaking a similar study with women from Black communities in the U.K.

PROBLEMS AND DIFFICULTIES

The problems facing the role of C.D.A. in educational change are of three orders: theoretical, methodological and practical. Firstly, there is the theoretical issue of whether critical discourse analysis is able to reveal relations of power inscribed in language use. It is not possible to pin down the complexity of relations between the social subject, text and social structures in any straightforward way. The critical linguists of the early 1980s were criticized for suggesting that social meaning can be read off directly from the linguistic characteristics of a text. Critical discourse analysts are claiming to do more than this: to explain the characteristics of text in terms of characteristics of the broader social context. But some argue that a critical analysis is merely one possible interpretation of the text, and does not recognize that there can be multiple interpretations (see

Widdowson, 1995). A pluralist, post-modern view of reading is that all interpretations are relative, creating a potentially infinite heterogeneity of possible worlds, possible positions, possible interpretations. In this view of heterogeneity there is no place for struggle over meaning, simply an endless diversity. C.D.A. also recognizes heterogeneity, both of linguistic resources and of interpretations. However, it takes a less neutral view of heterogeneity, claiming that it is actually constituted by struggle over meaning, and drawing attention to the way in which some interpretations gain greater acceptance than others because of the relative position of power of the different interpreters (as argued by Fairclough, 1996a and b).

So far, C.D.A. has been well developed in abstract theoretical terms, but this has not been accompanied by enough research. Too much attention has been paid to discourse as text and not enough to discourse practices. Critical discourse analysts have made assumptions about what people do and how they react. The methodological challenge facing C.D.A. is to develop ways of studying what real people do while producing and interpreting texts, what resources they draw on and how, and how these discourse practices relate to wider social structures and relations of power.

There are also several practical problems facing the introduction of insights from C.D.A. into the classroom in the form of CLA. Learners often argue that they, as people without social status, do not have the power to contribute to change, and therefore have no option other than to conform to discourse conventions and thereby reproduce the existing social order: a sort of 'If you can't beat them, join them' attitude. There is a tension between the pedagogical objective of helping learners to use statusful discourses which will be to their immediate advantage, and that of giving them the means to challenge those conventions which are disrespectful to or disempowering of any social group, thereby contributing to discoursal and social change. Some learners may not want to challenge the conventions, only to gain access to them. Associated with this is the unpalatable truth that raising awareness of the empowering and disempowering characteristics of discourses can have the opposite of the intended effect, giving people tools with which to linguistically abuse or oppress others.

A further practical problem is that the current social and educational climate, at any rate in Britain, is not conducive to critical language awareness-raising in mainstream educational settings. In 1993 the then Minister of Education for England and Wales banned the publication of the LINC project teacher development materials (LINC Coordinators, 1992), many of which were aimed at critical language awareness-raising (see the review by Donmall-Hicks in this volume). As teaching and learning is increasingly regulated and codified through a national curriculum, forms of assessment and adherence to particular materials, so there are less cracks into which teachers are able to introduce the insights of C.D.A. to their learners.

FUTURE DIRECTIONS

C.D.A. practitioners (for example, Fairclough, 1995, 1996b; The New London Group, 1996) have increasingly recognized the need to develop a more complex understanding of

1. the relationship and tension between issues of structural power and issues of identity;
2. the heterogeneity of texts and the interaction of interpretation, positioning and social relations;
3. the complex interaction between verbal and other sign systems in the ideological shaping of meaning;
4. the increasing commodification and technologization of language and the impact of this on language education in schools or the workforce (see reviews by Wortham and Malcolm in this volume).

These issues suggest some ways forward for CLA research and practice. One of the biggest and most urgent tasks is to develop a suitable and workable methodology for observing and probing interpretive practices. More research needs to be carried out into how people, particularly young people, negotiate their social identities, and into how they are socialized into the wider culture through the texts – spoken and written – which are made available to them (this sort of research has been pioneered by researchers such as Maybin, 1994; Rampton, 1995). Such research should inform the development of CLA tasks and materials which help learners to investigate what they actually do, how they take up, cut across, and resist positionings and how they negotiate their place in the world. Such activities could engage the learners themselves as co-researchers into the processes and outcomes of critical language awareness-raising.

Other critical linguists are attempting to make semiosis as a whole the object of their inquiry rather than focusing exclusively on language (see, for example, Kress & van Leeuwen, 1996). Future directions include identifying the ways in which the full range of sign systems combine to create and reinforce the cultural meaning systems that provide the backdrop for interpretations. Critical language awareness-raising in the future might include more attention to the way in which language interacts with visual, kinetic and musical modes of representation.

The heightened awareness of the role of language and other sign systems in the workplace (see the review by Malcolm in this volume) has significant implications for language education and provides opportunities for CLA. Instead of the construction of a workforce able to 'communicate effectively' in the interests of capital, CLA work can help the future workforce to understand the significance of language in constructing identities and social relations within structures of power, and the possibilities for resistance in the context of broader social change.

Lancaster University
England

REFERENCES

Benesch, S: 1993, 'Critical thinking: A learning process for democracy', *TESOL Quarterly* 27, 545–548.

Clarence, J.: 1994, *Black Students in an Open University: A Critical Exploration of Student Responses to a Selection of Texts Which Form Part of the Discourse of the University of Natal*, unpublished M.A. Dissertation, University of Natal, Pietermaritzburg.

Clark, R.: 1992, 'Principles and practice of CLA in the classroom', in N. Fairclough (ed.), 117–140.

Clark, R.: 1995, 'Developing critical reading practices', *Prospect: The Journal of Australian TESOL* 10, 65–81.

Clark, R. & Ivanič, R.: 1991, 'Consciousness-raising about the writing process', in P. Garrett & C. James (eds.), *Language Awareness in the Classroom*, Longman, London.

Clark, R., Fairclough, N., Ivanič, R. & Martin-Jones, M.: 1990, 'Critical language awareness. Part I: A critical review of three current approaches to language awareness', *Language and Education* 4, 249–260.

Clark, R., Fairclough, N., Ivanič, R. & Martin-Jones, M.: 1991, 'Critical language awareness. Part II: Towards critical alternatives', *Language and Education* 5, 41–54.

Clark, R., Constantinou, C., Cottey, A. & Yeoh, O.C.: 1990, 'Rights and obligations in student writing', in R. Clark et al. (eds.), 85–102.

Clark, R., Fairclough, N., Ivanič, R., Mcleod, N., Thomas, J. & Meara, P. (eds.): 1990, *British Studies in Applied Linguistics 5: Language and Power*, Centre for Information on Language Teaching, for the British Association for Applied Linguistics, London.

Clark, R. & Ivanič, R.: 1997, *The Politics of Writing*, Routledge, London.

Comber, B.: 1994, 'Critical literacy: An introduction to Australian debates and perspectives', *Journal of Curriculum Studies* 26, 655–668.

Department of Education and Science: 1989, *English for Ages 5–16*, H.M.S.O., London.

Fairclough, N.: 1989, *Language and Power*, Longman, London.

Fairclough, N.: 1992a, *Discourse and Social Change*, Polity Press, Cambridge.

Fairclough, N. (ed.): 1992b, *Critical Language Awareness*, Longman, London.

Fairclough, N.: 1995, *Critical Discourse Analysis*, Longman: London.

Fairclough, N: 1996a, 'A reply to Henry Widdowson's "discourse analysis: A critical view"', *Language and Literature* 5, 49–56.

Fairclough, N.: 1996b, *Discourse Across Disciplines: Critical Discourse Analysis in the Study of Social Change*, paper delivered as the keynote address to the Association Internationale de Linguistique Appliquée Congress, Jväskylä, Finland, August 1996.

Fairclough, N. & Ivanič, R.: 1989, 'Language education or language training? a Critique of the Kingman model of the English language', in J. Bourne. & T. Bloor (eds.), *Kingman and the Linguists*, C.L.I.E. Publications (Special Issue), Aston, 12–19.

Fowler, R., Hodge, R., Kress, G. & Trew, T.: 1979, *Language and Control*, Routledge, London.

Ivanič, R.: 1988, 'Critical language awareness in action', *Language Issues* 2, 2–7. (Reprinted in Carter R. (ed.), *Knowledge About Language and the Curriculum: The LINC reader*, Hodder and Stoughton, London, 1990, 122–132).

Ivanič, R.: 1994, 'I is for interpersonal: Discoursal construction of writer identities and the teaching of writing', *Linguistics and Education*, 6, 3–15.

Ivanič, R.: 1995, 'Writer identity', *Prospect: The Australian Journal of TESOL* 10, 1–31.

Ivanič, R.: forthcoming, *Writing and Identity*, Benjamins, Amsterdam.

Ivanič, R. & Roach. D.: 1990, 'Academic writing, power and disguise', in R. Clark et al. (eds.), 103–121.

Janks, H. (ed.): 1993a, *Critical Language Awareness Series*, Johannesburg: Hodder and Stoughton and Wits University Press.

Janks, H.: 1993b, 'Closed meanings in open schools', *Literacy for the New Millenium: Proceedings of the Australian Reading Association First International and 19th International Conference*, Carlton, Victoria: Australian Reading Association, 85–93.

Janks, H.: 1995, *The Research and Development of Critical Language Awareness Materials for Use in South African Secondary Schools*, unpublished Ph.D. Thesis, Department of Linguistics and Modern English Language, Lancaster University.

Kress, G.: 1982, *Learning to Write*, Routledge, London (second edition: 1994).

Kress, G.: 1985, *Linguistic Processes in Sociocultural Practice*, Deakin University Press, Victoria (reprinted by Oxford University Press, 1989).

Kress, G. & Hodge, R.: 1979, *Language as Ideology*, Routledge, London.

Kress, G. & van Leeuwen, T.: 1996, *Reading Images: The Grammar of Visual Design*, Routledge, London.

Hodge, R. & Kress, G.: 1988, *Social Semiotics*, Polity Press, Cambridge.

Lee, A. 1993: 'Whose geography? A feminist-poststructuralist critique of systemic 'genre'-based accounts of literacy and curriculum', *Social Semiotics* 3, 131–156.

LINC Coordinators: 1992, *Language in the National Curriculum: Materials for Professional Development*, Department of English Studies, University of Nottingham.

Maybin, J.: 1994, 'Children's voices: Talk, knowledge and identity', in D. Graddol, J. Maybin & B. Stierer (eds.), *Researching Language and Literacy in Social Context*, Multilingual Matters, Clevedon, 131–150.

The New London Group: 1996, 'A pedagogy of multiliteracies: Designing social futures', *Harvard Educational Review* 66, 60–92.

Rampton, B.: 1995, *Crossing: Language and Ethnicity among Adolescents*, Longman, London.

Widdowson, H.: 1995, 'Discourse analysis: A critical view', *Language and Literature* 4, 157–172.

DAVID CORSON

AWARENESS OF NON-STANDARD VARIETIES IN THE SCHOOLS

In many settings, the non-standard language of socially marginalized people is used unjustly as a guide to their potential for achievement and to their worth as human beings. This occurs in any stratified society where many variations in vocabulary, syntax, accent, and discourse style are socially marked, so that even a basic communicative exchange between individuals can suggest their place in the social structure. For example, to people from Philadelphia a change in one aspect of a single vowel in an utterance may be enough to make a White speaker sound Black, and a Black speaker sound White (Fasold, 1990).

In any language community, including all monolingual societies, there is a range of language varieties that is used by closely knit social or ethnic groups. These varieties are brought into the work of the school in one way or another. Children coming from these backgrounds may possess two or more varieties which they use in their everyday language, perhaps one variety used in the home, another in the peer group, and a third in the school. Largely as a result of the school's influence, this last variety may come to be very close to the standard variety. At the same time, many children arrive in schools with little or no contact with the more standard variety used as the language of formal education. Often these children are penalized for having a language variety that is different from the linguistic capital that has high status in the school (Corson, 1998).

In this review, I use the term 'language variety' to cover any non-standard form of a language, whether a geographical or social dialect, a patois, a creole, or some other code of a language. Most speakers of a language use a variety which differs in recognisable ways from 'the standard' variety; and none of these varieties is in any sense inherently inferior to the standard variety in grammar, accent, or phonology. At the same time, these sociocultural and geographical variations within a language are signalling matters of great importance to those who use them. Varieties serve valuable group identity functions for their speakers; they express interests that are closely linked to matters of self-respect and other psychological attributes. It follows that different language varieties deserve respect and recognition in education (see the review on this topic in Volume 1).

L. van Lier and D. Corson (eds), Encyclopedia of Language and Education,
Volume 6: Knowledge about Language, 229–240.
© *1997 Kluwer Academic Publishers. Printed in the Netherlands.*

EARLY CONTRIBUTIONS

The history of prejudice against non-standard users of a dominant language is probably as long as the history of language itself. In my review of 'Non-Standard Varieties and Educational Policy' in Volume 1, I discuss this history and the role of State policies in creating discrimination against non-standard varieties in and through education. This discrimination is so severe in some places that Claudine Dannequin (1987) describes very young students who are non-standard speakers of French as 'gagged children' in their own classrooms ('les enfants bâillonnés').

William Labov's early work (1966, 1971) found that the non-standard language varieties used by socioculturally diverse peoples in his studies varied systematically and consistently with their sociocultural backgrounds. In other words, the varieties were entirely regular but still distinct codes of the language. And they were in no sense inferior to the standard variety in matters of syntax, accent and pronunciation. At the same time, he explicitly allowed that certain key aspects of words and their meanings, including mastery of the very different morphosemantic features of Latinate words in English, may be critical attainments for educational success (Labov, 1972). Studies of the lexico-semantic range of adolescents from different sociocultural and language backgrounds suggest that Labov's guardedness on the matter of vocabulary was justified (Corson, 1995). Clearly educational experience and language experience itself are vital factors in shaping lexico-semantic range.

Along with other work, Labov's studies prompted official recognition of the need to give fairer treatment to non-standard varieties in education. This is best evidenced in the Bullock Report (DES, 1975) in Britain which recommended that schools begin to value whatever language variety children bring with them to school, while adding to it, in every case, those other forms, functions, styles, and registers that are necessary acquisitions for educated people to make. This watershed document prompted a search for ways to make teachers in many British Commonwealth countries more aware of their own prejudices about the non-standard, and of the range of non-standard language varieties that co-exist in monolingual societies. More recently it also led directly to the idea that students and teachers should become much more critically aware of language varieties, especially of their role in activating prejudices and stereotypes.

MAJOR ISSUES FOR TEACHING PRACTICE

Prejudices and Stereotypes

The evidence of language itself is central in confirming stereotypes and activating prejudices: Negative teacher attitudes towards the speech of culturally and socially different children undoubtedly affect teacher expectations, which in turn affect pupil performance (J. Edwards, 1989). A general and long-standing finding of research is that teachers' perceptions of children's non-standard speech produces negative expectations about the children's personalities, social backgrounds, and academic abilities (Giles et al., 1987). Studies suggest that although our awareness of this key injustice stretches back over a generation of research, in practice this has not lessened the injustice very much. For example in Britain in the 1990s, there remain grave doubts about teachers' ability to be objective when formally assessing oral language ability at senior school level. Findings there reveal that the standard variety is rated much more favourably than non-standard varieties, thus routinely discriminating against non-standard speakers (Corson, 1993). Moreover, it seems that teachers bring these stereotypes with them into the profession. Viv Edwards (1986) reports student-teacher evaluations of anonymous children's speech where both the academic and the interest level of speakers of non-standard varieties was viewed less favourably.

Remarkably, there is now much evidence that teacher attitudes to children's non-standard language use are more critical in judging the quality of language use than the children's language itself. There is even evidence to suggest that the stereotypes that beginning teachers from the majority culture hold about children from minority backgrounds causes them to 'hear' those children as non-standard in their language, regardless of how standard their speech actually is (Fasold, 1984). This complex phenomenon raises issues that have led to legal action in certain settings (see my review in Volume 1 and its discussion of Labov's involvement in the Ann Arbor Black English trial). The perseverance of these stereotypes can probably be blamed on simple ignorance among teachers about the range of varieties that can and do co-exist in a single linguistic space.

Some Relevant Research on Non-Standard Varieties

In line with Labov's early studies, Frederick Erickson (1984) reports that the African American non-standard variety, like other varieties discussed here, is a fully developed, internally coherent, and entirely effective system of language for its in-group members. But that variety's discourse structures also reveal a system far removed from the literate style of linear sequencing that is presently valued in educated discourse. Instead, the logic and systematic coherence is organized by audience/speaker interaction and by the consistent application of public aesthetic criteria for persuasion, often based on prosodic devices. I should add a rider to Erickson's conclusions, however. What he reports as a single variety is no doubt a great many varieties reaching across a continuum of variations. Diversity in language codes is much greater than the early researchers or their methods were ready to detect.

The patois used by many children in Britain of Caribbean origin provides a continuum of codes which the children often range across, switching their code depending on the context (V. Edwards, 1986). Examples of code switching of this kind are to be found to some extent in every community where modern schools operate. They offer a different dimension of language variation. For example, Hewitt (1989) identifies two kinds of 'creole' operating among Londoners of Caribbean descent: the relatively stable community language of the older generations of Caribbean immigrants into Britain; and the 'London-Jamaican' anti-language of the young. The former is a creatively developed community language, serving the normal range of everyday functions that community languages serve; the latter is a strategic and contextually variable use of Creole to mark race in the context of the daily anti-racist struggle that adolescents find themselves in. In fact, this form of Creole is structured to heighten its contrast with other forms of language. All this means that there is greater diversity in language varieties than most people realise. And this kind of language knowledge is highly local and context-specific. So sometimes it is not easy to make teachers aware of differences that only they themselves are in a position to discover.

Critical Awareness of Variety

Valuing non-standard varieties is not an easy thing for many people to do, especially if they are only vaguely aware that non-standard varieties exist. For experienced teachers, it may be contrary to a professional lifetime of tacit prejudice. But critical language awareness (CLA) asks teachers to go much further than this (Fairclough, 1992: also see the review by Clark & Ivanič in this volume, and by Janks in Volume 1). CLA certainly asks teachers to value the varieties that children bring to school. But for that 'valuing' of varieties to really count, it needs to be carried out in a genuinely *critical* context. In other words, children need to become aware of the social, political, and historical factors that combine to make one variety of the language seem more 'appropriate' in contexts of power and prestige, while allotting non-standard varieties appropriateness only along the margins of prestigious usage.

On the one hand, students need to be aware that their use of less prestigious forms and expressions will be judged unfavourably in many social contexts, and may cause them to be disadvantaged as individuals in those contexts. But at the same time, in the interests of their own critical language awareness, children need to know that non-standard language used regularly and systematically by people for their own purposes is not incorrect (or inappropriate). Perhaps children can be helped to grasp this difficult social paradox by some examples of language forms that are widely judged to be 'incorrect', but whose use is more frequent among language users even than the so-called correct versions. Among other examples, Andersson & Trudgill (1990) cite the form "I done it" which is usually regarded as a mistaken form of "I did it". This happens in spite of the fact that "I did it" is normally used by no more than 30% of native speakers of English. The more common form "I done it" is regarded as mistaken usually because of the social background of those who tend to use it: Its users are rarely those with wealth, status, power, prestige, and education; and their lowly regarded linguistic capital is unfairly stigmatized by those in possession of high status capital, which includes the power to say whose language is right (or appropriate), and whose is wrong.

Andersson & Trudgill offer a valuable instructional principle in this area: *while discrimination may result in many contexts from a use of forms like the above, which is reason enough to urge students to be aware of the stigma that may attach to them, students also need to be aware that by avoiding their use they are doing so for social reasons, and not for reasons of linguistic correctness.* Again children need to be aware of the social and historical factors that make one variety of the language more 'appropriate' in prestigious contexts, and others only in contexts at the margins of polite discourse. But Norman Fairclough (1992) asks teachers and others to think carefully about what we mean when we use this word 'appropriateness' to discuss the respective place of standard and non-standard varieties in schools. He sees the idea of 'appropriateness' itself as a compromise that allows the standard variety to maintain its position of prestige, thus confusing sociolinguistic reality with ideology.

Practical Classroom Knowledge

There are other areas of knowledge about varietal differences that are more straightforward. What knowledge do teachers need to have about the fair treatment of varieties to organise their own programs in reading, writing, listening and speaking in classrooms (Corson, 1993)?

When children are asked to read and listen to the standard variety in classrooms, this seems to create few practical problems for non-standard variety speakers. For all their lives, most modern children have constant exposure to the standard variety through daily contacts with the mass media. Evidence suggests that there are few practical difficulties for non-standard speakers in reading the standard variety. Joshua Fishman (1969) points to the high levels of literacy in the standard variety that non-standard speakers achieve in Japan, Germany, and Switzerland; and William Labov (1972a) argues that the range of structures unique to Black English Vernacular (BEV) would not account for the record of reading failure by these non-standard users in inner city schools.

But when children are asked to speak and write the standard variety, this can create specific difficulties that may disadvantage non-standard users.

This may occur even though non-standard varieties will typically have the standard variety as their written version. There are several ways in which the use of a non-standard variety can influence a student's competence in writing standard English. The evidence appears in studies of BEV in the USA (Whiteman, 1981) that trace non-standard features in writing back to their use in speech by the writer. Instances of direct interference are limited, but a generation ago at least, they seem to have been frequent.

More recent studies suggest that the above concerns are no longer as relevant. From her longitudinal surveys of academic writing, Geneva Smitherman (1992) reaches two conclusions: The use of BEV in writing has significantly declined since the late 1960s; and the use of BEV does not presently affect scores received when assessors are rating specific writing tasks. She sees the latter as testimony to the various forces in the USA that have combined to sensitize teachers about non-standard varieties. Teachers there now seem more willing to divorce assessment of success in writing from attention to dialect-related features of grammar. In a study of dialect interference in the writing of students in the Caribbean island-nation of St Lucia, Christopher Winch & John Gingell (1992) reach conclusions that may support Smitherman. At the very least, the conventional wisdom that creole interference causes St Lucian children problems with their academic writing needs careful re-examination. The most common errors that could be attributed to non-standard interference by dialect-speaking young people in this former British colony, also appear in studies of students in Britain, and probably have rather different causes.

There may be a stronger case to show that a non-standard variety can interfere with students' ability to monitor and edit the standard use of verb forms, inflectional endings, spelling and punctuation. This seems to happen because usually a non-standard variety is the children's first language, so they cannot always depend on their knowledge of that variety to tell them whether a piece of text in the standard variety is appropriate or not. Carroll Reed (in Whiteman, 1981) terms this situation 'linguistic insecurity'. My review in Volume 1 discusses these difficulties in self-assessment. In that review I also suggest that the written version of a language is probably the closest to any 'standard variety' of it that can really be said to exist.

At the same time, insisting that students use the standard variety in speech presents greater difficulties, both practical and ethical (Corson, 1993). Clearly attempts to force children to 'speak in the standard variety' against their wishes, risk devaluing their varieties, along with all those attributes of identity that the varieties represent. Extension into the spoken standard variety, not replacement by it, seems a fairer practice, if at all necessary. Over the years of schooling, most non-standard speakers experi-ence the standard variety in many contexts and this promotes a high degree of natural bidialectalism. In settings where more is possible, there are sensitive approaches for changing classroom practices in ways that extend children's language repertoire and also develop their communicative and analytic competence (Mehan, 1984; Young, 1992). Jim Cummins says that "if the teacher consistently uses the standard form while accepting student utterances" in the non-standard, then "students will gradually shift to using the standard in the school context" (1981, p. 35). This advice is consistent with a general sociolinguistic principle that Labov offers (1971): whenever speakers of a non-dominant language system are in contact with a more dominant one, those speakers will gradually change their speech to accommodate the features of the more dominant system.

Other Critical Knowledge About Varieties

Language varieties exist because of historical divisions, different patterns of behaviour, differences in power, and differences in language experience. Typically non-standard varieties are associated with the relatively power-less more often than with the empowered, but even the children of affluent people can be discriminated against if they use a geographical variety that differs from the norm. And because infants arrive in a language system that is already fully developed and functioning, there is a tendency for people to see the world of language as something stable and natural; as something which is not generated and controlled by social forces, by struggles, and by historical events. Because of this human tendency to take language for granted, it is easy for language communities to maintain an ideology of correctness in language, especially if it is in the interests of one dominant group or another to do so.

This ideology of correctness is maintained by the commonsense preju-dices of human beings themselves: the most difficult prejudices for educa-tion to overcome. Pierre Bourdieu describes a trait which is especially characteristic of the bourgeoisie (or of teachers who largely come from the middle classes): "the tendency to hyper-correction, a vigilance which overshoots the mark for fear of falling short and pounces on linguistic incorrectness, in oneself and others" (1984, p. 331). He sees this tendency as a particular trait of the *petit-bourgeois*, the lower middle classes, as they seek to cement their status within the dominant classes of a society. Historically, responding to pressure from dominant groups, schools have supported this ideology of correctness; and as long as schools have legiti-mated this ideology, dominant and non-dominant communities of speakers have accepted it normatively.

The ideology of correctness also creates problems for the majority of speakers who do not always use the standard variety. In the company of their friends and associates, they may have to rationalize the use of their non-standard variety. They sometimes do this by ironicizing its features, in much the same way as they poke fun at the features of the standard variety in some contexts. In order to explain away major differences in language use, people sometimes pillory variations in the language use of others; they describe differences that exist as poor or sloppy speech, arising from the speaker's ignorance, laziness, lack of education, or even perversity. These prejudiced notions, circulated in the discourse of language communities, reinforce the ideology of correctness and make the facts of the matter seem contrary to commonsense. But the facts are rather straightforward: We all make errors in our language use at some time or other, especially when speaking informally; but the 'errors' that people often perceive in the language of others (who are usually from slightly different sociocultural groups) are not really errors at all; they are evidence for the existence of a different variety of the language, a variety which preserves its features as systematically and regularly as any language variety.

Unfortunately schools almost everywhere uncritically uphold the ideology of correctness. They accept the standard variety as a high status form of cultural capital whose possession elevates the academic status of the holder. Because some children start out in schools with more of this linguistic resource than others and are consistently rewarded for its posses-sion, an injustice results for the many children who arrive in schools with less of the standard variety. For these children, the standard variety valued in schools represents more than a mere convention. It is the model of excellence against which their own varieties are measured; it is 'correct', while their own varieties are less correct. As a result, non-standard language users often come to perceive their own varieties as things of lesser worth.

WORK IN PROGRESS

Almost everywhere, classroom-related work is still in its infancy (Christian & Wolfram, 1989; Wolfram, 1993), so perhaps a sketch of developments in Canada will serve to illustrate what might be done in many places. Early Canadian interests span four areas: non-standard varieties of French in minority francophone settings; non-standard varieties of English in majority anglophone settings; non-standard varieties of official languages used by aboriginal peoples; and non-standard varieties of immigrant and refugee languages used in heritage language programs. Below I introduce some of the more exemplary work under the first three areas (for a complete review, see Corson & Lemay, 1996).

Based on her studies of franco-ontarian students, Monica Heller argues that the legitimizing ideology of French-language minority education is based on the "collective identity authenticated through Canadian French, a set of vernacular varieties", yet it moves "towards forms of social mobility legitimized through language standardization" (1994, pp. 2–3). Drawing on data comparing an advanced-level French class, consisting mostly of middle class students, with a general level class, consisting mostly of working class students, Heller argues that the interests of middle class students coincide with those of the school, which is directed towards language standardization. At the same time, school institutional processes marginalize working class students, along with their non-standard varieties. Also in Ontario, Morrison, Luther & McCullough (1991) introduced a special program to grade one children who were speakers of a Caribbean patois variety of English. The researchers' aim was to encourage free expression in a setting where standard English could be acquired while at the same time respecting and reinforcing the children's pride in their own variety. Results point to meaningful changes in the children's speaking, thinking, and writing in both varieties.

New aboriginal varieties of English are appearing as aboriginal peoples try to relate their own languages to English and French in Canada (or to English in Australia (Harris, 1991)). From a comparative study of 200 teachers in Saskatchewan and in the Australian state of Queensland, Blair (1986) concludes that older teachers with more experience tend to support a *deficit* model of non-standard language (i.e. they believe that non-standard varieties are in some way deficient in the forms and structures that schools need), while younger teachers tend to support a *difference* model of non-standard language (i.e. they believe that non-standard varieties are different from the language that is presently valued in schools). In spite of this, Blair reports that *neither young nor old teachers* are prepared to tolerate non-standard varieties from aboriginal students in their classrooms.

PROBLEMS AND DIFFICULTIES: FUTURE DIRECTIONS

If we generalize from Blair's rather unhopeful finding, then there seems very little that reformers can do to raise the awareness of practising teachers. There are probably too many teachers to mount the kind of extended dialogic process of teacher counselling that is needed. Joao Telles (1996) describes exactly this kind of shared reflective process as a tool that can foster critical awareness of variety. In his study as a teacher developer, his use of dialogue over an extended period helped a single teacher in a Portuguese-speaking school in Brazil to see how her own life history created the stereotyping attitudes that she held about her own students from non-standard speaking backgrounds. But opportunities for this kind of in-service work are few. The best place to begin seems to be teacher education itself. Blair (1986) provides teacher education guidelines for valuing varietal differences. In recommendations reminiscent of the Bullock Report, teachers need to:

- learn to appreciate non-standard varieties as assets rather than hindrances in the acquisition of the standard [variety]

- extend the range of children's skills by showing them that in certain situations it is appropriate to use certain forms of language, while others suit other contexts
- teach the features of the standard [variety] that do not exist in the children's variety, looking at genuine communication needs rather than teaching isolated features artificially
- pay attention to differences in the rules of interaction between the children's community environment and in the more formal environments where the standard [variety] is used
- learn as much as possible about the children's cultural and linguistic traditions
- avoid testing procedures that favour the standard [variety] since these may not reveal genuine ability, only knowledge of the standard [variety].

While there is much to agree with in these suggestions, workers in critical language awareness would want to take teachers-in-training way beyond this point. But there is always a tension in wedding abstract ideas from critical theory to everyday teacher practices. Perhaps the best way for beginning teachers to become critically aware of non-standard and standard issues, is for them to study the critical practices of critical practitioners themselves: to look at other teachers who have managed to put themselves 'inside' these issues, and managed to use that awareness to reconstruct the education they offer.

A major challenge for all teachers is to understand how language differences both construct and reflect ideologies and power relations. Since teachers and teachers-in-training are forced by the archaic structures of most forms of formal education to follow conservative patterns of professional behaviour, it is difficult to see widespread future change occurring rapidly. This is especially so since schools will always tend to accept that their role is to pass on the cultural heritage, including the standard version of the culture's language. Again the circle turns back fully to teacher education itself, and to the selection of those responsible for orientating teachers towards their professional practice. For change to occur, it is certain that a more explicit and thorough discussion of questions of power and social justice (Corson, 1993, 1998) needs to enter the curriculum of teacher education.

OISE, University of Toronto
Canada

REFERENCES

Andersson, L-G. & Trudgill, P.: 1990, *Bad Language*, Basil Blackwell, Oxford.

Blair, H.: 1986, 'Teacher's attitudes toward the oral English of indigenous children in Saskatchewan and Queensland', in *Mokakit: Selected Papers from the First Mokakit Conference, July 25–27, 1984*, Vancouver, 22–35.

Bourdieu, P.: 1984, *Distinction: A Social Critique of the Judgement of Taste*, Harvard University Press, Cambridge, Mass.

Christian, D. & Wolfram, W.: 1989, *Dialects and Education: Issues and Answers*, Prentice Hall, Englewood Cliffs, NJ.

Corson, D.: 1993, *Language, Minority Education, and Gender: Linking Social Justice and Power*, Multilingual Matters, Clevedon, Avon.

Corson, D.: 1995, *Using English Words*, Kluwer Academic Publishers, Dordrecht.

Corson, D.: 1998, *Changing Education for Diversity*, Open University Press, London.

Corson, D. & Lemay, S.: 1996, *Social Justice and Language Policy in Education: The Canadian Research*, OISE/University of Toronto Press, Toronto.

Cummins, J.: 1981, *Bilingualism and Minority Language Children*, Ontario Insitute for Studies in Education, Toronto.

Dannequin, C.: 1987, 'Les enfants baîllonnés: The teaching of French as mother tongue in elementary school', *Language and Education* 1, 15–31.

DES (Department of Education and Science): 1975, *A Language for Life* (The Bullock Report), HMSO, London.

Edwards, J.: 1989, *Language and Disadvantage: Studies in Disorders of Communication* (second edition), Cole & Whurr, London.

Edwards, V.: 1986, *Language in a Black Community*, Multilingual Matters, Clevedon, Avon.

Erickson, F.: 1984, 'Rhetoric, anecdote and Rhapsody: Coherence strategies in a conversation among Black American adolescents', in D. Tannen (ed.), *Coherence in Spoken and Written Discourse*, Ablex: Norwood, NJ.

Fairclough, N. (ed.): 1992, *Critical Language Awareness*, Longmans, London.

Fasold, R.: 1984, *The Sociolinguistics of Society*, Basil Blackwell, Oxford.

Fasold, R.: 1990, *The Sociolinguistics of Language*, Basil Blackwell, Oxford.

Fishman, J.: 1969, *Readings in the Sociology of Language*, Mouton, The Hague.

Giles, H. et al.: 1987, 'Research on language attitudes', in U. Ammon, N. Dittmar & K. Mattheier (eds.), *Sociolinguistics*, Walter de Gruyter, Berlin.

Harris, J.: 1991, 'Kriol – the creation of a new language', in S. Romaine (ed.), *Language in Australia*, Cambridge University Press, Sydney.

Heller, M.: 1994, *Crosswords: Language, Education and Ethnicity in French Ontario*, Mouton, Berlin.

Hewitt, R.: 1989, 'Creole in the classroom: Political grammars and educational vocabularies', in R. Grillo (ed.), *Social Anthropology and the Politics of Language*, Routledge, London.

Labov, W.: 1966, 'Finding out about children's language', *Working Papers in Communication* 1, 1–30.

Labov, W.: 1971, 'The notion of system in Creole studies', *Pidginization and Creolization of Languages*, Cambridge University Press, New York.

Labov, W.: 1972a, *Language in the Inner City*, University of Pennsylvania Press, Philadelphia.

Labov, W.: 1972b, 'The logic of non-standard English', in P.P. Giglioli (ed.), *Language and Social Context*, Penguin, Harmondsworth.

Mehan, H.: 1984, 'Language and schooling', *Sociology of Education* 57, 174–183.

Morrison, D., Luther, M. & McCullough, J.: 1991, 'Language programming with dialect students', *Orbit* 22, 8–9.

Smitherman, G.: 1992, 'Black English, diverging or converging?: The view from the national assessment of educational progress', *Language and Education* 6, 47–61.

Telles, J.: 1996, *Being a Language Teacher: Stories of Critical Reflection on Language and Pedagogy [in Brazil]*, unpublished PhD thesis. Ontario Institute for Studies in Education.

Whiteman, M. (ed.): 1981, *Writing: The Nature, Development and Teaching of Written Communication. Volume 1. Variation in Writing: Functional and Linguistic-Cultural Diferences*, Lawrence Erlbaum, Hillsdale, NJ.

Winch, C. & Gingell, J.: 1994, 'Dialect interference and difficulties with writing: An investigation in St Lucian primary schools', *Language and Education* 8, 157–182.

Wolfram, W.: 1993, 'Ethical considerations in language awareness programs', *Issues in Applied Linguistics* 4, 225–55.

Young, R.E.: 1992, *Critical Theory and Classroom Talk*, Multilingual Matters, Clevedon, Avon.

CATHERINE WALLACE

THE ROLE OF LANGUAGE AWARENESS IN CRITICAL PEDAGOGY

A critical pedagogy presupposes an approach to language education in which learners and teachers aim to achieve some critical distance from language use in a range of spoken and written texts. Conversely, approaches under the broad umbrella of critical language awareness need to be located within a critical pedagogy if they are to have credibility as educational practice. It will be assumed here that critical understanding can be understood at two broad levels: first, in the cognitive sense of 'conscious awareness'; secondly, – and this will be the understanding of critical pursued in this review – a deeper sense of 'critical' as the ability and willingness to critique the ideological bases of language choice and variation. The literature reviewed, drawn from linguistics, educational and social philosophy and classroom based studies, will deal with the way in which knowledge about language can be developed within a critically oriented pedagogy.

EARLY DEVELOPMENTS

There are two very broad fields of enquiry which are drawn upon by educators attempting to develop language awareness within critical pedagogy. One is constituted by studies in educational and social theory; the second emerges from studies in linguistics.

The first strand is broad and multi-faceted and arises from studies across a wide range of disciplines, to include work by European social philosophers such as Michel Foucault and Jurgen Habermas and educators with a strong interest in critical and social theory such as Michael Apple and Henry Giroux in the United States, Basil Bernstein in Britain, Paulo Freire in Brazil and Robert Young in Australia.

The second major influence on critical language awareness studies comes from the field of linguistics where the work of Michael Halliday (e.g. 1985) has been central, beginning with early work in critical linguistics (Fowler et al., 1979). There are understandable reasons for this choice of model. Firstly, Hallidayan functional/systemic grammar links description of specific textual features to a wider social context, by invoking a simple conceptual framework consisting of three macrofunctions which characterise any speech event: Field, Tenor and Mode of discourse. These relate

L. van Lier and D. Corson (eds), Encyclopedia of Language and Education,
Volume 6: Knowledge about Language, 241–249.
© *1997 Kluwer Academic Publishers. Printed in the Netherlands.*

respectively to what is going on in the event, the relationships between participants and the role which language itself is playing in constructing the text. However, although Hallidayan grammar is premised on the necessary link between micro features of texts and their social function, one is still left with the task of matching up a theory of language with a wider social theory. How do the global social structures which, for instance, reinforce racism, sexism and classism in particular societies relate to the micro level of text analysis?

In the attempt to answer this question contemporary critical linguists such as Kress (1985) and Fairclough (1989) have looked to the work of social philosophers, such as Pierre Bourdieu and most notably, Michel Foucault, as well as, to a lesser extent, Jurgen Habermas.

The particular contribution of Foucault (for example in 1972) has been an understanding of discourse as constitutive of society. Following the Foucaultian position, Kress (1985) argues that discourses are sets of statements which give expression in specific texts to the largely taken for granted meanings and values of social institutions such as medicine, education and the law. In short, texts arise out of discourses (Lemke, 1995, p. 7). This view represents a departure from mainstream applied linguistic accounts of discourse as exemplifed, for instance, in Widdowson's work whereby discourses are constructed by individual readers or listeners from texts; 'we interpret texts into discourses in different ways' (Widdowson, 1992, p. 192). Moreover, a key feature of the Foucaultian position, as opposed to applied linguistic ones is that there is an ideological foundation to discourses in the sense that the ways of using language characteristic of the major institutional bases of any society both reflect and continually recreate relations of power.

Clark et al. (1990, 1991), influenced by the developments in critical discourse analysis of Fairclough, Fowler and Kress, set out an agenda for a language education which would look at language behaviour and phenomena in more critical ways than had previous language awareness approaches (e.g. Hawkins, 1984). Clark et al. argued that although issues of social diversity were addressed in orthodox language awareness study what was missing was close attention to the unequal relations of power which led to one kind of language being favoured over another in particular social settings. Following the publication of these papers, critical language awareness as a distinctive concept was created. It might best be described as the pedagogic arm of critical discourse analysis.

MAJOR CONTRIBUTIONS

Over the last decade language awareness work which can be placed broadly within a critical pedagogic framework has taken on different inflections in different countries, drawing variously on the work of scholars introduced in the previous section.

In the United States contemporary educational philosophers such as Michael Apple (1990) have drawn on a neo-Marxist and largely European tradition. Other educators have continued to favour the tradition of John Dewey as one of the early progressivist educators in the United States. A liberal/humanist discourse which emphasises individual motivation, diversity and scepticism for elitist European traditions is evident, for instance, in Shor (1987) and, with a postmodern emphasis, Lemke (1995). Their work differs in that while Lemke is one of the few American scholars to draw on a Hallidayan framework for textual analysis, Shor has been strongly influenced by the Brazilian educator Paulo Freire, (e.g. Freire, 1972) whose agenda for a critical pedagogy has also been espoused by other U.S. educators such as Donaldo Macedo, who has collaborated with Paulo Freire in one influential publication (Macedo & Freire, 1987).

Elsa Auerbach, who has worked largely in adult literacy, has drawn also on a Freirean philosophy which is based on a critical understanding of the social contexts of education and the need for action to change oppressive conditions. Auerbach & Wallerstein (1987) devised a specific Freirean procedure in language teaching materials where a problem-posing approach is taken to language data in the form of written texts, visuals or simple dialogues. The texts are seen, in Freire's terms, as codes which invite students to problematise the situations presented through a series of open questions.

In Australia there was a reaction in the late nineteen eighties against what was felt to be an overly individualist progressivist philosophy, particularly apparent in the United States, which gave undue emphasis to student-centredness and experiential learning. Kalantzis et al. (1990), for instance argue:

in its more unrestrained use in disadvantaged schools it (progressivism) is often unhelpful in failing to be explicit about knowledge and in failing to explain and justify its own epistemological appropriateness. (1990, p. 243)

In the light of such misgivings, many Australian educators began to espouse a more explicit and less naturalistic pedagogy. This differently focused pedagogy is encapsulated in the term 'genre'.

As argued by Martin (1989) the genre movement counsels a high degree of teacher intervention and explicitness, particularly the need to be explicit about the distinctive features of different texttypes, especially texts which carry power in the wider society, – what Martin and others in the genre school have called the 'genres of power.' The general aim has been to make the power bases of society visible in ways which the essentially implicit, student-centred and experiential approaches have failed to do, it is argued. Linked to the need to make features of texts explicit both at sentence level and beyond has been a concern to present a specific grammatical model which can be introduced to students. The one opted for was Hallidayan functional grammar which has been adapted in a number of language curricula for Australian schools.

In Britain, practical pedagogic proposals of those working in critical pedagogy have drawn variously on both the Freirean and Hallidayan orientation, but have built particularly on the work of Fairclough and Kress. A number of practical proposals for critical language awareness are included in a an edited collection entitled Critical Language Awareness (Fairclough (ed.), 1992) which range in their focus from critical challenge to academic writing (Clark, 1992) to the developing of specific procedures for the development of critical language awareness in secondary school (Lancaster & Taylor, 1992) and a more specifically text-based focus in a critical literacy programme for adult ESL learners (Wallace, 1992). This takes a genre-based approach in that students are progressively presented with different, socially recognisable types of text, ranging from advertisements to newspaper reports and travel brochures. Students are then asked, by referring to a framework for analysis adapted from Hallidayan grammar, to evaluate the ideological effect of the dominant discourses within texts through an identification of a writer's key linguistic choices.

A critical language awareness orientation was also evident in the materials produced as part of the Language in the National Curriculum project. This was an inservice teacher education programme (1989–1992), whose official publication was vetoed by the British Conservative Government of the time, although the material remains available in the form of desk-top versions. One reason for the failure to gain official approval for publication was a perceived over-emphasis on the social circumstances of language use. Another is likely to have been the proposal for a differently focused grammar, what Carter (1990) calls the 'New Grammar Teaching' which would aim to teach students:

not simply to look through language, to the content of a message but rather to see through language and be empowered better to understand and explain the ways in which messages are mediated or shaped, very often in the interests of preserving a particular view point or of reinforcing existing ideologies. (1990, p. 108)

This interest in the specific ideological effect of linguistic choice in texts was echoed at around the same time by other linguists interested in proposing a New Grammar (e.g. Stubbs, 1990).

WORK IN PROGRESS

It is possible to identify, among the work of current theorists and practitioners, accounts of language awareness at different levels of generality. On the one hand there is work which explores language and literacy practices within and across different cultures; on the other is work which centres on the specific linguistic choices in texts. Both levels might form part of a language awareness syllabus within a critical pedagogy, as Lankshear (1994) proposes.

Language awareness at the macro level of observing ways in which language is used in communities and societies is the concern of scholars in anthropology and ethnography. One of the most influential examples of this work is Brice Heath's book (1983) which describes language and literacy practices across three communities, one black, working class, the second, white and working class, the third middle class town dwellers, in the United States. British scholars who pursue this ethnographic tradition include Brian Street (1995) and David Barton. Barton & Padmore (1991) for instance, describe the literacy practices in peoples' everyday lives in a small northern English town.

One application of this work for critical language awareness in an educational context has been to devise simple ethnographies which students themselves carry out, aimed to help them discover who speaks, reads or writes what language or kind of language to whom in what kind of situation. This kind of work has been given a cross-cultural emphasis by a team of researchers based in West London and Durham (Barro et al., 1993) where, respectively, first year undergraduate students and secondary school students were asked to carry out home ethnographies – that is, observation studies of familiar language events – prior to doing similar observations of the foreign cultural setting during a period of study abroad. The aim is to achieve some critical distance on familar practices in order to better understand the unfamiliar – to make the familar strange and the strange familar in ethnographic terms.

This kind of language awareness work can be seen as preparatory and complementary to critical language analysis study of specific texts of the kind carried out by Wallace (op cit). Work at this second, more text-focused level, aims to proceduralise principles of critical language awareness in actual teaching programmes. Thus Malischewski (1990), based in Canada, but drawing largely on Australian work, and taking a strong Hallidayan perspective, presents a proposed pedagogy for critical reading for ESL/EFL students reading for academic purposes at University level. Kamler (1994), among a number of other scholars in Australia, where there is a particularly strong interest in the pedagogic applications of critical linguistics, has devised text analytic tools for the analysis of media texts in a secondary school context. A rare example of actual published material which takes an explicit critical language awareness stance is a series of small books edited by Hilary Janks and her colleagues in South Africa (Janks (ed.), 1994) These books, as the general introduction to the series states:

deal with the relationship between language and power ... the materials attempt to raise awareness of the way language can be used and is used to maintain and to challenge existing forms of power.

There is growing interest in developing language awareness in the very early stages of schooling. Thus in Luke, O'Brien & Comber (1994) O'Brien talks of the way that everyday texts can be problematised through a classroom procedure which draws attention to the conditions of production of certain genres – often related to commercial interests – and to the representations of participants in texts. The example she gives is of work done with a class of 5–7 year olds in a school located in a mixed-race, lower socio-economic area and centres around junk mail which comes uninvited into peoples homes around Mothers Day, advertising 'Mothers Day' products. Even young children, O'Brien argues, can become aware – and, more importantly, learn to articulate this awareness – of ways in which mothers are stereotypically represented in such material.

Other researchers (cf Wallace forthcoming) note the need to subject to critical scrutiny the 'classroom' text in which any exploration of specific texts takes place; language awareness within a critical pedagogy must offer up to inspection the language used by both teacher and students to talk about texts as well as the language of texts themselves, in order to examine the processes by which interpretations are socially constructed in the classroom. Further questions to be addressed include the impact of factors in the wider sociocultural setting beyond the classroom which may set limits on the ability and willingness to critique texts.

PROBLEMS AND DIFFICULTIES

There are a number of dilemmas and contradictions around both the theory of critical discourse analysis and its practical pedagogic applications as critical language awareness. One question, as Hammersley (1996) points out, which remains inadequately addressed is what the term 'critical' adds to the phrase 'discourse analysis'? By the same token, we could extend this to ask the same question regarding 'critical pedagogy' and 'critical language awareness'. It is reasonable to ask whether critical pedagogy is not simply good pedagogy. One answer to such questions is that critical pedagogy has clear emancipatory objectives; put simply, 'by acting on the basis of critical theory we can change the world for the better' (Hammersley, 1996, p. 4). However, such aspirations, as Hammersley, sceptical of aspects of the critical discourse movement, notes, only raise further questions around varying judgements about what might constitute a better world. There is also the clear danger that a strongly committed pedagogy (underpinned by a clear political agenda) might simply replace the tyranny of the dominant, typically unchallenged text with the tyranny of the most powerful interpretative voice in the classroom, likely to be that of the teacher. Moreover, if all language is ideologically suspect, then all our interpretations are also equally suspect. We are consequently left with the dilemma that, if there is no real world or ultimate truth beyond discourse, then what is the point of producing discourses of critique which are as suspect as those targeted for criticism in the first place? A similar dilemma is presented by the work of Foucault which, as Eagleton (1991) points out, in positing that 'power constitutes us to our very roots' (Eagleton, 1990, p. 47) does not allow the subject a position outside or distant from such construction to resist the effect of power.

Corson (1997) argues the case for an emancipatory pedagogy which, before it can aspire to change the world, needs first to establish adequate interpretations of the world from the point of view of its relevant actors. The reasons and accounts of people really exist. Corson, drawing largely on the work of the English philosopher Bhaskar who presents the case for 'critical realism', is interested in reinstating notions of realism or truth. This position resonates with Habermas's notion of a universal pragmatics (Habermas, 1979) by which communities of speakers negotiate consensual interpretations around notions of what is factually verifiable or sincerely meant, taking their bearings against a universal understanding of an ideal speech situation. In this way Habermas aims to reclaim the pursuit of truth and truthfulness as feasible human goals.

FUTURE DIRECTIONS

One might expect future directions at the theoretical level to address more fully some of the objections and dilemmas raised in the previous section. Indeed critical discourse analysts, aware for instance of the dilemma presented by Foucault's relativism, are beginning to look to social theorists who take a more optimistic view of the possibility of interpretations being arrived at rationally and consensually around notions of truth and truthfulness. Habermas's Universal Pragmatics and Bhaskar's Critical Realism hold promise here.

It follows that, at the practical level, future studies will need to attend more to negotiated interpretations of texts in the classroom setting. Also we should expect to be able to point to distinctive kinds of awareness and growth in understanding experienced by students, if the concept of critical language awareness or critical pedagogy is to retain any credibility. This is likely to involve much closer inspection of the language data which arises in pedagogic contexts, both of the ways in which specific responses to language phenomena might be called 'critical' and the actual processes by which critical understanding is achieved.

University of London, Institute of Education
England

REFERENCES

Apple, M.: 1990, *Ideology and Curriculum* (second edition), Routledge, New York and London.

Auerbach, E. & Wallerstein, N.: 1987, *ESL for Action: Problem Posing for the Workplace*, Addison and Wesley Hall, New York.

Barro, A., Byram, M., Grimm, H., Morgan, C. & Roberts, C.: 1993, 'Cultural studies for advanced language learners', in *Language and Culture*, British Studies in Applied Linguistics 7, in association with Multilingual Matters, Clevedon, 55–70.

Barton, D. & Padmore, S.: 1991, 'Roles, networks, and values in everyday writing', in D. Barton & R. Ivanic (eds.), *Writing in the Community*, Sage, London, 58–77.

Brice-Heath, S.: 1983, *Ways with Words*, Cambridge University Press, Cambridge.

Carter, R.: 1990, 'The new grammar teaching', in R. Carter (ed.), *Knowledge about Language and the Curriculum*, Hodder and Stoughton, London, 104–121.

Clark, R., Fairclough, N., Ivanic, R. & Martin-Jones, M.: 1990, 'A critical review of three current approaches to language awareness', *Language and Education* 4(4), 249–260.

Clark, R., Fairclough, N., Ivanic, R. & Martin-Jones M.: 1991, 'Critical language awareness. Part 2: Towards critical alternatives', *Language and Education* 5(1), 41–54.

Clark, R.: 1992, 'Principles and practice of CLA in the classroom', in N. Fairclough (ed.), *Critical Language Awareness*, Longman, London, 117–140.

Corson, D.: 1997, 'Critical realism: An emancipatory philosophy for applied linguistics?', *Applied Linguistics* 18(2), 166–188.

Eagleton, T.: 1991, *Ideology*, Verso, London and New York.

Fairclough, N.: 1989, *Language and Power*, Longman, London.

Fairclough, N. (ed): 1992, *Critical Language Awareness*, Longman, London.

Foucault, M.: 1972, *The Archaeology of Knowledge*, Tavistock, London.

Fowler, R. Hodge, B., Kress, G. & Trew, T: 1979, *Language and Control*, Routledge and Kegan Paul, London.

Freire, P.: 1972, *Pedagogy of the Oppressed*, Penguin Middlesex, England.

Freire, P. & Macedo, D.: 1987, *Literacy: Reading the Word and the World*, Routledge, London.

Habermas, J.: 1979, *Communication and the Evolution of Society*, Heinemann, London.

Halliday, M.A.K.: 1985, *An Introduction to Functional Grammar*, Edward Arnold, London.

Hammersley, M.: 1996, unpublished paper *On the Foundations of Critical Discourse Analysis*.

Hawkins, E.: 1984, *Awareness of language: an introduction*, Cambridge University Press, Cambridge.

Janks, H. (ed): 1994, *Critical Language Awareness Series*, Hodder and Stoughton London in association with Witwatersrand University Press, Johannesburg, S. Africa.

Kalantzis, M., Cope, B., Noble, G. & Poynting, S.: 1990, *Cultures of Schooling: Pedagogies for Cultural Difference and Social Access*, Falmer Press, London.

Kamler, B.: 1994, 'Lessons about language and gender', *Australian Journal of Language and Literacy* 17(2), 129–138.

Kress, G.: 1985, *Linguistic Processes as Sociocultural Practice*, Deakin Press, Deakin University, Australia.

Lancaster, L. & Taylor, R.: 1992, 'Critical approaches to language, learning and pedagogy: A case study', in N. Fairclough (ed.), *Critical Language Awareness*, Longman, London, 256–284.

Lankshear, C.: 1994, *Critical literacy*, Occasional Paper No 3, Australian Curriculum Studies Association.

Lemke, J.: 1995, *Textual Politics: Discourse and Social Dynamics*, Taylor and Francis, London.

Luke, A., O'Brien, J. & Comber, B.: 1994, 'Making community texts objects of study', *Australian Journal of Language and Literacy* 17(2), 139–149.

Malischewski, E.: 1990, 'Reinterpreting reading: From techniques to critical distance', in *TESL '90, Reading into the Future: Proceedings of the 1990 TESL Ontario Conference*.

Martin, J.: 1989, *Factual Writing: Exploring and Challenging Social Reality*, Oxford University Press, Oxford.

Shor I.: 1987, 'Educating the educators: A Freirean approach to the crisis in teacher education', in I. Shor (ed.), *Freire for the Classroom*, Boynton Cook Heinemann, Portsmouth NH, 7–32.

Street, B.: 1995, *Social Literacies. Critical Approaches to Literacy in Development, Ethnography and Education*, Longman, London.

Stubbs, M.: 1990, *Knowledge about Language: Grammar, Ignorance and Society*, University of London Institute of Education, London.

Wallace, C.: 1992, 'Critical literacy awareness in the EFL classroom', in N. Fairclough (ed.), *Critical Language Awareness*, Longman, London, 59–92.

Wallace, C.: (forthcoming) PhD thesis: *Critical Language Awareness in the Second Language Classroom*.

Widdowson, H:. 1992, *Practical Stylistics*, Oxford University Press, Oxford.

STANTON E.F. WORTHAM

THE COMMODIFICATION OF CLASSROOM DISCOURSE

Marx (1867/1978) presents "the commodity" as the organizing principle of capitalist society. This review describes research on classroom discourse which shows that – although classroom language use seems removed from the marketplace – verbal practice in schools is often commodified. A clearer understanding of Marx' concept can help us better understand language use in contemporary schools, and how schools fit into the social system.

Different traditions in social theory, however, have interpreted Marx' "commodity" in different ways. Before describing research on classroom discourse, we must clarify these interpretations. This review presents four theoretical interpretations of the commodity, from the Frankfurt School (Horkheimer & Adorno, 1944/1972; Postone, 1993), Habermas (1981/1984), Foucault (1975/1979), and Bourdieu (1991), all of which have inspired important research on the commodification of classroom discourse.

COMMODIFICATION: ITS ORIGINS IN SOCIAL THEORY

Marx' "commodity form" is not just a type of product, but the basic unit of capitalist society. This form of social relations arose historically in societies where goods are not produced primarily for their use value – which varies according to purposes and context – but are produced primarily for exchange. Goods are exchanged through a quasi-objective market system, which introduces two features unique to capitalism: idiosyncratic aspects of goods come to be ignored or flattened out, as people concern themselves primarily with how much money they can get for the good; and products seem to have a mysterious, objective value (because they are worth money), which people attribute to the objects' natural properties – while forgetting that it was in fact human labor that produced the goods. (See Postone, 1993, for a comprehensive discussion of Marx' argument.)

Members of the Frankfurt School elaborated Marx' analysis of the commodity, and adapted it to the twentieth century (Adorno, 1938/1978; Horkheimer & Adorno, 1944/1972). They also showed that cultural products like music and art were themselves becoming increasingly

L. van Lier and D. Corson (eds), Encyclopedia of Language and Education,
Volume 6: Knowledge about Language, 251–260.
© 1997 Kluwer Academic Publishers. Printed in the Netherlands.

commodified. Drawing also on Weber (1922/1968), they elaborated Marx'
insights about the flattening or decontextualization of products into a
concept of "standardization." Adorno, for instance, describes the standardization of modern music. Many songs are simply commonplace formulae
into which clichés are slotted. This contrasts with great music, in which
particular aspects force listeners to rethink their conception of the whole.
Commodified music has little part-whole tension, and thus consumers
can digest it with little thought. They engage in "quotational listening":
listening for catchy moments provided by unrelated pieces of the work.
However, and this is the second aspect of Marx' argument, consumers
often perceive standardized commodities as unique and spontaneous.
Consumers of contemporary music often claim that songs express genuine
immediacy and intimacy. Thus consumers "reify" standardized products,
misperceiving their standardized character as natural and genuine. (See
Wortham, 1995, for further description of standardization and reification.)
This review will present evidence that, like cultural products, classroom
discourse has become commodified.

All the social theorists discussed in this review agree that standardized
and reified goods characterize capitalist society. Particular interpretations
vary, however. Habermas (1981/1984) criticizes Horkheimer & Adorno's
(1944/1972) pessimism – as they provide no vision of how we might get
beyond commodification. As an alternative Habermas posits, instead of
one social system with the commodity as its organizing principle, two
realms: the productive system, organized by labor, which has in fact
become commodified in late capitalism; and the interpersonal system,
organized by communication. He explains commodified cultural products by claiming that the commodified productive system is "colonizing"
domains formerly organized by communicative (as opposed to technical)
rationality. This perspective offers the possibility of social change, as we
retain the potentially uncommodified communicative realm. It pays the
price of positing realms of labor and communication which supposedly
exist in all times and places. Foucault (1975/1979) leaves open the possibility of change in a different way. He criticizes Adorno and Habermas'
characterizations of society as too monolithic. Foucault tries instead to
explain standardization ("discipline" and "technologies of the self") and
reification ("regimes of truth") in terms of more fragmented and contextualized practices. Bourdieu (1991) analyzes standardization and reification
in terms of the relations among social groups which compete for status and
power. The next section reviews Bourdieu's work on classroom discourse.
Work on classroom discourse inspired by the other theorists is reviewed
subsequently.

CONNECTING SOCIAL THEORY TO CLASSROOM DISCOURSE: MAJOR CONTRIBUTIONS

Commodification as a Function of Social Group

One important line of work on the commodification of classroom discourse interprets reification as a veil for group interests. Bourdieu (1991; Bourdieu & Passeron, 1970/1977), for instance, posits "linguistic markets." Members of different social groups use language in different ways, and when they speak they "sell" their manner of speech for its symbolic value. Different ways of speaking carry more or less symbolic value, and thus speakers from different groups can "buy" different amounts of status and access to lucrative institutional settings. The state and the schools establish a "standard" language, which is closer to the speech style of dominant groups. Children from these groups thus gain more prestige from their manner of speaking, and gain easier access to information taught in school – because the school uses standard speech, and children are evaluated in part based on the symbolic value of their speech style.

So Bourdieu claims that classroom speech is assessed partly in terms of its value in an exchange system, a system based in group distinctions of the larger society. Thus classroom speech is "standardized," because its value comes from stereotypes associated with certain groups' speech. Bourdieu also describes the "reification" of classroom discourse, in his claim that teachers and students "misrecognize" the value of standard speech. Although the speech styles of dominant groups are not inherently better or worse than others', people tend to perceive standard speech as logically superior and communicatively more efficient. Furthermore, they often perceive speakers of the standard style as mentally more developed and ethically more refined. This creates obvious problems for students who do not control dominant speech styles: in school they are often considered morally and intellectually inferior, because society has reified an arbitrary difference of communicative conventions into a "natural" difference that symbolizes character and intelligence (for more on the treatment of standard and non-standard varieties in education, see the reviews by Corson in this volume and in Volume 1).

Several others have developed theories of classroom discourse similar in structure to Bourdieu's – with a description of how different speech styles are valued more or less highly on the school "market," and how dominant groups' ways of speaking are "naturalized" as inherently superior. Bernstein's (1971, 1996) theory of middle-class and working-class communicative "codes" provides an example. Bernstein gives an account of how working class and middle class styles derive from their positions in the division of labor, and how the school favors middle class styles as naturally superior. In his later work he also gives a more elaborate description of the different "codes." His describes middle-class codes as a more abstract communicative style, which seems more standardized than working class styles. This raises the possibility that middle class speech is more commodified, while working class speech is less so. Such a theory would challenge Marx' (1867/1978) and Postone's (1993) claim that the commodity characterizes all social relations in capitalism.

Hasan (1993) follows up this suggestion of Bernstein's, in an interesting direction. Wedding a much more systematic linguistic theory to Bernstein's sociology, she describes two "fashions of speaking" or "semantic orientations" associated with middle and working-class speakers. Drawing on a large corpus of mother-child and classroom conversation, Hasan finds middle-class mothers much more prone to indirect and suggestive commands, to reasons that cite natural facts instead of social power relations, and to remarks that express confidence in the child's ability to act reasonably. Middle-class children, then, are socialized through language use to believe that they are unique individuals with their own discretion, and that social power is not a major factor. Working-class children are socialized to recognize more explicit control over their actions by authority figures. Hasan concludes that middle-class discourse patterns mask power relations, while working-class patterns do not. Thus she extends Bernstein's suggestion that middle-class discourse is more commodified, by adding that middle-class discourse might also involve greater misrecognition of social power relations as apparently natural.

The perspective developed by Bourdieu, Bernstein, and others – which describes how the commodification of classroom discourse systematically disadvantages children from non-dominant groups – underlies much recent work. Three examples will have to suffice here. In literacy research Gee (1990) gives detailed descriptions of non-dominant communicative "discourses," especially those characteristic of American blacks, and shows how these ways of using language are devalued by mainstream schools. He also describes how mainstream communicative practices are reified, and how minority children are thus cast as "naturally" inappropriate or unintelligent. In work on classroom science discourse, Lemke (1990) describes how only members of certain groups, especially men from mainstream backgrounds, are empowered to master scientific talk. Because of science's value as high-status knowledge, those not initiated into successful science talk often think of themselves as unintelligent, and are excluded from many careers. Singh (1993) provides a case study that illustrates Lemke's point. She uses categories from Bernstein to show how girls are constructed as technologically illiterate in a particular classroom.

Such work that presents commodification as a function of social grouping, has been criticized in recent years. Collins (1993) argues that Bourdieu's account tends toward determinism, with one's social group inevitably leading to one's success in school and sense of self. This criticism clearly applies to work that presents social groups as monolithic – as if groups were naturally associated with stable styles of speaking, and as if their social positions were mechanically determined by these. Tyler (1995), for instance, criticizes Bernstein for using social class in this sort of static, mechanical way. Following Foucault (1975/1979), Tyler sees power as more fragmentary and less dependent on structural mechanisms than Bernstein. Bourdieu, however, focuses not only on socioeconomic class but also on more subtly delineated social and cultural groups. He also claims to avoid a determinist structural account, by describing how social distinctions emerge in practice. Collins (1993) denies this latter claim, arguing that Bourdieu does not adequately recognize the contextually-specific connections between particular instances of classroom discourse and the constitution of (and resistance to) social groups.

What is clear is that Bourdieu's analyses depend on two claims that are denied by other theories of commodification. First, the "market" for Bourdieu is an exchange system on which different groups' symbolic capital – for instance, their ways of speaking – is valued differently. Using this construct, Bourdieu's explanations center around a set of social groups struggling for domination. Horkheimer & Adorno (1944/1972) and Postone (1993) offer a divergent interpretation of the market. They do not deny the existence of struggles between social groups, but they claim that all of capitalist society is organized by standardization engendered by the market. On their account, the commodity form (derived from the market and exchange value) is the central organizing principle of social relations, for members of all groups. Bourdieu's second claim is to explain folk accounts of social phenomena primarily as misperceptions that function to veil group interests and reproduce relations of domination among groups. Again, Horkheimer & Adorno (1944/1972) and Postone (1993) claim that reification characterizes capitalist society as a whole, and does not function primarily for the benefit of certain groups. All of us misrecognize the products of human labor as natural, whether this benefits certain groups in particular cases or not. It is beyond the scope of this review to resolve this theoretical dispute. But important empirical work on commodification in classroom discourse has been done from both theoretical perspectives. Work that has been inspired by Horkehimer and Adorno, and by Habermas and Foucault, is discussed in the next section.

Standardized Classroom Discourse

The classic work on standardization in classroom discourse was done by Sinclair & Coulthard (1975) and Mehan (1979). They describe a common pattern in classroom discourse: the "IRF" or "IRE" (teacher initiation, student response, teacher feedback or evaluation) sequence. This organization of classroom talk occurred more commonly than any other Mehan observed (during classroom lessons, 53% of all teacher-initiated sequences had this form). It favors the transmission of facts, and discourages idiosyncratic interpretations. The IRE structure is standardized in two ways: it represents a standard organization for classroom talk, where the student needs only to fill in the slot; and it favors the transmission of standardized knowledge. Poole (1994) elaborates this insight into standardized classroom discourse, giving a more complex linguistic account of how classroom talk presents knowledge as "discrete and measurable units of information" free from affect or values. She shows how classroom talk, even in non-technical fields like social studies, often presents knowledge as discrete, incontrovertible facts that unproblematically represent the world. She also analyzes testing as a classroom practice particularly prone to standardize knowledge and then reify it.

Other work has explicitly connected this standardization of classroom discourse to social theories of commodification. Wortham (1995) argues that "experience-near" classroom teaching often seems experiential only because of reification – that we misperceive standardized descriptions of students' experience as genuinely personal and unique. This analysis draws explicitly on Adorno's (1938/1978) discussion of cultural commodities, and argues that an analogous structure exists in classroom discourse. Fairclough (1993) draws on Habermas (1981/1984) and Foucault's (1975/1979) analyses, to argue that school discourse has been "colonized" recently by market and technological discourses. He describes discursive patterns characteristic of market discourse that have recently become common in educational settings – like "synthetic personalization," the discussion of personal content in public settings where it becomes artificial despite the appearance of genuineness. Collins (1989) also draws on Foucault, describing the development of regimented, unified standards and tests of literacy. He shows how people reify practice that conforms to these standards, as naturally superior. Luke's analyses of classroom discourse (1992, 1995) draw on Foucault as well. He describes how, even in apparently creative activities, controlling, regulating discourse patterns often force students to reproduce standardized responses. Apparently innocuous literacy curricula become "a form of moral and political discipline." Luke also describes how standardized, mainstream values and identities are naturalized, behind the façade of teaching universal literacy skills.

Textbooks and Technological Literacy

One further area of research deserves mention: work on the commodification of written classroom materials. Apple (1986, 1993) analyzes textbooks as commodities. He documents the standardization of knowledge that takes place as certain views become sanctioned in textbooks. Textbooks elide the complex political and scientific struggles that lead to the acceptance of belief, and present a univocal version of "official knowledge." This version then gets perceived as "naturally" correct. Apple also describes the standardization of the school workplace that has happened largely through textbook-based curricula – a process through which teachers are "deskilled," as improvisation and independent judgment are discouraged by prescriptive curricula. These aspects of Apple's analyses seem inspired more by Horkheimer and Adorno's perspective. But Apple also attends to the struggle among social groups. In selecting certain versions as official, textbook companies and educational bureaucrats select some groups' cultural capital as more legitimate than others. Furthermore, the development of "teacher-proof" curricula and related attempts to control and limit teachers' judgment connect with the "feminization" and devaluing of teaching.

De Castell & Luke's (1989) analysis of textbooks picks up many of the same themes as Apple, and provides further evidence of how textbooks can lead to standardization and reification in classrooms. They sketch the history of standardized textbook-based curricula and the role of scientific psychology in this history. Literacy is treated by psychology and multinational textbook manufacturers as a "universal, culturally-neutral information processing skill." Thus literacy curricula can be standardized – one product fits all. De Castell and Luke describe how standardized curricula dampen critical thinking, turning teachers into technicians and students into passive recipients. A curriculum "packaged" even to the point of "prespecified linguistic exchanges" robs teachers and students of initiative. Like a consumer of the commodified songs described by Adorno (1938/1978), a student learning to read through these commodified curricula has few opportunities for initiative and innovation: the texts require "mere recognition" rather than reasoning.

Recent work from several disciplinary traditions has reinforced and supplemented these analyses of textbooks and commodification. Bazerman (1988), Klamer (1990) and Myers (1992) describe the alienating and naturalizing aspects of scientific writing (including science textbooks). They show how the texts engineer an image of objective truth by claiming simply to record the "natural facts", and by hiding rhetorical structure and social context. They describe rhetorical devices through which textbooks present theories as established facts. Such textbooks invite readers simply to "consume" the finished products instead of thinking critically. Kenway, Fitzclarence, Collier & Bigum (1997) go beyond textbooks to study the commodification of educational technology. They also introduce feminist themes into analyses of commodification – by focusing on how educational commodities differentially affect women, and by studying people's subjective experience of commodification as well as more abstract structural factors.

Recent work on "technological literacy" has provided even more linguistically sophisticated analyses of how science textbooks and classroom speech alienate many students and present scientific knowledge as transparent representations of the natural world. Lemke (1990) describes how science talk creates a dichotomy between the apparently impersonal, objective facts described by science and the ordinary, personal world. This alienates many students from science, as it seems unconnected to familiar contexts. Halliday & Martin (1993) give detailed linguistic analyses of written scientific discourse, describing how it presents nature as a collection of impersonal things. They argue that scientific discourse naturalizes a particular view of the world, as a fixed edifice of facts. Lemke (1995) connects this more sophisticated linguistic analysis back to the political uses of language, describing how technical discourse can be used to naturalize and obscure the evaluative bases of policy disputes.

PROBLEMS AND FUTURE DIRECTIONS

The discovery of standardization and reification in so many aspects of classroom discourse indicates the value of connecting social theories of commodification with analyses of classroom language use. Three substantial problems remain, however. The first concerns apparently incompatible accounts of the commodity form. Bourdieu claims that social groups are central. Horkheimer, Adorno and Postone claim that group-based analyses fail to explain the historically particular sort of standardization and reification we see in capitalism, and that we must instead study how the commodity organizes all groups and practices in capitalist society. Habermas agrees that we should not over-emphasize social groups, but claims that Horkheimer and Adorno do not explain how we might escape commodified practices. In his alternative, however, Habermas posits transhistorical realms of labor and communication that are difficult to justify empirically or conceptually. Foucault criticizes all analyses like Bourdieu's, Adorno's and Habermas', as inattentive to the fragmented and interactionally constituted character of power and ideology; and all of them criticize Foucault as inattentive to larger structural realities. How can future research on commodification proceed, with such theoretical disagreement about the basic concept? I have two brief thoughts on this. First, as I hope this review has shown, the concepts of standardization and reification can help organize research on commodification – from any of the theoretical perspectives. This is not to say further theoretical work would not help, but theoretical proliferation should not paralyze empirical researchers. Second, research on classroom discourse might play a role in empirical examination of the various theories. One study is unlikely to disprove any social theory, but empirical work can nonetheless lead to theoretical advances.

The second problem for future research concerns the difficulty of establishing a standpoint for critique. Analyses of classroom commodification claim that teachers and students misperceive their experience – thinking that their practices are genuine and valuable when the analyst claims they are standardized. But where does the analyst stand, to make such a claim? What genuine standards does s/he have, to judge people's claims against? Marx' solution, applied to classrooms by Wortham (1995), was an "immanent critique" – a critique that does not claim ahistorical standards, but only that people violate standards they themselves espouse. Luke (1995) claims that we can acknowledge the limitations of all knowledge-claims, including our own, and use critique as merely a "tool" to disrupt common sense. Further work is needed here, to help us avoid teacher-bashing without abandoning a critical stance.

The third problem involves the "micro-macro gap." Social theory is so abstract, and good research on classroom discourse so empirically rich, that it seems difficult to connect the two. How can we do more than simply line up abstract concepts with details of classroom talk and claim that the two connect? More work will certainly be needed to bridge this gap, but some contemporary research is both good social theory and good empirical linguistics. Sophisticated frameworks like those developed by Fairclough (1993), Lemke (1995), and Luke (1995) leave room for optimism.

Bates College
USA

REFERENCES

Adorno, T.: 1938/1978, 'On the Fetish-character in music and the regression of listening', in A. Arato & E. Gebhardt (eds.), *The Essential Frankfurt School Reader*, Basil Blackwell, Oxford.

Apple, M.: 1986, *Teachers and Texts*, Routledge, New York.

Apple, M.: 1993, *Official Knowledge*, Routledge, New York.

Bazerman, C.: 1988, *Shaping Written Knowledge*, University of Wisconsin, Madison.

Bernstein, B.: 1971, *Class, Codes and Control, Volume 1*, Routledge, New York.

Bernstein, B.: 1996, *Pedagogy, Symbolic Control and Identity*, Taylor & Francis, Bristol PA.

Bourdieu, P.: 1991, *Language and Symbolic Power* (J. Thompson, ed., G. Raymond & M. Adamson, translators), Harvard University, Cambridge MA.

Bourdieu, P. & Passeron, J.: 1970/1977, *Reproduction in Education, Society and Culture*, (R. Nice, translator), Sage, Beverly Hills.

Collins, J.: 1989, 'Hegemonic practice', *Journal of Education* 171, 9–34.

Collins, J.: 1993, 'Determination and contradiction', in C. Calhoun, E. LiPuma & M. Postone (eds.), *Bourdieu: Critical Perspectives*, University of Chicago, Chicago, 116–138.

DeCastell, S. & Luke, A.: 1989, 'Literacy instruction', in S. de Castell, A. Luke & C. Luke (eds.), *Language, Authority, and Criticism*, Falmer, Bristol PA, 77–95.

Fairclough, N.: 1993, 'Critical discourse analysis and the marketization of public discourse', *Discourse & Society* 4, 133–168.

Foucault, M.: 1975/1979, *Discipline and Punish* (A. Sheridan, translator), Vintage Books, New York.

Gee, J.: 1990, *Social Linguistics and Literacies*, Falmer, Bristol PA.

Habermas, J.: 1981/1984, *The Theory of Communicative Action* (T. McCarthy, translator), Beacon, Boston.

Halliday, M.A.K. & Martin, J.: 1993, *Writing Science*, University of Pittsburgh, Pittsburgh.

Hasan, R.: 1993, 'Contexts for meaning', in J. Alatis (ed.), *Language, Communication, and Social Meaning*, Georgetown University, Washington DC, 79–103.

Horkheimer, M. & Adorno, T.: 1944/1972, *Dialectic of Enlightenment* (John Cumming, translator), Herder & Herder, New York.

Kenway, J., Fitzclarence, L., Collier, J. & Bigum, C.: 1997, 'Consumer contexts, culture-sand kids', in B. Green, L. Fitzclarence & J. Kenway (eds.), *Changing Education*, Deakin University, Geelong, Australia.

Klamer, A.: 1990, 'The textbook presentation of economic discourse', in W. Samuels (ed.), *Economics as Discourse*, Kluwer, Boston, 129–154.

Lemke, J.: 1990, *Talking Science*, Ablex, Norwood NJ.

Lemke, J.: 1995, *Textual Politics*, Taylor & Francis, Bristol PA.

Luke, A.: 1992, 'The body literate', *Linguistics and Education* 4, 107–129.

Luke, A.: 1995, 'Text and discourse in education', in M. Apple (ed.), *Review of Research in Education* 21, American Educational Research Association, Washington DC, 3–48.

Marx, K.: 1867/1978, *Capital, Volume 1* (S. Moore & E. Aveling, translators), in R. Tucker, *The Marx-Engels Reader* (second edition), Norton, New York.

Mehan, H.: 1979, *Learning Lessons*, Harvard University, Cambridge MA.

Myers, G.: 1992, 'Textbooks and the sociology of scientific knowledge', *English for Specific Purposes* 11, 3–17.

Poole, D.: 1994, 'Routine testing practices and the linguistic construction of knowledge', *Cognition and Instruction* 12, 125–150.

Postone, M.: 1993, *Time, Labor, and Social Domination*, Cambridge, New York.

Sinclair, J. & Coulthard, M.: 1975, *Towards an Analysis of Discourse*, Open University, London.

Singh, P.: 1993 'Institutional discourse and practice', *British Journal of the Sociology of Education* 14, 39–58.

Tyler, W.: 1995, 'Decoding school reform', in A. Sadovnik (ed.), *Knowledge and Pedagogy*, Ablex, Norwood NJ, 237–258.

Weber, M.: 1922/1968, *Economy and Society* (E. Fischoff, translator), Bedminster, New York.

Wortham, S.E.F.: 1995, 'Experience-near classroom examples as commodities', in D. Corson, *Discourse and Power in Educational Organizations*, Hampton, Cresskill NJ, 283–300.

KAYE MALCOLM

LANGUAGE USE AND AWARENESS IN THE MULTICULTURAL WORKPLACE

The field of research into language use and awareness in the multicultural workplace is a young, but rapidly expanding one. This is because the growth of cross-national movement by workers has meant that workplaces are increasingly multicultural and communication has become more evidently problematic. Literature on the topic can be categorised along two dimensions, its source and its focus. With respect to source, the literature is from business specialists on the one hand and language specialists on the other, with by far the greater amount of research coming from the latter source. The focus of the literature is on description on the one hand and pedagogical application on the other, with the greater contribution having the latter focus. This review will reflect such an emphasis (also see the review by Auerbach in Volume 2).

EARLY DEVELOPMENTS

Although educational language programs began in multicultural workplaces in the early 1970s, there is little literature from that time. Such programs were a response to a perceived need that minority group workers were unable to communicate in the majority group language to such an extent that problems emerged. Literature describing these programs did not appear until a few years after the work had actually begun.

Industrial English: An example of theory and practice in functional language teaching, by Jupp & Hodlin (1975) is one of these early works. It describes the program developed by the Industrial Language Training Service in England. Courses were developed to meet the specific functional needs of companies who employed Asian workers.

In the USA early workplace programs also had their roots in functionalism. In 1975 an adult performance level project identified the competencies required to function in workplaces in the USA. This led to the development of English competency-based workplace programs. While such programs were essentially work-centred, rather than worker-centred, the ground was being laid at the same time for a more participatory, critical language awareness approach. Paulo Freire's work, though not specifically addressing multicultural workplace issues, was drawn on for more worker and social action-centred programs. An example of this is Moriarity & Waller-

L. van Lier and D. Corson (eds), Encyclopedia of Language and Education,
Volume 6: Knowledge about Language, 261–269.
© *1997 Kluwer Academic Publishers. Printed in the Netherlands.*

stein's (1979) *Student/teacher/learner: A Freire Approach to ABE/ESL.* As in the USA, in Canada, Freire's influence was strong from the seventies onwards.

In Australia, workplace programs began in 1973. They were responses to immediate needs resulting from a growing number of migrants in the workforce. In Europe, language training in some countries had been mandatory for many years. In Sweden, for example, foreign workers had, since the 1970s, to receive 240 hours of language instruction in company time.

Generally, literature from the seventies comes from language specialists with a pedagogical focus. It describes programs which were work-centred, non-participatory, seen as separate from general literacy, adult education or work-skill programs and designed to make minority group workers more efficient.

MAJOR CONTRIBUTIONS IN THE 1980S

Over the 1980s, literature continued to come mainly from language specialists. Holden (1987) reports on a survey of 500 English language management texts, finding that only a small percentage treated language issues, and that when they were treated, it was with brevity and with little evidence of linguistic knowledge.

Holden (1989) contributes to the small volume of literature from the eighties which is descriptive, rather than pedagogical in focus. He is interested in the international, rather than the intranational multicultural work situation. He develops what he calls a functional typology of languages of international business, identifying languages of market contact, market languages and languages of marketing value. Also descriptive is the work of Gumperz (1982), some of which is focussed on workplace settings. Gumperz uses an interpretive sociolinguistic approach to examine the role of communication in the exercise of power and control in intergroup relationships.

The more pedagogical literature of the eighties falls into four categories. There is literature in the form of philosophical discussions, of manuals, of descriptive reports on language programs, and of evaluative reports.

Philosophical discussions include those like Hernandez's (1989) article on the move from what he calls 'existence' to 'participation' (a Freirean concept).

The manuals are for teachers and for students. Belfiore & Burnaby (1984), for example, have a manual for teachers with practical chapters on: the participants, negotiations, needs analysis, designing a syllabus, developing materials, classroom sequences and assessment and evaluation. These chapters are underpinned by the Freirean philosophy that teachers and learners should be seen as equal partners in the planning and delivery of courses. Auerbach & Wallerstein's (1987) manual, *ESL for Action: Problem Posing at Work*, also draws on Freire, suggesting a three stage development in lessons: listening, dialoguing, acting. Students are provided with English relevant to wider social issues which affect them, and they are encouraged to think critically and to engage in strategies which will enable them to make changes to their situations. Australian workplace teachers were provided with an English in the Workplace curriculum guide in 1989.

Descriptive reports include, for example, that of Bell (1982), who describes the development of a curriculum which seeks to engage learners as active participants. Brooks & Roberts (1985) describe the work of the Industrial Language Training Service in England over the decade from 1975. The Service evaluated its early approach, considering such matters as whether the work-focussed functional training could have long term effects on people's life chances and on relationships in the workplace. Changes were made during the eighties and are described in the report.

Evaluative reports include Finnan's (1981) and Miltenyi's (1989). Finnan reports that in most low wage jobs in the eighties there was little need to use a new workplace language and no provision to learn it. Miltenyi examines four English in the workplace programs in Australia to discover whether gains have been made with respect to eleven factors. These include: the improvement of macro language skills for workers, the impact on social functioning in the workplace and productivity.

In general, literature from the eighties is more conscious of a developing field with respect to language use in the workplace. This is indicated in the presence of some reflective literature alongside the practical manuals.

WORK IN PROGRESS

During the nineties interest in the multicultural workplace, and hence literature on the topic, has burgeoned.

From business education specialists there is now a wealth of material on *the new workplace* and on how to introduce workplace reform. Such material frequently contains advice on how to improve communication, and some work, such as that of Loden & Rosener (1991), focusses entirely on how communication should take account of diversity, although the diversity they refer to is not limited to that of culture and language.

Output on language topics from some well known business journals remains low, however. The journal *Training* includes 'Multicultural issues' in its subject index, and *Training and Development* has 'Cross cultural training'. However the *Academy of Management Journal*, in a special 1995 issue on 'Intercultural and International Management Research', includes nothing on language use or awareness. A review of issues of eleven other journals in the years 1990–1996 reveals no reference to language issues.

Language specialist literature with a more descriptive focus is beginning to emerge. Clyne (1994) examines cultural variation in English discourse and the role of verbal communication patterns in successful and unsuccessful workplace interactions. Meeuwis (1994) describes a similar project in a Belgian company, where all the subjects are non-native speakers. Hagen (1992) describes language use (that is, which languages are used) in the European workplace and predicts future language requirements. Nair-Venugopal (1993) gives an account of language choice in a Malaysian workplace.

The pedagogically focussed literature appears to fall into three categories: manuals, reports, and a new category, discussion of the place of language training in various wider contexts.

Manuals now include, as well as those for teachers and students, those for supervisors of language learners and for management. Migliorino, Miltenyi & Robertson's (1994) manual for managers analyses what often occurs in areas such as workplace communication, what the impact of a multicultural workforce is on this area, and suggests ways of improving problem situations. A training manual for managers using a competency framework is available in Australia (Baylis & Thomas, 1994).

Reports can be divided into two groups. Many are reports of particular projects undertaken in one area or workplace; others are reports describing general trends over time or a certain geographical area. Both the particular and the more general reports may describe content and/or philosophies behind programs, and may be descriptive and/or evaluative.

Most of the reports on particular projects describe programs which teach a majority group language to a minority language group. These reports come from many countries. For example, there is a successful problem-based program in a multinational company in Thailand and Snoeken (1993) reports on the implementation of a training model to teach Dutch in the Workplace to non-native speakers in The Netherlands. Not all programs are 'successful', and Peirce, Harper & Burnaby (1993) analyse the reasons for 'drop-out' at a Canadian workplace. There are few references to the teaching of minority group languages to majority group workers, or to the sort of assistance which might be given to native speakers to assist in communication with non native speakers.

Reports describing general trends include those of McGroarty & Scott (1993), Wrigley (1993) and Grognet (1994) These categorize language programs according to the approach or philosophy behind them. McGroarty & Scott's categories are: pre-workplace programs, work-centred programs and worker-centred programs. They say that many agencies now favour the last of these approaches, being more holistic, participatory and exhibiting critical language awareness. Wrigley, on the other hand, says that most programs would fit into the second category, supporting the philosophy of social and economic adaptation and reproducing inequalities in society. The debate over which philosophy does and will dominate programs is engaging researchers worldwide. See, for example, Hampel (1992), examining the Australian situation, and Kerfoot (1993) the South African context.

Roberts, Davies & Jupp's (1992) book, *Language and Discrimination*, is a further report on the work of the Industrial Language Training Service in the United Kingdom. This book describes communication practices in the workplace and examines how they contribute to discrimination. It outlines the programs developed to combat discrimination and racism.

The third area of pedagogic literature is that which discusses the place of multicultural workplace language education in a wider context. Firstly, where education is for non-native speakers, there is its relation to the whole area of second language teaching. Chisman, Wrigley & Ewen (1993) see it as one of seven types of ESL. Secondly, there is its relation to general adult basic education and vocational skills training. Bean (1994) is one of many who advocate the integration of these three areas. This integration is in fact occurring. In Australia, for example, there is now a combined adult literacy, ESL and communication studies workplace education programme. Also, language and literacy competencies are being incorporated into industry standards. Thirdly there is its place in the area of crosscultural awareness and education. Cope, Pauwels, Slade, Brosnan & Neil (1994) suggest that a focus on language is one of six approaches to crosscultural training in the workplace. Fourthly, it is considered in relation to the rapidly changing nature of workplace organization. In democratic countries, the workplace is undergoing its most fundamental change since the industrial revolution. Technological advances, new consumer demands, a global marketplace, and the growth of the social justice movement have meant that employees need to be multiskilled, and competent in new oral and written communicative genres in order to take part in the more participative, democratic workplaces. Mawer (1992) discusses how these greater demands impact upon workers who have to meet them in a language which is not native to them.

In general, work in progress in the nineties is both theoretical and practical, is rapidly increasing both in volume and extent, and is beginning to result in sharing of ideas and resources among researchers and practitioners.

PROBLEMS AND DIFFICULTIES

Grognet (1994) outlines six problems facing immigrant workplace education in the United States. It is claimed that, first, the very extent of the task is daunting; second, resources for both federal and state-funded programs are limited; third, delivery is fragmented, with no generally agreed on courses and no recognized accountability system; fourth, there is little networking of information and insights; fifth, there is still insufficient research and development; sixth, there is a conflict between what Grognet terms 'education' and 'training' on the one hand and 'workplace' and 'workforce' programs on the other. 'Education' is described as long term, sequential, decontextualized, knowledge oriented and connected, while 'training' is short term, non sequential, contextualized, goal oriented and disconnected. Grognet claims that most workplace programs offer 'training'. 'Workplace' programs focus on the tasks of the workplace and 'workforce' programs focus on the needs of the workers.

Other writers refer to further problems. McKay (1993) says that there may be resistance by workers to joining programs for fear of hostility by co-workers. She refers also to the problem of program control. If management controls the program, it may want a course design which increases efficiency, but ignores workers' goals. There may be a management fear that if workers become linguistically competent they will become too active in unions, or leave the present job for better prospects.

Some, but not all of these problems occur in other countries. Australia, for example, does not face the third problem, having published national guidelines for the development of competencies for the workplace (National Training Board, 1992). The Board subsequently issued a report entitled *Incorporating Language and Literacy Competencies into Industry Standards* (1993).

Other countries have their own particular problems. Goldstein (1994) says that in Canada learning and using the majority group language does not always mean economic gain, and for this reason workers may resist programs. She says that people with, for example, four years schooling in their home country cannot achieve excellent English and Grade 12 education with only two hours language training each week. Excellent English and Grade 12 education is what she says is required for higher paying jobs in Canada. Further, workers may not find that speaking English provides them with any social gain. She quotes the case of Portuguese workers in Canada who prefer to speak Portuguese because it is a symbol of solidarity on the production floor. In fact there are risks in *not* using Portuguese, the use of English being seen as an insult. Other Canadian writers make points similar to Goldstein's.

Kerfoot (1993) says that in South Africa, most teachers have little training or experience, and most material is still written by whites, for blacks.

It appears that the focus on the multicultural workplace is bringing with it a growing awareness of many problems.

FUTURE DIRECTIONS

If awareness of the importance of language issues in the multicultural workplace is to have practical outcomes, business specialists will need to work together with language specialists and to give more recognition to the latter's input. Whether this will happen is debatable. A 1989 conference in the United States, for example, entitled *Building a Quality Workforce: A National Priority for the Twenty First Century*, in spite of having the keynote address on the topic of *The Glory and Power of the Multicultural Workforce*, had not one of the other 140 papers dealing with language issues. On the other hand, language specialists will need to acquaint themselves more thoroughly with the business world. Chisman, Wrigley & Ewen (1993) point out that language providers often have little experience in working with companies.

Judging by recent trends, the descriptive focus in workplace literature will begin to catch up with the pedagogical focus. According to Grognet (1994) this is very necessary, at least in the United States, where there has been little work done on discourse patterns and styles in the workplace. In answer to her own question, 'What are the linguistic tasks?' Grognet says, 'We don't really know', because there is no real corpus of work available in the USA (Grognet, 1994, p. 6).

Grognet further suggests that quality programs in the future will be demonstrated by such evidence as: good needs analyses, the 'buy-in' of management and unions, curriculum decisions based on a consideration of the needs analysis as well as funding and timing, attention to cross cultural issues, an articulation system between language personnel and workplace supervisory personnel, demonstration of results by changes in linguistic and cultural competence and the ability to get funds. This last point is supported by Hampel (1992), who says that there needs to be a commitment by governments to allocate funds to achieve goals enshrined in declared policies such as social justice.

Goldstein (1994) says that what is needed for the future is a "critical pedagogy" which attempts to challenge workers' subordinate position by providing them with a means of thinking about their position in society and of ways of increasing access to economic, social and personal power.

As with problems and difficulties, future directions may differ from country to country. Hagen (1992) says that in Europe the majority of companies will be owned across borders and staffed by different nationalities. Multilingual discussion will require participants to use whatever languages they have to create functional communication. He suggests that this will require people to speak English and at least two other languages. Jones & Jiang (1995) see four needs in Fiji. They say that language needs and a common business language for managers should be systematically investigated nationally, that language skills should include skills audits, that adult literacy and ESL programs in urban areas need a workplace focus, and that interpreter and translator training should be investigated. Kerfoot (1993) says that in South Africa there needs to be a coherent theoretical model which incorporates literacy, English language teaching and adult basic education. There also needs to be an infrastructure which avoids support only for the manufacturing workforce and a co-operation between small scale action research and national initiatives.

Future directions for literature on language use and awareness in the multicultural workplace will continue to involve not only discussion of the effects of multiculturalism on the workplace, but on a workplace which is itself changing dramatically. Also of interest will be the effects of the workplace on multiculturalism and multilingualism. Thus, attention to language use and awareness will demand attention from all parties involved in work in the twenty-first century.

Adult Migrant Education Service
Western Australia

REFERENCES

Auerbach, E.R. & Wallerstein, N.: 1987, *ESL for action: Problem Posing at Work*, Addison-Wesley, Reading, MA.

Baylis, P. & Thomas, G.: 1994, *English in the Workplace: Competency Framework*, AMES, New South Wales.

Bean, R.: 1994, 'Integrating communication and skill training', *Open Letter* 5(1), 17–30.

Belfiore, M.E. & Burnaby, B.: 1984, *Teaching English in the Workplace*, Ontario Institute for Studies in Education & Hodder & Stoughton Ltd, Ontario.

Bell, J.: 1982, 'The Levi Strauss project: Development of a curriculum', *TESL Talk* 13(4), 83–91.

Brooks, T. & Roberts, C.: 1985, 'No Five fingers are all alike: Managing change and difference in the multi-ethnic workplace', in C.J. Brumfit (ed.), *English as a Second Language in the United Kingdom*, Pergamon Press, Oxford, 111–130.

Chisman, F., Wrigley, H.S. & Ewen, D.: 1993, *ESL and the American Dream: A Report on an Investigation of English as a Second Language Service for Adults*, Southport Institute for Policy Analysis, USA.

Clyne, M.: 1994, *Intercultural Communication at Work: Cultural Values in Discourse*, Cambridge University Press, Cambridge.

Cope, B., Pauwels, A., Slade, D., Brosnan, D. & Neil, D.: 1994, *Local Diversity, Global Connections, Volume 1, Six Approaches to Cross Cultural Training*, Australian Government Publishing Service, Canberra.

Finnan, C.R.: 1981, 'Occupational assimilation of refugees', *International Migration Review* 15(1), 292–309.

Goldstein, T.: 1994, ' "We are all sisters, so we don't have to be polite" Language choice and English language training in the multilingual workplace', *TESL Canada Journal* 11(2), 30–45.

Grognet, A.G.: 1994, *ESL and the Employment Connection*, paper presented at the Office of Refugee Resettlement English Language Training Consultations, USA.

Gumperz, J.: 1982, *Language and Social Identity*, Cambridge University Press, Cambridge.

Hagen, S.: 1992, 'Foreign language needs in the European workplace, *ARAL* 15(1), 107–124.

Hampel, B.: 1992, 'Social justice and English as a second language provision in Melbourne: Some considerations from the literature', *Journal of Intercultural Studies* 13(1), 1–15.

Hernandez, C.: 1989, 'Beyond existence, towards participation', *TESL Talk* 19(1), 62–64.

Holden, N.: 1987, 'The treatment of language and linguistic issues in the current English language international management literature', *Multilingua* 6(3), 233–246.

Holden, N.: 1989, 'Toward a functional typology of languages of international business', *Language Problems and Language Planning* 13(1), 1–8.

Jupp, T.C. & Hodlin, S.: 1975, *Industrial English: An Example of Theory and Practice in Functional Language Teaching*, Heinemann Educational Books, London.

Kerfoot, C.: 1993, 'Participatory education in a South African context: contradictions and challenges', *TESOL Quarterly* 27(3), 431–447.

Loden, M. & Rosener, J.: 1991, *Workforce America: Managing Employee Diversity as a Vital Resource*, Business One Irwin, Homewood, Illinois.

Mawer, G.: 1992, 'Developing new competencies for workplace education', *Prospect* 7(2), 7–27.

McGroarty, M. & Scott, S.: 1993, *Workplace ESL Instruction: Varieties and Constraints*, ERIC Clearing House for ESL Literacy Education, Washington.

McKay, S.L.:1993, *Agendas for Second Language Literacy*, Cambridge University Press, Cambridge.

Meeuwis, M.: 1994, 'Non native – non native intercultural communication: An analysis of instruction sessions for foreign engineers in a Belgian company', *Multilingua* 13(1/2), 59–82.

Migliorino, P., Miltenyi, G. & Robertson, H.: 1994, *Best Practice in Managing a Culturally Diverse Workplace: A Manager's Manual*, Australian Government Public Service, Canberra.

Miltenyi, G.: 1989, *English in the Workplace: A Shrewd Economic Investment*, a report prepared for the Office of Multicultural Affairs, Department of the Prime Minister and Cabinet, Canberra.

Moriarity, P. & Wallerstein, N.: 1979, 'Student/teacher/learner: A Freire approach to ABE/ESL', *Adult Literacy and Basic Education* (Fall).

National Training Board: 1992, *National Competency Standards, Policy and Guidelines* (second edition), National Capital Printing, Canberra.

Nair-Venugopal, S.: 1993, *Language Choice in Training: A Cross-cultural Perspective*, paper presented at Communication in the Workplace Conference: Culture, Language and Organizational Change, Sydney.

Peirce, B.N., Harper, H. & Burnaby B.: 1993, 'Workplace ESL at Levi Strauss: "Dropouts" speak out', *TESL Canada* 10(2), 9–30.

Roberts, C., Davies, E. & Jupp, T.: 1992, *Language and Discrimination: A Study of Communication in Multi-ethnic Workplaces*, Longman, London & New York.

Snoeken, H.: 1993, *Research into Language Needs Analysis in the Workplace*, paper presented to Communication in the Workplace Conference: Culture, Language and Organizational Change, Sydney.

Wrigley, H.S: 1993, 'One size does not fit all: Educational perspectives and program practices in the United States', *TESOL Quarterly* 27(3), 449–466.

SUBJECT INDEX

271

NAME INDEX

279

TABLE OF CONTENTS

VOLUME 1: LANGUAGE POLICY AND POLITICAL ISSUES IN EDUCATION

TABLE OF CONTENTS

TABLE OF CONTENTS

VOLUME 2: LITERACY

TABLE OF CONTENTS

Section 3: Focus on the Social Context of Literacy

Section 4: Focus on Selected Regions

TABLE OF CONTENTS

VOLUME 3: ORAL DISCOURSE AND EDUCATION

TABLE OF CONTENTS

TABLE OF CONTENTS

VOLUME 4: SECOND LANGUAGE EDUCATION

TABLE OF CONTENTS

TABLE OF CONTENTS

VOLUME 5: BILINGUAL EDUCATION

TABLE OF CONTENTS

TABLE OF CONTENTS

VOLUME 7: LANGUAGE TESTING AND ASSESSMENT

TABLE OF CONTENTS

TABLE OF CONTENTS

TABLE OF CONTENTS

VOLUME 8: RESEARCH METHODS IN LANGUAGE AND EDUCATION

TABLE OF CONTENTS

Encyclopedia of Language and Education

Set ISBN Hb 0-7923-4596-7; Pb 0-7923-4936-9

1. R. Wodak and D. Corson (eds.): *Language Policy and Political Issues in Education.* 1997
   ISBN Hb 0-7923-4713-7
   ISBN Pb 0-7923-4928-8

2. V. Edwards and D. Corson (eds.): *Literacy.* 1997
   ISBN Hb 0-7923-4595-0
   ISBN Pb 0-7923-4929-6

3. B. Davies and D. Corson (eds.): *Oral Discourse and Education.* 1997
   ISBN Hb 0-7923-4639-4
   ISBN Pb 0-7923-4930-X

4. G.R. Tucker and D. Corson (eds.): *Second Language Education.* 1997
   ISBN Hb 0-7923-4640-8
   ISBN Pb 0-7923-4931-8

5. J. Cummins and D. Corson (eds.): *Bilingual Education.* 1997
   ISBN Hb 0-7923-4806-0
   ISBN Pb 0-7923-4932-6

6. L. van Lier and D. Corson (eds.): *Knowledge about Language.* 1997
   ISBN Hb 0-7923-4641-6
   ISBN Pb 0-7923-4933-4

7. C. Clapham and D. Corson (eds.): *Language Testing and Assessment.* 1997
   ISBN Hb 0-7923-4702-1
   ISBN Pb 0-7923-4934-2

8. N.H. Hornberger and D. Corson (eds.): *Research Methods in Language and Education.* 1997
   ISBN Hb 0-7923-4642-4
   ISBN Pb 0-7923-4935-0

KLUWER ACADEMIC PUBLISHERS – DORDRECHT / BOSTON / LONDON